Swahili

phrasebooks
and
Dr Martin Benjamin

Swahili phrasebook
3rd edition – September 2005

Published by
Lonely Planet Publications Pty Ltd ABN 36 005 607 983
90 Maribyrnong St, Footscray, Victoria 3011, Australia

Lonely Planet Offices
Australia Locked Bag 1, Footscray, Victoria 3011
USA 150 Linden St, Oakland CA 94607
UK 72-82 Rosebery Ave, London, EC1R 4RW

Cover illustration
Soulful Swahilian by Wendy Wright

ISBN 1 86450 282 7

text © Lonely Planet Publications Pty Ltd 2005
cover illustration © Lonely Planet Publications Pty Ltd 2005

  10 9 8 7 6 5 4 3 2

Printed through Colorcraft Ltd, Hong Kong
Printed in China

acknowledgments

Editor Branislava Vladisavljevic would like to acknowledge the following people for their contributions to this phrasebook:

Dr Martin Benjamin for the translations, cultural information, and writing a concise guide to Swahili grammar. Martin is an anthropologist who has lived and worked in Tanzania for many years as a researcher and consultant on issues of development, health and gender. In addition to teaching Swahili and Anthropology at Wesleyan University, he is the founder and editor of the Kamusi Project Internet Living Swahili Dictionary at Yale University. Readers who wish to advance their Swahili can use the online lessons that he is developing in the 'Learning Guide' at www.yale.edu/swahili, and all travellers to East Africa are invited to visit http://research.yale.edu/swahili/serve_pages/photouploader.php to learn how to contribute their pictures to the cause of Swahili education.

Martin wishes to thank Charles Mironko and Anne Geoghegan for their work on the previous edition of this phrasebook – many of their words have found their way into the current edition. Thanks also to Ben and Branislava for all their work preparing and editing this book. My deepest thanks for making it possible for me to (almost) meet my deadlines go to my wife Veronica, who yielded me to this project in the weeks right after our wedding.

Lonely Planet Language Products

Publishing Managers: Karin Vidstrup Monk & Chris Rennie
Commissioning Editor: Ben Handicott
Editor: Branislava Vladisavljevic
Assisting Editors: Meladel Mistica, Jodie Martire & Francesca Coles
Layout Designer: Margie Jung

Managing Editor: Annelies Mertens
Production Manager: Jo Vraca
Layout Manager: Adriana Mammarella
Series Designer: Yukiyoshi Kamimura
Cartographer: Wayne Murphy
Project Manager: Annelies Mertens

make the most of this phrasebook ...

Anyone can speak another language! It's all about confidence. Don't worry if you can't remember your school language lessons or if you've never learnt a language before. Even if you learn the very basics (on the inside covers of this book), your travel experience will be the better for it. You have nothing to lose and everything to gain when the locals hear you making an effort.

finding things in this book

For easy navigation, this book is in sections. The Tools chapters are the ones you'll thumb through time and again. The Practical section covers basic travel situations like catching transport and finding a bed. The Social section gives you conversational phrases, pick-up lines, the ability to express opinions – so you can get to know people. Food has a section all of its own: gourmets and vegetarians are covered and local dishes feature. Safe Travel equips you with health and police phrases, just in case. Remember the colours of each section and you'll find everything easily; or use the comprehensive Index. Otherwise, check the two-way traveller's Dictionary for the word you need.

being understood

Throughout this book you'll see coloured phrases on each page. They're phonetic guides to help you pronounce the language. You don't even need to look at the language itself, but you'll get used to the way we've represented particular sounds. The pronunciation chapter in Tools will explain more, but you can feel confident that if you read the coloured phrase slowly, you'll be understood.

communication tips

Body language, ways of doing things, sense of humour – all have a role to play in every culture. 'Local talk' boxes show you common ways of saying things, or everyday language to drop into conversation. 'Listen for ...' boxes supply the phrases you may hear. They start with the language (so local people can point out what they want to say to you) and then lead in to the pronunciation guide and the English translation.

introduction 8

tools 11

practical 47

social 107

CONTENTS

7

swahili

national language
widely spoken

For more details, see the **introduction**.

Swahili is one of the most widely spoken African languages and is internationally recognised as the key language of communication in the East African region. It belongs to the Bantu group of languages from the Niger-Congo family and can be traced back to the first millenium AD. This Bantu origin is clearly visible in the distinctive grammar and sound system of Swahili.

Although the number of speakers of Swahili throughout East Africa is estimated to be well over 50 million, it's the mother tongue of only about 4–5 million people, and is predominantly used as a second language or a lingua franca by speakers of other African languages. Swahili is the national language of Tanzania and Kenya and is widely used in Uganda, Rwanda and Burundi, as well as in the eastern part of the Democratic Republic of Congo and on the Indian Ocean islands of Zanzibar and the Comoros. There are speakers of Swahili in the southern parts of Ethiopia and Somalia, the northern regions of Mozambique and Zambia, and even on the northwestern coast of Madagascar.

The development of Swahili through time is an interesting story of contact between nations, reflecting many political and social changes in this part of the world. Originally spoken by indigenous people along the coast and on the

---

at a glance ...

language name: Swahili

name in language:
Kiswahili kee·swa·hee·lee

language family:
Niger-Congo

key countries:
Tanzania, Kenya

approximate number of speakers: 4–5 million as first language, over 50 million as second language or lingua franca

close relatives:
Bantu languages (eg Pokomo, Mijikenda, Comorian)

donations to English:
safari, simba (lion)

islands, it was the main language of coastal trade, and therefore from the 7th century heavily influenced by Arabic, principally in the vocabulary – the word 'Swahili' itself comes from an Arabic word for 'coastal'. With the arrival of European explorers and colonisers and the rise of the slave trade in the 19th century, Swahili spread inland. Apart from Arabic, there are influences from Persian, Portuguese, and of course, English (words like *baisikeli*, *penseli* and *kompyuta* have only been adapted slightly to reflect Swahili pronunciation).

It's hardly surprising that in an area as vast as East Africa many different dialects of Swahili can be found, but you shouldn't have problems being understood if you stick to the standard coastal form, as used in this book. Standard Swahili developed from the urban dialect of Zanzibar City, dominant from pre-colonial times. The missionaries and colonial governments in Kenya and Tanzania used it first to communicate with the locals and later encouraged its use in administration, which led to its official status in the post-colonial period.

Even though Swahili grammar can seem a bit daunting, you should find the pronunciation pretty much straightforward. The writing system is based on the Roman alphabet, which will make using this phrasebook and learning Swahili much easier.

So wherever you go throughout the East African region, you'll find Swahili greatly useful and attempts to communicate with locals in the language will be greatly appreciated. This book gives you the practical phrases you need to get by, as well as the fun, spontaneous phrases that lead to a better understanding of East African people and their culture. Local knowledge, new relationships and a sense of satisfaction are on the tip of your tongue. So don't just stand there, say something!

abbreviations used in this book:

a	adjective	n	noun
adv	adverb	pl	plural
f	feminine	prep	preposition
Ken	Kenya	sg	singular
m	masculine	Tan	Tanzania
lit	literal translation	v	verb

TOOLS > pronunciation

matamshi

The pronunciation of Swahili is relatively simple, since most of the sounds in this language are also found in English. Once you learn a few basic rules you won't have any problems reading or pronouncing it, but we've included a pronunciation guide throughout this book to make it even easier.

vowel sounds

Vowels are short and each one is pronounced clearly, even when not stressed. There are no diphthongs in Swahili (ie vowel sound combinations, like in English 'how' or 'day').

symbol	english equivalent	swahili example	transliteration
a	father	*dada*	*da·da*
ay	may	*wewe*	*way·way*
ee	bee	*sisi*	*see·see*
oh	role	*moja*	*moh·ja*
oo	moon	*duka*	*doo·ka*

consonant sounds

Most consonants in Swahili have equivalents in English. The only one that might be a bit unusual for an English speaker is the sound ng. It can be a bit tricky at first, but with a little practice it should come easily – try saying 'sing along' a few times and then dropping the 'si', and that's how it sounds at the beginning of a word.

pronunciation

The sounds th and dh occur only in words borrowed from Arabic.
Swahili speakers make only a slight distinction between r and l.
Instead of the hard 'r', try pronouncing a light 'd'.

symbol	english equivalent	swahili example	transliteration
b	**b**ig	*betri*	*bay*·tree
ch	**ch**illi	*chakula*	cha·*koo*·la
d	**d**in	*duka*	*doo*·ka
dh	**th**is	*dhambi*	*dham*·bee
f	**f**un	*sufu*	*soo*·foo
g	**g**o	*gari/ghali*	*ga*·ree/*ga*·lee
h	**h**at	*tarehe*	ta·*ray*·hay
j	**j**am	*jiwe*	*jee*·way
k	**k**ick	*ukuta*	oo·*koo*·ta
l	**l**oud	*uliza*	oo·*lee*·za
m	**m**an	*mwanamume*	m·wa·na·*moo*·may
n	**n**o	*nunua*	noo·*noo*·a
ng	si**ng**	*ng'ombe*	ng·*ohm*·bay
ny	ca**ny**on	*nyasi*	*nya*·see
p	**p**ig	*chupa*	*choo*·pa
r	**r**un (but softer, more like a light 'd')	*dirisha*	dee·*ree*·sha
s	**s**o	*kisu*	*kee*·soo
sh	**sh**ip	*shida*	*shee*·da
t	**t**in	*tochi*	*toh*·chee
th	**th**ing	*thelathini*	thay·la·*thee*·nee
v	**v**an	*vumbi*	*voom*·bee
w	**w**in	*wazo*	*wa*·zoh
y	**y**es	*yoyote*	yoh·*yoh*·tay
z	**z**oo	*ziwa*	*zee*·wa

TOOLS

regional variations

Being used over a huge geographical area, Swahili has many dialectical variations, which can be grouped as northern, central and southern dialects, with a further basic distinction between urban and rural dialects. The form of Swahili in this phrasebook is the standard form which is based on Kiunguja, the coastal dialect spoken in Zanzibar City. When you travel across East Africa, you should be understood using this book, as all the regional variations are generally mutually intelligible and also increasingly influenced by this standard form, which is used in all the media.

word stress

In Swahili, words are almost always stressed on the second-last syllable. There are only a handful of words that break this rule, and these are mostly loanwords. In our pronunciation guide, the stressed syllable is always in italics.

stressing the point

• Changing the stress in a word can sometimes make a whole lot of difference. Make sure to get the stress in the right place on *barabara* ba·ra·*ba*·ra (amazing). If you say ba·ra·*ba*·ra, you're simply saying 'road'!

• Many words in Swahili come from English, but the pronunciation changed slightly. Be sure to stress the second-last syllable in the word *tiketi* tee·*kay*·tee (ticket), rather than the first syllable (*tee*·kay·tee) as you would in English. *Tikiti* tee·*kee*·ti is used instead of *tiketi* in many areas – listen to the locals' pronunciation and follow their lead.

reading & writing

Swahili was traditionally written in a modified Arabic script (used mostly for writing epic poetry). The Roman-based alphabet, in use since the mid-19th century, was formalised in the 1930s. It consists of 24 letters (all the letters of the English alphabet except 'q' and 'x').

The correspondence between the written language and the pronunciation is consistent. As a general rule, every written letter is pronounced. When two vowels appear together, each one must be pronounced separately. For example, *kawaida* (usual) is pronounced ka·wa·*ee*·da. However, if the same vowel is repeated twice at the end of a word, it's pronounced as one syllable and the stress falls on that (last) syllable, rather than the second-last one: *sikukuu* see·koo·*koo* (holiday).

There are only a few two-letter combinations in written Swahili that don't follow the general rule of pronouncing every letter separately: *ch*, *dh*, *gh*, *ng*, *ny*, *sh* and *th* all represent single sounds (see **consonant sounds**, page 12). Our coloured pronunciation guides indicate the correct pronunciation so don't worry if you can't remember these rules.

The symbol ' which appears in written Swahili after the letter combination *ng*, as in *ng'ombe* ng·*ohm*·bay (cow), is called a glottal stop, which is similar to the tightening of the throat that happens when you cough. You can also hear it in the word 'bottle' when the double 't' is swallowed. It's not represented in the pronunciation guide, as it only serves to show in writing that *ng'* should be pronounced as one syllable. Without it, these two letters belong to separate syllables, as in *changu* chan·goo (finger).

alphabet					
A a a	*B b* bee	*C c* see	*D d* dee	*E e* ay	*F f* ayf
G g jee	*H h* *ay*·chee	*I i* ee	*J j* jay	*K k* kay	*L l* ayl
M m aym	*N n* ayn	*O o* oh	*P p* pee	*R r* ar	*S s* ays
T t tee	*U u* oo	*V v* vee	*W w* *dab*·al·yoo	*Y y* *wa*·ee	*Z z* *zayd*·ee

contents

The index below shows the grammatical structures you can use to say what you want. Look under each function – listed in alphabetical order – for more information on how to build your own phrases. For example, to tell the taxi driver where your hotel is, look for **giving directions/orders** and you'll be directed to information on **location**, **prepositions** and **requests**. A glossary of grammatical terms is also included at the end of this chapter. The label 'survival Swahili' used after some forms in this chapter means that the form won't be fully correct, but will generally be understood. You can find detailed explanations and grammar exercises in the *Learning Guide* at www.yale.edu/swahili.

adjectives & adverbs

describing things

Adjectives always come after the noun they describe.

good news   *habari nzuri*   ha·*ba*·ree n·*zoo*·ree
             (lit: news good)

Many adjectives in the **dictionary** (page 195) have a hyphen in front. The hyphen indicates the space for a prefix, which varies depending on certain qualities of the thing being described. The rules are complicated and there are many exceptions, but the basic groups are listed here.

noun qualities	prefix	swahili example	english example
person or animal sg	*m-*	*mtoto mzuri* m·*toh*·toh m·*zoo*·ree *tembo mkubwa* *taym*·boh m·*koo*·bwa	good child big elephant
person or animal pl	*wa-*	*watoto wazuri* wa·*toh*·toh wa·*zoo*·ree *tembo wakubwa* *taym*·boh wa·*koo*·bwa	good children big elephants
object sg&pl (survival swahili)	*n-* or *j-* or no prefix	*habari nzuri* ha·*ba*·ree n·*zoo*·ree *pikipiki kubwa* pee·kee·*pee*·kee *koo*·bwa	good news big motorcycle

Many Swahili nouns can become adjectives by using the word 'of' before them. The word used for 'of' changes depending on the qualities of the thing being described, as shown in the table on the next page. The word 'of' is also used to express possession. (For more details on the forms for 'of' see also **possession**.)

noun qualities	'of'	swahili example	english example
person or animal sg&pl	wa	*tembo wa kijivu* taym·boh wa kee·*jee*·voo	**gray elephant**
		mbu wa jioni m·boo wa jee·*oh*·nee	**evening mosquitos**
object sg (survival swahili)	ya	*baisikeli ya kisasa* ba·ee·see·*kay*·lee ya kee·*sa*·sa	**modern bike**
object pl (survival swahili)	za	*boti za mbao* boh·tee za m·*ba*·oh	**wooden boats**

Adverbs also go after the verb they're modifying. Often, the word *kwa* appears before the adverb – in that case, *kwa* resembles the English suffix '-ly' (eg 'nicely').

I walked a lot.
  Nilitembea sana.   nee·lee·taym·*bay*·a *sa*·na
  (lit: I-*past*-walk much)

She speaks in a hurry.
  Anasema kwa haraka.   a·na·*say*·ma kwa ha·*ra*·ka
  (lit: she-*present*-talk with hurry)

articles

describing things • naming things/people

Swahili doesn't have articles (a/an, the). To refer to a specific object (ie 'the' thing), use a demonstrative pronoun ('this' book) or a possessive pronoun ('his' book) (see **demonstratives & possession**). To refer to 'a' thing (ie an unspecified thing in a generic sense), use the adjective *-moja* for 'one' (preferably with the appropriate prefix – see **adjectives & adverbs**):

a flower   *ua moja*   oo·a *moh*·ja
                      (lit: flower one)

'Some' is expressed with the phrase *baadhi ya*, which is used before the noun, or *kadhaa*, which comes after the noun.

some people   *baadhi ya watu*   ba·dhee ya *wa*·too
                   (lit: some people)
                   watu kadhaa   *wa*·too ka·*dha*
                   (lit: people some)

be

doing things • making a statement • negating

In the present tense, the verb 'be' (*kuwa*) is incredibly easy. No matter what the subject, the word for 'am/is/are' is *ni*.

I am English.
   Mimi ni Mwingereza.   mee·mee nee mween·gay·*ray*·za
   (lit: I am English)

We are Africans.
   Sisi ni Waafrika.   see·see nee wa·a·*free*·ka
   (lit: we are Africans)

It's just as easy to form negative statements – the form of 'be' is *si* for all persons in singular and plural.

I am not a doctor.
   Mimi si daktari.   mee·mee see dak·*ta*·ree
   (lit: I am-not doctor)

We are not students.
   Sisi si wanafunzi.   see·see see wa·na·*foon*·zee
   (lit: we are-not students)

However, many things that you can 'be' in English are things you can 'have' in Swahili (see **have**).

In the past and future tenses the verb 'to be' has a different form for each person, as shown in the next table.

past tense			
I	was	*nilikuwa*	nee·lee·*koo*·wa
you sg	were	*ulikuwa*	oo·lee·*koo*·wa
he/she (person)*		*alikuwa*	a·lee·*koo*·wa
it (object) (survival swahili)	was	*ilikuwa*	ee·lee·*koo*·wa
we		*tulikuwa*	too·lee·*koo*·wa
you pl		*mlikuwa*	m·lee·*koo*·wa
they (person)*	were	*walikuwa*	wa·lee·*koo*·wa
they (object) (survival swahili)		*zilikuwa*	zee·lee·*koo*·wa

future tense			
I		*nitakuwa*	nee·ta·*koo*·wa
you sg		*utakuwa*	oo·ta·*koo*·wa
he/she (person)*		*atakuwa*	a·ta·*koo*·wa
it (object) (survival swahili)	will be	*itakuwa*	ee·ta·*koo*·wa
we		*tutakuwa*	too·ta·*koo*·wa
you pl		*mtakuwa*	m·ta·*koo*·wa
they (person)*		*watakuwa*	wa·ta·*koo*·wa
they (object) (survival swahili)		*zitakuwa*	zee·ta·*koo*·wa

* or animal(s)

demonstratives

naming things/people · pointing things out

When you want to point something out (eg 'this thing' or 'those things'), remember that in Swahili the demonstrative comes after the noun it refers to:

this child	*mtoto huyu* (lit: child this)	m·*toh*·toh *hoo*·yoo
those giraffes	*twiga wale* (lit: giraffes those)	*twee*·ga *wa*·lay

noun qualities	this/these	that/those
person or animal sg	*huyu* hoo·yoo	*yule* yoo·lay
person or animal pl	*hawa* ha·wa	*wale* wa·lay
object sg (survival swahili)	*hii* hee	*ile* ee·lay
object pl (survival swahili)	*hizi* hee·zee	*zile* zee·lay

huyo

have

doing things · making a statement · possessing

In Swahili, the verb 'have' (*kuwa na*) is very similar to the verb 'be' (*kuwa*) – essentially, it translates as 'to be with'. Many things that you 'are' in English are things that you 'have' in Swahili:

I am hungry.
   Nina njaa.   *nee*·na n·*ja*
   (lit: I-have hunger)

She is cold.
   Ana baridi.   *a*·na ba·*ree*·dee
   (lit: she-has cold)

In the present tense, the verb is irregular, but not difficult, as you can see in the tables that follow. In the past and future tenses, simply add the word *na* after the correct form of the verb 'be' in the table on page 20.

I	have	*nina*	*nee*·na
you sg		*una*	*oo*·na
he/she (person or animal)	has	*ana*	*a*·na
it (object) (survival swahili)		*ina*	*ee*·na
we	have	*tuna*	*too*·na
you pl		*mna*	m·*na*
they (person or animal)		*wana*	*wa*·na
they (object) (survival swahili)		*zina*	*zee*·na

I		*sina*	*see*·na
you sg	don't have	*huna*	*hoo*·na
he/she (person)*	doesn't have	*hana*	*ha*·na
it (object) (survival swahili)		*haina*	*ha·ee*·na
we		*hatuna*	*ha·too*·na
you pl	don't have	*hamna*	*ham*·na
they (person)*		*hawana*	*ha·wa*·na
they (object) (survival swahili)		*hazina*	*ha·zee*·na

* or animal(s)

location

giving directions/orders • indicating location

To say that something is 'here' or 'there' requires two parts – variations on the verb 'be' and a locative suffix (ie a verb ending that indicates location). Swahili divides location into three general areas – 'here', 'there', and 'inside', with these corresponding suffixes:

here	-po	·poh
there	-ko	·koh
inside	-mo	·moh

I will be at the market at noon.

| *Nitakuweko* | nee·ta·koo·*way*·koh |
| *sokoni saa sita.* | soh·*koh*·nee sa *see*·ta |

(lit: I-*future*-be-there market-at hour six)

In addition, if something is at a specific place, the word for that place will often take the suffix -ni:

| **store** | *duka* | *doo*·ka |
| **at the store** | *dukani* | doo·*ka*·nee |

In the present tense, the locative suffixes are used with the subject prefixes in the table below, depending on the person or thing whose location is pointed out:

subject prefixes used when making statements			
I	*ni-*	we	*tu-*
you sg	*u-*	you pl	*m-*
he/she (person)*	*yu-*	they (people)*	*wa-*
it (object) (survival swahili)	*i-*	they (objects) (survival swahili)	*zi-*

subjects prefixes used for negating			
I	*si-*	we	*hatu-*
you sg	*hu-*	you pl	*ham-*
he/she (person)*	*hayu-*	they (people)*	*hawa-*
it (object) (survival swahili)	*hai-*	they (objects) (survival swahili)	*hazi-*

* or animal(s)

Is she at school?
Yuko shuleni?   yoo·koh shoo·*lay*·nee
(lit: she-there school-at)

She is not here.
Hayupo.   ha·*yoo*·poh
(lit: she-not-here)

For past and future tenses, use the forms of the verb 'be' from page 20 and attach the suffix directly to the verb. Adding the locative suffix will always change the stress of the verb to the syllable immediately before the suffix. Swahili speakers often change the final *-wa* to *-we* before adding the locative suffix.

Was he at the hotel?
Alikuwako gestini?   a·lee·koo·*wa*·koh gay·*stee*·nee
(lit: he-*past*-be-there hotel-at)

We won't be here tomorrow.
Hatutakuwepo kesho.   ha·too·ta·koo·*way*·poh *kay*·shoh
(lit: not-we-*future*-be-here tomorrow)

negatives

Negative verbs are formed in a similar way to positive verbs (see **verbs**), but with different subject prefixes and different tense markers.

negative subject prefixes			
I	*si-*	we	*hatu-*
you sg	*hu-*	you pl	*ham-*
he/she (person)*	*ha-*	they (person)*	*hawa-*
it (object) (survival swahili)	*hai-*	they (object) (survival swahili)	*hazi-*

* or animal(s)

Negative tense markers for past and future tense are *-ku-* and *-ta-* respectively:

I didn't know.	*Sikujua.*	see·koo·*joo*·a
	(lit: not-me-*past*-know)	
It won't rain.	*Haitanyesha.*	ha·ee·ta·*nyay*·sha
	(lit: not-it-*future*-rain)	

In the present tense, however, no tense marker is used, but there's a twist – if the verb ends in an *-a*, that final *-a* changes to an *-i*.

know	*-jua*	·*joo*·a
I don't know.	*Sijui.*	see·*joo*·ee
	(lit: not-me-know)	

For negative forms of the verb **be**, see page 19.

nouns

describing things • naming things/people

Nouns in Swahili are divided into groups with similar qualities or characteristics called 'noun classes'. What noun class something belongs to determines many other things in a sentence – for example, the subject prefix or object infix of the verb, the prefix of any associated adjectives, and the demonstrative and possessive pronouns to use.

Although Swahili has 16 noun classes, you can get by with the basic sets of rules shown in all the tables of this chapter. The others cover concepts you can explore if you're inspired to study Swahili in greater depth. Most noun classes come in pairs for the singular and the plural (with a different prefix for the two forms). The prefixes for noun classes that will allow you to get by are given in pairs below:

noun classes			
prefix sg	example	prefix pl	example
m- (person or animal)	**mke** m·kay wife	wa- (person or animal)	**wake** wa·kay wives
m-	**mto** m·toh river	mi-	**mito** mee·toh rivers
no prefix	**embe** aym·bay mango	ma-	**maembe** ma·aym·bay mangoes
ji-	**jicho** jee·choh eye	ma-	**macho** ma·choh eyes
ki-	**kiatu** kee·a·too shoe	vi-	**viatu** vee·a·too shoes
ch-	**choo** choh toilet	vy-	**vyoo** vyoh toilets
u-	**ukuta** oo·koo·ta wall	no prefix	**kuta** koo·ta walls

Many nouns are the same in the singular and the plural – the only way to tell whether a speaker is referring to one or several things is by looking at the associated grammatical elements within the sentence:

This bird flies.

> *Ndege huyu anaruka.* n·*day*·gay hoo·yoo a·na·*roo*·ka
> (lit: bird this it-*present*-fly)

These birds fly.

> *Ndege hawa wanaruka.* n·*day*·gay *ha*·wa wa·na·*roo*·ka
> (lit: bird these they-*present*-fly)

personal pronouns

doing things · making a statement

Personal pronouns in Swahili have just one form for both subject (eg 'I', 'they') and object ('me', 'them') in a sentence.

I/me	mimi	mee·mee
you sg	wewe	way·way
he/she/him/her/it	yeye	yay·yay
we/us	sisi	see·see
you pl	ninyi/nyinyi	nee·nyee/nyee·nyee
they/them	wao	wa·oh

Personal pronouns are often not necessary as subject of a sentence, as the form of Swahili verbs already indicates who that is. Using the personal pronoun in such a case often has the same effect as putting an exclamation point at the end of your sentence:

I want food.

> *Ninataka chakula.* nee·na·*ta*·ka cha·*koo*·la
> (lit: I-*present*-want food)

I want food!

> *Mimi ninataka chakula.* *mee*·mee nee·na·*ta*·ka cha·*koo*·la
> (lit: I I-*present*-want food)

You can sometimes, however, use the personal pronoun instead of a verb construction in answer to a direct question:

Who wants food?

   Nani anataka chakula?   na·nee a·na·*ta*·ka cha·*koo*·la

   (lit: who *third-person-sg-present*-want food)

I do.

   Mimi.   *mee*·mee

   (lit: me)

possession

naming things/people • possessing

To say that a thing belongs to someone or something, you can either use the word 'of' with the name of the possessor, or you can use a possessive pronoun. The possessive pronouns have a prefix and a suffix, which change according to different patterns. The suffix changes according to who or what is the possessor:

english equivalent	pronoun suffix	
my	*-angu*	*an* goo
your sg	*-ako*	·*a*·koh
his/her/its	*-ake*	·*a*·kay
our	*-etu*	·*ay*·too
your pl	*-enu*	·*ay*·noo
their	*-ao*	·*a*·oh

This is our camera.

   Hii ni kemra yetu.   hee nee *kaym*·ra *yay*·too

   (lit: this be camera our)

Both the possessive pronoun prefix and the word 'of' change according to the noun class qualities of the thing being possessed:

noun qualities	pronoun prefix	'of'	swahili example	english example
person or animal sg&pl	w-	wa	*mtoto wangu* m·*toh*·toh *wan*·goo	**my child**
object sg (survival swahili)	y-	ya	*pikipiki yako* pee·kee·*pee*·kee *ya*·koh	**your motorcycle**
object pl (survival swahili)	z-	za	*nyumba zetu* nyoom·ba *zay*·too	**our houses**

If you use the word 'of' instead of the pronoun, this word and the name of the possessor always go after the thing being possessed:

today's news *habari za leo* ha·*ba*·ree za *lay*·oh
(lit: news of today)

prepositions

giving directions/orders • indicating location

Prepositions always come before the word they go with:

since yesterday *tangu jana* *tan*·goo *ja*·na

across from, opposite	*ng'ambo ya*	ng·*am*·boh ya
after	*baada ya*	ba·*a*·da ya
at	*kwenye*	*kway*·nyay
before	*kabla*	*ka*·bla
from	*kutoka*	koo·*toh*·ka
in	*katika*	ka·*tee*·ka
on	*juu ya*	joo ya
since	*tangu*	*tan*·goo
to	*hadi*	*ha*·dee

questions

asking a question

To ask a question in Swahili, use the word *je*. It essentially means 'hey, I'm asking a question' and can go either at the beginning or the end of a sentence:

What's your name?
  Jina lako ni nani, je?   jee·na *la*·koh nee *na*·nee jay
  (lit: name your be who *question*)

The word *je* has one other function – if you attach it directly to the verb in a sentence, it serves as the question word 'how?':

How do you say …?
  Unasemaje …?   oo·na·say·*ma*·jay …
  (lit: you-*present*-say-how)

You can also turn most statements into questions simply by raising intonation at the end of a sentence.

  For question words, see the **dictionary** (page 195). To answer a direct question, see **personal pronouns**.

requests

giving directions/orders

Basic requests are very easy. To tell one person to do something, simply use the verb stem (dictionary form of a verb). To tell more than one person to do something, add the suffix *-ni* to the verb stem (if the verb stem ends in an *-a*, it changes to an *-e*).

english	verb stem	request sg	request pl
run	*-kimbia* keem·*bee*·a	*kimbia* keem·*bee*·a	*kimbieni* keem·bee·*ay*·nee
return	*-rudi* roo·dee	*rudi* roo·dee	*rudini* roo·*dee*·nee
speak	*-sema* say·ma	*sema* say·ma	*semeni* say·*may*·nee

A few verbs have irregular request forms:

english	verb stem	request sg	request pl
come	*-ja* ·ja	*njoo* n·joh	*njooni* n·joh·nee
go	*-enda* ·ayn·da	*nenda* nayn·da	*nendeni* nayn·day·nee

there is/are

making a statement · negating · pointing things out

The word *kuna* corresponds to both 'there is' and 'there are'. The word *hakuna* is used for 'there isn't' and 'there aren't'.

There are two passengers.
Kuna abiria wawili.   koo·na a·bee·*ree*·a wa·*wee*·lee
(lit: there-are passengers two)

There isn't any toilet paper.
Hakuna karatasi ya choo.   ha·*koo*·na ka·ra·*ta*·see ya *choh*
(lit: there-are-not paper of toilet)

verbs

doing things

Most verbs in Swahili follow a very regular (although often quite complex) set of rules. The Swahili verb has slots for different elements. A basic verb consists of a subject prefix, a tense marker and a verb stem. The table below shows these and other slots (such as object infix and suffix) that can be filled within the structure of a verb:

verb slots				
subject prefix	tense marker	object infix	verb stem	suffix
a-	*-na-*	*-tu-*	*-pik(a)-*	*-ia*

He is cooking for us.

    Anatupikia.   a·na·too·peek·*ee*·a

    (lit: he-now-us-cooks-for)

As you can see in the table below, the subject prefix changes depending on the noun class of the subject ('he'), while the object infix depends on the noun class of the object ('us').

noun qualities	subject prefix	negative subject prefix	object infix
I/me	*ni-*	*si-*	*-ni-*
you sg	*u-*	*hu-*	*-ku-*
he/she (person or animal – often begins with *m*-)	*a-*	*ha-*	*-m-/-mw-*
it (object) (survival swahili)	*i-*	*hai-*	*-i-*
we/us	*tu-*	*hatu-*	*-tu-*
you pl	*m-*	*ham-*	*-wa-*
they (person or animal – often begins with *wn*-)	*wa-*	*hawa-*	*-wa-*
they (object) (survival swahili)	*zi-*	*hazi-*	*-zi-*

As the example below shows, both the direct object ('the book') and the indirect object ('me') use the same set of infixes, although if you have both a direct and an indirect object in the sentence, only the indirect object will be marked in the object slot within the verb.

He gave the book to me.

    Alinipa kitabu.   a·lee·*nee*·pa kee·*ta*·boo

    (lit: he-*past*-me-give book)

He gave it.

    Alikipa.   a·lee·*kee*·pa

    (lit: he-*past*-it-give)

The following are the most common tense markers that you'll come across:

tense	tense marker	swahili example	english example
present	-na-	*ninasoma* nee·na·*soh*·ma	I am reading
past (completed action)	-li-	*nilisoma* nee·lee·*soh*·ma	I read
past (recent or ongoing action)	-me-	*nimesoma* nee·may·*soh*·ma	I have read
future	-ta-	*nitasoma* nee·ta·*soh*·ma	I will read

If you take one subject prefix, one tense marker, and one verb stem, you can make a basic verb:

He said ... *Alisema ...* a·lee·*say*·ma ...
(lit: he-*past*-say)

If your sentence has an object, put the appropriate infix between the tense marker and the verb stem.

I will marry you. *Nitakuoa.* nee·ta·koo·*oh*·a
(lit: I-will-you-marry)

For information on negative verbs, see **negatives**.

word order

making a statement

Swahili sentences are usually constructed in the order subject-verb-object, just like in English:

The elephants eat grass.
Tembo wanakula nyasi. *taym*·boh wa·na·*koo*·la *nya*·see
(lit: elephants eat grass)

For word order in questions and negative statements, see **questions** and **negatives**.

glossary

adjective	a word that describes something – 'a **long** journey'
adverb	a word that explains how an action was done – 'he walked **slowly**'
article	the words 'a/an' and 'the'
demonstrative pronoun	a word like 'this/these' or 'that/those' used to point something out
infix	syllable(s) inserted in the middle of a word, eg to show what the object in the sentence is
locative suffix	syllable(s) added to the end of a word to indicate location
noun	a thing, person or idea, eg 'table'
object	the thing or person in the sentence that has the action directed to it, eg in 'Please bring me the menu', 'the menu' is the direct object and 'me' is the indirect object
possesive pronoun	a word that conveys the meaning 'mine', 'yours', 'ours', 'theirs', etc
prefix	syllable(s) added to the beginning of a word, eg to show who the subject in the sentence is
preposition	a word like 'from' or 'after' in English
pronoun	a word that means 'you', 'she', etc

subject	the thing or person in the sentence that does the action – '**I** took the train'
suffix	syllable(s) added to the end of a word to modify its meaning, eg **-ly** is added to 'happy' to make 'happily'
tense marker	*infix* in a verb which shows the time an action takes place, ie past, present, future
verb	the word that tells you what action happened – eg 'I **saw** the book'
verb stem	the dictionary form of a verb, which doesn't change – 'search' in 'searched' and 'searching'

Do you speak (English)?
Unasema (Kiingereza)? oo·na·*say*·ma (kee·een·gay·*ray*·za)

Does anyone speak (English)?
Kuna mtu yeyote *koo*·na m·too yay·*yoh*·tay
kusema (Kiingereza)? koo·*say*·ma (kee·een·gay·*ray*·za)

Do you understand?
Unaelewa? oo·na·ay·*lay*·wa

Yes, I understand.
Ndiyo, naelewa. n·*dee*·yoh na·ay·*lay*·wa

No, I don't understand.
Hapana, sielewi. ha·*pa*·na see·ay·*lay*·wee

I understand.
Naelewa. na·ay·*lay*·wa

I don't understand.
Sielewi. see·ay·*lay*·wee

speaking sheng

While travelling around Kenya, you might come across Sheng, a mixture of Swahili and English with a fair sprinkling of other local languages. It's spoken almost exclusively by young people. Unless you're reasonably fluent in Swahili, you probably won't even realise Sheng is being spoken, so listen out for *sassa sa*·sa (distinctive greeting between friends). The response can be either *besht* baysht, *mambo mam*·boh or *fit* feet (all variations of 'hello').

I speak (English).
Nasema (Kiingereza). na·*say*·ma (kee·een·gay·*ray*·za)

I don't speak (Swahili).
Sisemi (Kiswahili). see·*say*·mee (kee·swa·*hee*·lee)

I speak a little.
Nasema kidogo. na·*say*·ma kee·*doh*·goh

What does 'asante' mean?
Neno 'asante' lina *nay*·noh a·*san*·tay *lee*·na
maana gani? ma·*a*·na *ga*·nee

How do you …?		
pronounce this	*Unatamkaje?*	oo·na·tam·*ka*·jay
write *'asante'*	*Unaandikaje*	oo·na·an·dee·*ka*·je
	'asante'?	a·*san*·tay

Could you please …?	*Tafadhali …*	ta·fa·*dha*·lee …
repeat that	*sema tena*	*say*·ma *tay*·na
speak more	*sema pole*	*say*·ma *poh*·lay
slowly	*pole*	*poh*·lay
write it down	*andika*	an·*dee*·ka

---

knock knock!

The word for 'stranger' in Swahili, *mgeni* m·*gay*·nee, is also the word for 'guest', and many East Africans enjoy welcoming strangers as guests not only to their countries but to their homes too.

You'll always be greeted with *karibu* ka·*ree*·boo (welcome). It's an all-purpose word, used to welcome visitors to the home, the business or even the country. It also means 'you're welcome' (when someone thanks you).

When entering someone's home or office, you should always announce your presence and your intent to come in by calling out *hodi* hoh·dee (Hello, may I enter?) before crossing the threshold. It can be accompanied by knocking on the door. Even if you're being escorted in by the inhabitant, it's polite to pause at the door and say *hodi*.

numbers & amounts

cardinal numbers

namba kamili

0	*sifuri*	see·*foo*·ree
1	*moja*	*moh*·ja
2	*mbili*	m·*bee*·lee
3	*tatu*	*ta*·too
4	*nne*	n·nay
5	*tano*	*ta*·noh
6	*sita*	*see*·ta
7	*saba*	*sa*·ba
8	*nane*	*na*·nay
9	*tisa*	*tee*·sa
10	*kumi*	*koo*·mee
11	*kumi na moja*	*koo*·mee na *moh*·ja
12	*kumi na mbili*	*koo*·mee na m·*bee*·lee
13	*kumi na tatu*	*koo*·mee na *ta*·too
14	*kumi na nne*	*koo*·mee na n·nay
15	*kumi na tano*	*koo*·mee na *ta*·noh
16	*kumi na sita*	*koo*·mee na *see*·ta
17	*kumi na saba*	*koo*·mee na *sa*·ba
18	*kumi na nane*	*koo*·mee na *na*·nay
19	*kumi na tisa*	*koo*·mee na *tee*·sa
20	*ishirini*	ee·shee·*ree*·nee
21	*ishirini na moja*	ee·shee·*ree*·nee na *moh*·ja
30	*thelathini*	thay·la·*thee*·nee
40	*arobaini*	a·roh·ba·*ee*·nee
50	*hamsini*	ham·*see*·nee
60	*sitini*	see·*tee*·nee
70	*sabini*	sa·*bee*·nee
80	*themanini*	thay·ma·*nee*·nee
90	*tisini*	tee·*see*·nee
100	*mia moja*	*mee*·a *moh*·ja
1,000	*elfu*	*ayl*·foo
100,000	*laki*	*la*·kee

ordinal numbers

For persons and animals, use *wa* wa. For objects, use *ya* ya before the cardinal number – '1st' and '2nd' are irregular though:

1st	*wa/ya kwanza*	wa/ya *kwan*·za
2nd	*wa/ya pili*	wa/ya *pee*·lee
3rd	*wa/ya tatu*	wa/ya *ta*·too
4th	*wa/ya nne*	wa/ya *n*·nay
5th	*wa/ya tano*	wa/ya *ta*·noh

fractions

a quarter	*robo moja*	*roh*·boh *moh*·ja
a third	*theluthi moja*	thay·*loo*·thee *moh*·ja
a half	*nusu*	*noo*·soo
three-quarters	*robo tatu*	*roh*·boh *ta*·too
all	*jumla*	*joom*·la
none	*hakuna*	ha·*koo*·na

useful amounts

How much?	*Kiasi gani?*	kee·*a*·see *ga*·nee
How many?	*Ngapi?*	n·*ga*·pee
(Please) give me ...	*(Tafadhali) nipe ...*	(ta·fa·*dha*·lee) *nee*·pay ...
less	*chache zaidi*	*cha*·chay za·*ee*·dee
(just) a little	*kidogo (tu)*	kee·*doh*·goh (too)
a lot	*kingi*	*keen*·gee
more	*zaidi*	za·*ee*·dee
some	*kiasi*	kee·*a*·see

telling the time

The word for time, *saa* sa, also means 'hour', 'watch' and 'clock'. Time and hours are distinguished by different noun classes, so *saa mbili* sa m·*bee*·lee (lit: clocks two) means '2 o'clock Swahili time/8 o'clock European time' while *masaa mawili* ma·*sa* ma·*wee*·lee (lit: hours two) means 'two hours'. (For more on noun classes, see the **phrasebuilder**.)

What time is it?
 Ni saa ngapi? — nee sa n·*ga*·pee

It's (ten) o'clock.
 Ni saa (nne). — nee sa (*n*·nay)

Five past (ten).
 Ni saa (nne) na tano. — nee sa (*n*·nay) na *ta*·noh

Quarter past (ten).
 Ni saa (nne) na robo. — nee sa (*n*·nay) na *roh*·boh

Half past (ten).
 Ni saa (nne) na nusu. — nee sa (*n*·nay) na *noo*·soo

Quarter to (ten).
 Ni saa (nne) kasarobo. — nee sa (*n*·nay) ka·sa·*roh*·boh

Twenty to (ten).
 Ni saa (nne) kasoro ishirini. — nee sa (*n*·nay) ka·*soh*·roh ee·she·*ree*·nee

what's the time?

The Swahili time system starts six hours later compared to the international one. It begins at sunrise which occurs at about 6am all year round. This system causes endless confusion for visitors to East Africa, especially as many people set their watches using the international system and then try to read them according to the Swahili system. Your best bet is to verify which system is being used – international time, *saa za kizungu* sa za kee·zoon·goo, or Swahili time, *saa za kiswahili* sa za kee·swa·hee·lee. Since people usually specify what period of the day they're talking about, you can determine which time system they're using from context.

International time		Swahili time
midnight	6	*saa sita usiku*
1am	7	*saa saba usiku wa manane*
2	8	*saa nane usiku wa manane*
3	9	*saa tisa usiku wa manane*
4	10	*saa kumi alfajiri*
5	11	*saa kumi na moja alfajiri*
6am (sunrise)	12	*saa kumi na mbili asubuhi*
7	1	*saa moja asubuhi*
8	2	*saa mbili asubuhi*
9	3	*saa tatu asubuhi*
10	4	*saa nne asubuhi*
11	5	*saa tano asubuhi*
noon	6	*saa sita mchana*
1pm	7	*saa saba mchana*
2	8	*saa nane mchana*
3	9	*saa tisa mchana*
4	10	*saa kumi mchana*
5	11	*saa kumi na moja jioni*
6pm (sundown)	12	*saa kumi na mbili jioni*
7	1	*saa moja jioni*
8	2	*saa mbili usiku*
9	3	*saa tatu usiku*
10	4	*saa nne usiku*
11	5	*saa tano usiku*
midnight	6	*saa sita usiku*

morning	*asubuhi*	a·soo·*boo*·hee
afternoon	*mchana*	m·*cha*·na
evening	*jioni*	jee·*oh*·nee
At what time ...?	*... saa ngapi?*	... sa n·*ga*·pee
At (ten).	*Saa (nne).*	sa (*n*·nay)
At (7.57pm).	*Saa (mbili*	sa (m·*bee*·lee
	kasoro dakika	ka·*soh*·roh da·*kee*·ka
	tatu jioni).	*ta*·too jee·*oh*·ni)

the calendar

kalenda

days

Monday	*Jumatatu*	joo·ma·*ta*·too
Tuesday	*Jumanne*	joo·ma·*n*·nay
Wednesday	*Jumatano*	joo·ma·*ta*·noh
Thursday	*Alhamisi*	al·ha·*mee*·see
Friday	*Ijumaa*	ee·joo·*ma*
Saturday	*Jumamosi*	joo·ma·*moh*·see
Sunday	*Jumapili*	joo·ma·*pee*·lee

months

Swahili has two systems for counting months: one consisting of English soundalikes that foreigners like to use and the one that Swahili speakers commonly use. It's best, however, to use the second system, which simply counts months as ordinal numbers starting with January. At a pinch, though, many people will understand the English version.

January	mwezi wa kwanza	mway·zee wa kwan·za
February	mwezi wa pili	mway·zee wa pee·lee
March	mwezi wa tatu	mway·zee wa ta·too
April	mwezi wa nne	mway·zee wa n·nay
May	mwezi wa tano	mway·zee wa ta·noh
June	mwezi wa sita	mway·zee wa see·ta
July	mwezi wa saba	mway·zee wa sa·ba
August	mwezi wa nane	mway·zee wa na·nay
September	mwezi wa tisa	mway·zee wa tee·sa
October	mwezi wa kumi	mway·zee wa koo·mee
November	mwezi wa kumi na moja	mway·zee wa koo·mee na moh·ja
December	mwezi wa kumi na mbili	mway·zee wa koo·mee na m·bee·lee

dates

What date is it today?
   Leo ni tarehe gani?   lay·oh nee ta·ray·hay ga·nee

It's (18 October).
   Ni (tarehe kumi na   nee (ta·ray·hay koo·mee na
   nane, mwezi wa kumi).   na·nay mway·zee wa koo·mee)

seasons

The seasons in East Africa don't correspond to those of other parts of the world. They vary greatly depending on altitude and latitude. *Kiangazi* kee·an·ga·zee (lit: dry-season), which roughly corresponds to June, July and August, can be cold in the southern highlands of Tanzania, pleasant on the coast and hot in the northern regions of Kenya. People may refer to the following seasons but have different times of year in mind:

... season	kipindi ...	kee·peen·dee ...
cold	cha baridi	cha ba·ree·dee
harvest	cha kuvuna	cha koo·voo·na
hot	cha joto	cha joh·toh
rainy	cha mvua	cha m·voo·a

present

now	*sasa*	*sa*·sa
today	*leo*	*lay*·oh
tonight	*leo usiku*	*lay*·oh oo·*see*·koo
this...		
morning	*asubuhi hii*	a·soo·*boo*·hee hee
afternoon	*mchana huu*	m·*cha*·na hoo
week	*wiki hii*	*wee*·kee hee
month	*mwezi huu*	*mway*·zee hoo
year	*mwaka huu*	*mwa*·ka hoo

past

day before yesterday	*juzi*	*joo*·zee
(three) days ago	*siku (tatu) zilizopita*	*see*·koo (*ta*·too) zee·lee·zo·*pee*·ta
(three) months ago	*miezi (mitatu) iliyopita*	mee·*ay*·zee (mee·*ta*·too) ee·lee·yoh·*pee*·ta
since (May)	*tangu (mwezi wa tano)*	*tan*·goo (*mway*·zee wa *ta*·noh)
last ...		
night	*jana usiku*	*ja*·na oo·*see*·koo
week	*wiki jana*	*wee*·kee *ja*·na
month	*mwezi uliopita*	*mway*·zee oo·lee·oh·*pee*·ta
year	*mwaka uliopita*	*mwa*·ka oo·lee·oh·*pee*·ta
yesterday ...	*jana ...*	*ja*·na ...
morning	*asubuhi*	a·soo·*boo*·hee
afternoon	*mchana*	m·*cha*·na
evening	*jioni*	jee·*oh*·nee

time & dates

43

future

day after tomorrow	kesho kutwa	kay·shoh koot·wa
in (six days)	baada ya (siku sita)	ba·a·da ya (see·koo see·ta)
until (June)	mpaka (mwezi wa sita)	m·pa·ka (mway·zee wa see·ta)
next ...	... kesho	... kay·shoh
week	wiki	wee·kee
month	mwezi	mway·zee
year	mwaka	mwa·ka
tomorrow ...	kesho ...	kay·shoh ...
morning	asubuhi	a·soo·boo·hee
afternoon	mchana	m·cha·na
evening	jioni	jee·oh·nee

during the day

afternoon	mchana	m·cha·na
dawn	alfajiri	al·fa·jee·ree
day	siku	see·koo
evening	jioni	jee·oh·nee
midday	saa sita mchana	sa see·ta m·cha·na
midnight	saa sita usiku	sa see·ta oo·see·koo
morning	asubuhi	a·soo·boo·hee
night	usiku	oo·see·koo
sunrise	macheo	ma·chay·oh
sunset	magharibi	mag·ha·ree·bee

How much is it?
Ni bei gani?   ni bay *ga*·nee

It's free.
Ni bure.   nee *boo*·ray

It's (500) shillings.
Ni shilingi (mia tano).   nee shee·*leen*·gee (*mee*·a ta·noh)

Can you write down the price?
Andika bei.   an·*dee*·ka bay

There's a mistake in the bill.
Kuna kosa kwenye bili.   koo·na koh·sa *kwayn*·yay *bee*·le

Do you accept …?	*Mnakubali …*	m·na·koo·*ba*·lee …
credit cards	*kadi ya benki*	*ka*·dee ya *bayn*·kee
travellers	*hundi ya*	*hoon*·dee ya
cheques	*msafiri*	m·sa·*fee*·ree
I'd like to …	*Nataka …*	na·*ta*·ka …
cash a cheque	*kulipwa fedha*	koo·*leep*·wa *fay*·dha
	kutokana	koo·toh·*ka*·na
	na hundi	na *hoon*·dee
change a	*kubadilisha*	koo·ba·dee·*lee*·sha
travellers	*hundi ya*	*hoon*·dee ya
cheque	*msafiri*	m·sa·*fee*·ree
change money	*kubadilisha*	koo·ba·dee·*lee*·sha
	hela	*hay*·la
get a cash	*kupata hela*	koo·*pa*·ta *hay*·la
advance	*ya awali*	ya *a*·wa·lee
withdraw money	*kuondoa hela*	koo·ohn·*doh*·a *hay*·la

Where's ...?	... iko wapi?	... ee·koh wa·pee
an automated teller machine	mashine ya kutolea pesa	ma·shee·nay ya koo·toh·lay·a pay·sa
a foreign exchange office	foreks	foh·rayks

What's the ...?	... ni nini?	... nee nee·nee
charge	gharama yake	ga·ra·ma ya·kay
exchange rate	kiwango cha kubadilisha hela	kee·wan·goh cha koo·ba·dee·lee·sha hay·la

I'd like ..., please.	Nataka ..., tafadhali.	na·ta·ka ... ta·fa·dha·lee
a refund	unirudishie hela	oo·nee·roo·dee·shee·ay hay·la
a receipt	risiti	ree·see·tee
my change	chenji yangu	chayn·jee yan·goo
to return this	kurudisha kitu hiki	koo·roo·dee·sha kee·too hee·kee

coast, island or town?

The Swahili name for Zanzibar Island is Unguja. It's often used locally to distinguish the island from the Zanzibar Archipelago (which also includes Pemba), as well as from Zanzibar Town (called Mji Mkongwe or Stone Town).

The word 'Zanzibar' comes from the Arabic Zinj el-Barr (lit: Land of the Blacks). It was used by Arab traders from the 8th century to refer to both the archipelago and the adjacent coast. Now, the name refers exclusively to the archipelago.

getting around

kutembea

Which ... goes to (Mbeya)?	... ipi huenda (Mbeya)?	... ee·pee hoo·ayn·da (m·bay·a)
Is this the ... to (Mombasa)?	Hii ni ... kwenda (Mombasa)?	hee nee ... kwayn·da (mohm·ba·sa)
boat	Boti	boh·tee
bus	Basi	ba·see
ferry	Kivuko	kee·voo·koh
minibus	Daladala/ Matatu **Tan/Ken**	da·la·da·la/ ma·ta·too
train	Treni	tray·nee

When's the ... bus?	Basi ... itaondoka lini?	ba·see ... ee·ta·ohn·doh·ka lee·nee
first	ya kwanza	ya kwan·za
last	ya mwisho	ya mwee·shoh
next	ijayo	ee·ja·yoh

Is the ... going today/tomorrow?
... itaenda leo/kesho?   ... ee·ta·ayn·da lay·oh/kay·shoh

What time does it leave?
Itaondoka saa ngapi?   ee·ta·ohn·doh·ka sa n·ga·pee

What time does it get to (Kisuma)?
Itafika (Kisumu)   ee·ta·fee·ka (kee·soo·moo)
saa ngapi?   sa n·ga·pee

How long will it be delayed?
　Itachelewa kwa　　　　　　ee·ta·chay·lay·wa kwa
　muda gani?　　　　　　　　moo·da ga·nee

Is this seat free?
　Kuna nafasi hapa?　　　　　koo·na na·fa·see ha·pa

That's my seat.
　Hiki ni kiti changu.　　　　hee·kee nee kee·tee chan·goo

Please tell me when we get to (Moshi).
　Niambie tukifika　　　　　nee·am·bee·ay too·kee·fee·ka
　(Moshi).　　　　　　　　　(moh·shee)

Please stop here.
　Simama hapa,　　　　　　see·ma·ma ha·pa
　tafadhali.　　　　　　　　ta·fa·dha·lee

How long do we stop here?
　Tutakaa hapa kwa　　　　too·ta·ka ha·pa kwa
　muda gani?　　　　　　　moo·da ga·nee

I'm sorry, I've changed my mind.
　Samahani,　　　　　　　sa·ma·ha·nee
　nimebadili nia.　　　　　nee·may·ba·dee·lee nee·a

hop on, hop off

The most common word people call out to get a bus to stop is *shusha* *shoo*·sha (drop off). It's also considered slang. Pay attention to the way East Africans deliver the line. If you casually call *shusha* the same way when you want to get off, you can sometimes bring an entire bus to laughter.

On the other hand, if you're standing by the side of the road and you want to get a local bus to stop, simply extend your arm fully and flap your hand like a whale's tail.

tickets

A ... ticket	Tiketi moja	tee-*kay*-tee *moh*-ja
to (Iringa).	ya ... kwenda (Iringa).	ya ... *kwayn*-da (ee-*reen*-ga)
1st-class	daraja la kwanza	da-*ra*-ja la *kwan*-za
2nd-class	daraja la pili	da-*ra*-ja la *pee*-lee
child's	mtoto	m-*toh*-toh
one-way	kwenda tu	*kwayn*-da too
return	kwenda na kurudi	*kwayn*-da na koo-*roo*-dee
student	mwanafunzi	mwa-na-*foon*-zee

I'd like a/an ... seat.	Nataka kiti ...	na-*ta*-ka *kee*-tee ...
aisle	jirani ya njia	jee-*ra*-nee ya n-*jee*-a
nonsmoking	kutovuta sigara	koo-toh-*voo*-ta see-*ga*-ra
smoking	kuvuta sigara	koo-*voo*-ta see-*ga*-ra
window	jirani ya dirisha	jee-*ra*-nee ya dee-*ree*-sha

Is there (a) ...?	Kuna ...?	*koo*-na ...
air conditioning	a/c	*ay*-see
blanket	blanketi	blan-*kay*-tee
sick bag	mfuko wa kutapikia	m-*foo*-koh wa koo-ta-pee-*kee*-a
toilet	choo	choh

Where do I buy a ticket?

| Ninunue tiketi wapi? | nee-noo-*noo*-ay tee-*kay*-tee *wa*-pee |

Do I need to book?

| Ni lazima nifanye buking? | nee *la*-zee-ma nee-*fa*-nyay *boo*-keeng |

How much is it?

| Ni bei gani? | nee bay *ga*-nee |

How long does the trip take?

Safari huchukua
muda gani?
sa·*fa*·ree hoo·choo·*koo*·a
moo·da *ga*·nee

Is it a direct route?

Njia ni moja
kwa moja?
n·*jee*·a nee *moh*·ja
kwa *moh*·ja

Can I get a stand-by ticket?

Naweza kununua
tiketi kutumia kama
nafasi ikipatikana?
na·*way*·za koo·noo·*noo*·a
tee·*kay*·tee koo·too·*mee*·a *ka*·ma
na·*fa*·si ee·kee·pa·tee·*ka*·na

Can I get a sleeping berth?

Naweza kupata
kitanda?
na·*way*·za koo·*pa*·ta
kee·*tan*·da

What time should I check in?

Ripoting ni saa ngapi?
ree·*pot*·eeng nee sa n·*ga*·pee

I'd like to … my ticket, please.	Nataka … tiketi yangu tafadhali.	na·*ta*·ka … tee·*kay*·tee yan·goo ta·fa·*dha*·lee
cancel	kufuta	koo·*foo*·ta
change	kubadilisha	koo·ba·dee·*lee*·sha
confirm	kuhakikisha	koo·ha·kee·*kee*·sha

---

listen for ...

dirisha la tiketi	dee·*ree*·sha la tee·*kay*·tee	**ticket window**
hii	hee	**this one**
hiyo	hee·yoh	**that one**
imeche leweshwa	ee·may·chay lay·*waysh*·wa	**delayed**
imefutwa	ee·may·*foot*·wa	**cancelled**
imejaa	ee·may·*ja*	**full**
mgomo	m·*goh*·moh	**strike**
ratiba	ra·*tee*·ba	**timetable**
stendi	*stayn*·dee	**platform**
uwakala wa safiri	oo·*wa*·ka·la wa sa·*fee*·ree	**travel agent**

luggage

mizigo

Where can I find ...?	... iko wapi?	... ee·koh wa·pee
the baggage claim	Sehemu ya kuchukulia mizigo	say·hay·moo ya koo·choo·koo·lee·a mee·zee·goh
the left-luggage office	Chumba cha kuwekea mizigo	choom·ba cha koo·way·kay·a mee·zee·goh
a luggage locker	Sanduku la kuhifadhia mizigo	san·doo·koo la koo·hee·fa·dhee·a mee·zee·goh
a trolley	Kigari	kee·ga·ree

My luggage	Mizigo	mee·zee·goh
has been ...	yangu ...	yan·goo ...
damaged	imeharibiwa	ee·may·ha·ree·bee·wa
lost	imepotea	ee·may·poh·tay·a
stolen	imeibwa	ee·may·eeb·wa

That's mine.
Ni yangu.   nee yan·goo

That's not mine.
Si yangu.   see yan·goo

Can I put my bag here?
Naweza kuweka   na·way·za koo·way·ka
mzigo wangu hapa?   m·zee·goh wan·goo ha·pa

Can I have some coins?
Nataka sarafu.   na·ta·ka sa·ra·foo

plane

ndege

Where does flight (number 432) arrive/depart?
Ndege (namba mia   n·day·gay (nam·ba mee·a
nne thelathini   n·nay thay·la·thee·nee
na mbili) itafika/   na m·bee·lee) ee·ta·fee·ka/
itaondoka wapi?   ee·ta·ohn·doh·ka wa·pee

I'd like to charter a plane to ...
Nataka kukodisha   na·ta·ka koo·koh·dee·sha
ndege kwenda ...   n·day·gay kwayn·da ...

Where's (the) ...?	... iko wapi?	... ee·koh wa·pee
airport	Basi ya uwanja	ba·see ya oo·wan·ja
shuttle	wa ndege	wa n·day·gay
arrivals hall	Wanaofika	wa·na·oh·fee·ka
departures hall	Wanaoondoka	wa·na·oh·ohn·doh·ka
duty-free shop	Duty-free	doo·tee·free
gate (3)	Mlango (tatu)	m·lan·goh (ta·too)

bus & coach

mabasi

Can you recommend a reliable/safe bus company?

Kampuni gani ina mabasi yenye uaminifu/usalama?   kam·*poo*·nee *ga*·nee *ee*·na ma·*ba*·see *yay*·nyay oo·a·mee·*nee*·foo/oo·sa·*la*·ma

How often do buses come?

Mabasi hufika muda gani?   ma·*ba*·see hoo·*fee*·ka *moo*·da *ga*·nee

What time is this bus leaving?

Basi hili litaondoka saa ngapi?   *ba*·see *hee*·lee lee·ta·ohn·*doh*·ka sa n·*ga*·pee

Does it stop at (Tanga)?

Linasimama (Tanga)?   lee·na·see·*ma*·ma (*tan*·ga)

What's the next stop?

Kipi ni kituo kijacho?   *kee*·pee nee kee·*too*·oh kee·*ja*·choh

transport

53

I'd like to get off at (Bagamoyo).

Nataka kushusha (Bagamoyo). — na·*ta*·ka koo·*shoo*·sha (ba·ga·*moh*·yoh)

Drop me off here!

Nishushe hapa! — nee·*shoo*·shay *ha*·pa

city bus	daladala/ matatu **Tan/Ken**	da·la·*da*·la/ ma·*ta*·too
express bus	basi ya moja kwa moja	*ba*·see ya *moh*·ja kwa *moh*·ja
intercity	baini ya miji	ba·*ee*·nee ya *mee*·jee
local bus	basi linalosimama katika kila kituo	*ba*·see lee·na·loh·see·*ma*·ma ka·*tee*·ka *kee*·la kee·*too*·oh

train

What station is this?

Hiki ni stesheni gani? — *hee*·kee nee stay·*shay*·nee *ga*·nee

What's the next station?

Stesheni ijayo itakuwa mji gani? — stay·*shay*·nee ee·*ja*·yoh ee·ta·*koo*·wa m·jee *ga*·nee

Does it stop at (Dodoma)?

Itasimama (Dodoma)? — ee·ta·see·*ma*·ma (doh·*doh*·ma)

Do I need to change?

Itabidi nibadilishe? — ee·ta·*bee*·dee nee·ba·dee·*lee*·shay

Is it ...?	Ni ...?	nee ...
direct	treni hii kwa safari nzima	*tray*·nee hee kwa sa·*fa*·ree n·*zee*·ma
express	moja kwa moja kwa haraka	*moh*·ja kwa *moh*·ja kwa ha·*ra*·ka

Which carriage is (for) ...?	Behewa gani ni (kwa) ...?	bay·*hay*·wa *ga*·nee nee (kwa) ...
1st class	daraja la kwanza	da·*ra*·ja la *kwan*·za
dining	kula	*koo*·la
Tabora	Tabora	ta·*boh*·ra

express train	*treni ya moja kwa moja kwa haraka*	*tray*·nee ya *moh*·ja kwa *moh*·ja kwa ha·*ra*·ka
ordinary train	*treni ya kawaida*	*tray*·nee ya ka·wa·*ee*·da

boat

boti

What's the sea like today?
Bahari ikoje leo? ba·*ha*·ree ee·*koh*·jay *lay*·oh

Are there life jackets?
Kuna jaketi la kuokolea? *koo*·na ja·*kay*·tee la koo·oh·koh·*lay*·a

Which island is this?
Hiki ni kisiwa gani? *hee*·kee nee kee·*see*·wa *ga*·nee

Which beach is this?
Huu ni ufukwe gani? hoo nee oo·*fook*·way *ga*·nee

I feel seasick.
Nahitaji kutapika. na·hee·*ta*·jee koo·ta·*pee*·ka

boat	*boti*	*boh*·tee
cabin	*kibini*	kee·*bee*·nee
car deck	*sitaha ya magari*	see·*ta*·ha ya ma·*ga*·ree
deck	*sitaha*	see·*ta*·ha
ferry n	*kivuko*	kee·*voo*·koh
lifeboat	*mashua ya kuokolea*	ma·*shoo*·a ya koo·oh·koh·*lay*·a
life jacket	*jaketi la kuokolea*	ja·*kay*·tee la koo·oh·koh·*lay*·a
row boat	*mtumbwi*	m·*toom*·bwee
ship n	*meli*	*may*·lee
small wooden boat	*mashua*	ma·*shoo*·a
traditional sailing boat	*dhau*	*dha*·oo
yacht	*mashua ya anasa*	ma·*shoo*·a ya a·*na*·sa

taxi

The majority of taxis in East Africa have no signs. As taxis can be scarce, it's not unusual to share a taxi with strangers, and each person usually agrees on a price individually. Another option is to hire a *bodaboda/teksi ya baisikeli* Ken/Tan boh·da·*boh*·da/ *tayk*·see ya ba·ee·see·*kay*·lee – a short-haul bicycle taxi.

I'd like a taxi ...	Nataka teksi ...	na·*ta*·ka *tayk*·see ...
at (9am)	saa (tatu asubuhi)	sa (*ta*·too a·soo·*boo*·hee)
now	sasa	*sa*·sa
tomorrow	kesho	*kay*·shoh
for the whole day	kwa siku nzima	kwa *see*·koo n·*zee*·ma
for (three) hours	kwa masaa (matatu)	kwa ma·*sa* (ma·*ta*·too)
to run various errands	kufanya shughuli mbalimbali	koo·*fa*·nya shoo·*goo*·lee m·*ba*·lee·m·*ba*·lee
to the airport	kwenda kwenye uwanja wa ndege	*kwayn*·da *kway*·nyay oo·*wan*·ja wa n·*day*·gay
to the harbor	kwenda bandarini	*kwayn*·da ban·da·*ree*·nee

Where's the taxi rank?
Stendi ya teksi
iko wapi?
stayn·dee ya *tayk*·see
ee·koh *wa*·pee

Is this taxi free?
Teksi hii
inapatikana?
tayk·see hee
ee·na·pa·tee·*ka*·na

Please take me to (this address).
Tafadhali niendeshe ta·fa·*dha*·lee nee·ayn·*day*·shay
mpaka (anwani hii). m·*pa*·ka (an·*wa*·nee hee)

Please put the meter on.
Tumia mita ya too·*mee*·a *mee*·ta ya
kupima nauli. koo·*pee*·ma na·*oo*·lee

How much should I expect to pay to …?
Nitarajie kulipa nee·ta·ra·*jee*·ay koo·*lee*·pa
shilingi ngapi shee·*leen*·gee n·*ga*·pee
kwenda …? *kwayn*·da …

How much is it to …?
Ni bei gani kwenda …? nee bay *ga*·nee *kwayn*·da …

How much is it?
Ni shilingi ngapi? nee shee·*leen*·gee n·*ga*·pee

That's too expensive!
Ni ghali mno! nee *ga*·lee m·noh

Please lower the price.
Punguza bei, tafadhali. poon·*goo*·za bay ta·fa·*dha*·lee

Would you like to share a taxi to …?
Ungependa kugawa oon·gay·*payn*·da koo·*ga*·wa
teksi kwenda …? *tayk*·see *kwayn*·da …

Can we share a taxi?
Tugawe teksi? too·*ga*·way *tayk*·see

Please … *Tafadhali …* ta·fa·*dha*·lee …
  slow down *endesha* ayn·*day*·sha
     polepole poh·lay·*poh*·lay
  stop here *simama hapa* see·*ma*·ma *ha*·pa
  wait here *subiri hapa* soo·*bee*·ree *ha*·pa

car & motorbike hire

Are you willing to hire out …?	Unaweza kunikodisha …?	oo·na·*way*·za koo·nee·koh·*dee*·sha …
your car	gari lako	ga·ree *la*·koh
your motorbike	pikipiki yako	pee·kee·*pee*·kee ya·koh

I'd like to hire a/an …	Nataka kukodi …	na·*ta*·ka koo·*koh*·dee …
4WD	forbaifor	fohr·ba·ee·fohr
automatic	otomatiki	oh·toh·*ma*·tee·kee
car	gari	ga·ree
manual	kwa mkono	kwa m·*koh*·noh
motorbike	pikipiki	pee·kee·*pee*·kee

With …	Kwenye …	*kway*·nyay …
air conditioning	a/c	ay·*see*
a driver	dereva	day·*ray*·va

How much for … hire?	Ni bèi gani kukodi kwa …?	nee bay *ga*·nee koo·*koh*·dee kwa …
daily	siku	*see*·koo
hourly	saa	sa
weekly	wiki	*wee*·kee

Does that include insurance/mileage?

Bei inazingitia bima/umbali?
bay ee·na·zeen·gee·*tee*·a *bee*·ma/oo·m·*ba*·lee

Do you have a guide to the road rules in English?

Mna mwongozo wa sheria za barabara kwa Kiingereza?
m·na mwohn·*goh*·zoh wa shay·*ree*·a za ba·ra·*ba*·ra kwa kee·een·gay·*ray*·za

Do you have a road map?

Mna ramani?
m·na ra·*ma*·nee

on the road

What's the speed limit?
Mwendo gani   mwayn·doh ga·nee
unaruhusiwa?   oo·na·roo·hoo·see·wa

Is this the road to (Embu)?
Hii ni barabara   hee nee ba·ra·ba·ra
kwenda (Embu)?   kwayn·da (aym·boo)

Where's a petrol station?
Kituo cha mafuta   kee·too·oh cha ma·foo·ta
kiko wapi?   kee·ko wa·pee

Please fill it up.
Jaza tangi/tanki.   ja·za tan·gee/tan·kee

I'd like … litres.
Nataka lita …   na·ta·ka lee·ta …

diesel	*dizeli*	dee·zay·lee
leaded	*na risasi*	na ree·sa·see
regular	*kawaida*	ka·wa·ee·da
premium unleaded	*super*	soo·payr
unleaded	*isiyo na risasi*	ee·see·yoh na ree·sa·see

windscreen
kiwambo upepo
kee·wam·boh
oo·pay·poh

petrol/gas
mafuta
ma·foo·ta

battery
betri
bay·tree

engine
injini
een·jee·nee

tyre
tairi
ta·ee·ree

headlight
taa ya mbele
ta ya m·bay·lay

Can you check the ...?	*Angalia ...?*	an·ga·*lee*·a ...
oil	*mafuta*	ma·*foo*·ta
tyre pressure	*upepo*	oo·*pay*·poh
water	*maji*	ma·jee

(How long) Can I park here?

Naweza kuegesha   na·*way*·za koo·ay·*gay*·sha
hapa (kwa muda gani)?   *ha*·pa (kwa *moo*·da *ga*·ni)

Do I have to pay?

Ni lazima nilipe?   nee *la*·zee·ma nee·*lee*·pay

listen for ...		
bure	*boo*·ray	**free**
kilomita	kee·loh·*mee*·ta	**kilometres**
laiseni	la·ee·*say*·nee	**drivers licence**

problems

I need a mechanic.

Nahitaji fundi.   na·hee·*ta*·jee *foon*·dee

I've had an accident.

Nimepata ajali.   nee·me·*pa*·ta a·*ja*·lee

The car/motorbike has broken down (at Chalinze).

Gari/Pikipiki   *ga*·ree/pee·kee·*pee*·kee
imeharibika (Chalinze).   ee·may·ha·ree·*bee*·ka (cha·*leen*·zay)

The car/motorbike won't start.

Gari/Pikipiki haiwaki.   *ga*·ree/pee·kee·*pee*·kee ha·ee·*wa*·kee

I have a flat tyre.

Nina pancha.   *nee*·na *pan*·cha

I've lost my car keys.

Nimepoteza   nee·may·poh·*tay*·za
funguo za gari.   foon·*goo*·oh za *ga*·ree

I've locked the keys inside.

Nimefunga	nee·may·*foon*·ga
funguo ndani.	foon·*goo*·oh n·*da*·ni

I've run out of petrol.

Mafuta yamekwisha.	ma·*foo*·ta ya·may·*kwee*·sha

Can you fix it (today)?

Utaweza	oo·ta·*way*·za
kuitengeneza (leo)?	koo·ee·tayn·gay·*nay*·za (*lay*·oh)

How long will it take?

Itachukua muda gani?	ee·ta·choo·*koo*·a *moo*·da *ga*·nee

bicycle

baisikeli

I'd like ...	Nataka ...	na·*ta*·ka ...
my bicycle	kutengeneza	koo·tayn·gay·*nay*·za
repaired	baisikeli yangu	ba·ee·see·*kay*·lee *yan*·goo
to buy a	kununua	koo·noo·*noo*·a
bicycle	baisikeli	ba·ee·see·*kay*·lee
to hire a	kukodisha	koo·koh·*dee*·sha
bicycle	baisikeli	ba·ee·see·*kay*·lee
I'd like	Nataka	na·*ta*·ka
a ... bike.	baisikeli ...	ba·ee·see·*kay*·lee ...
mountain	yenye gia	*yay*·nyay *gee*·a
	kupanda	koo·*pan*·da
	milima	mee·*lee*·ma
racing	yenye gia	*yay*·nyay *gee*·a
	kukimbia	koo·keem·*bee*·a
	mbio	m·*bee*·oh
second-hand	isiyo mpya	ee·*see*·yoh m·pya
How much is	Ni bei gani	nee bay *ga*·nee
it per ...?	kwa ...?	kwa ...
day	siku	*see*·kuu
hour	saa	sa

Do I need a helmet?

Ni lazima nivai helmeti? — nee *la*·zee·ma nee·*va*·ee hayl·*may*·tee

Is there a bicycle-path map?

Kuna ramani ya njia za baisikeli? — *koo*·na ra·*ma*·nee ya n·*jee*·a za ba·ee·see·*kay*·lee

I have a puncture.

Nina pancha. — *nee*·na *pan*·cha

local transport

Can I pay for a ride in your truck?

Naweza kulipa kwa lifti katika lori lako? — na·*way*·za koo·*lee*·pa kwa *leef*·tee ka·*tee*·ka *loh*·ree *la*·koh

How much to …?

Ni bei gani kwenda …? — nee bay *ga*·nee *kwayn*·da …

Are you waiting for more people?

Unangojea watu wengine? — oo·na·n·goh·*jay*·a *wa*·too wayn·*gee*·nay

How many people can ride on this?

Watu wangapi wanaweza kusafirishwa kwa hili? — *wa*·too wan·*ga*·pee wa·na·*way*·za koo·sa·fee·*ree*·shwa kwa *hee*·lee

Could I ride in the front?

Naomba kukaa mbele. — na·*ohm*·ba koo·*ka* m·*bay*·lay

I don't want to ride on top.

Sitaki kukaa juu. — see·*ta*·kee koo·*ka* joo

Could I contribute to the petrol cost?

Naweza kuchangia sehemu ya bei ya mafuta? — na·*way*·za koo·chan·*gee*·a say·*hay*·moo ya bay ya ma·*foo*·ta

Thanks for the ride.

Asante kwa lifti. — a·*san*·tay kwa *leef*·tee

border crossing

kuvuka mpaka

I'm ...	*Mimi ni ...*	*mee·mee nee ...*
in transit	*safarini*	sa·fa·*ree*·nee
on business	*kwa biashara*	kwa bee·a·*sha*·ra
on holiday	*kwa likizo*	kwa lee·*kee*·zoh
I'm here for ...	*Nipo kwa ...*	*nee*·poh kwa ...
(three) days	*siku (tatu)*	*see*·koo (*ta*·too)
(four) months	*miezi (minne)*	mee·*ay*·zee (mee·*n*·nay)
(two) weeks	*wiki (mbili)*	*wee*·kee (m·*bee*·lee)
Do I require a/an ...?	*Ni lazima niwe na ...?*	nee la·zee·ma nee·way na ...
I have a/an ...	*Nina ...*	*nee*·na ...
entry permit	*hati ya kuingia*	*ha*·tee ya koo·een·*gee*·a
customs form	*fomu ya forodha*	*foh*·moo ya foh·*roh*·dha
health certificate	*cheti cha afya*	*chay*·tee cha *af*·ya
pass/permit	*cheti*	*chay*·tee
police report	*ripoti ya polisi*	ree·*poh*·tee ya poh·*lee*·see

listen for ...

familia	fa·mee·*lee*·a	**family**
kundi	*koon*·dee	**group**
pasipoti	pa·see·*poh*·tee	**passport**
peke yake	*pay*·kay *ya*·kay	**alone**
visa	*vee*·sa	**visa**

I'm going to (Malindi).
Naenda (Malindi).   na·*ayn*·da (ma·*leen*·dee)

I'm staying at (the Pendo Inn).
Nakaa (Pendo Inn).   na·*ka* (*payn*·doh een)

The children are on this passport.
Watoto wanasafiri   wa·*toh*·toh wa·na·sa·*fee*·ree
kwenye pasipoti.   *kway*·nyay pa·see·*poh*·tee hee

at customs

I have nothing to declare.
Sina ya kutaja.   *see*·na ya koo·*ta*·ja

I have something to declare.
Ninacho kitu cha kutaja.   nee·*na*·cho *kee*·too cha koo·*ta*·ja

Do I have to declare this?
Ni lazima nitaje hiki?   nee *la*·zee·ma nee·*ta*·jay *hee*·kee

That's (not) mine.
Hiki ni (si) changu.   *hee*·kee nee (see) *chan*·goo

I didn't know I had to declare it.
Sikujua ilibidi   see·koo·*joo*·a ee·lee·*bee*·dee
kuitaja.   koo·ee·*ta*·ja

I didn't know I couldn't take this out of the country.
Sikujua kwamba   see·koo·*joo*·a *kwam*·ba
hairuhusiwi   ha·ee·roo·hoo·*see*·wee
kuchukua kitu   koo·choo·*koo*·a *kee*·too
hiki nje ya nchi.   *hee*·kee *n*·jay ya *n*·chee

signs		
Duty-Free	doo·tee·*free*	**Duty-free**
Forodha	foh·*roh*·dha	**Customs**
Karantini	ka·ran·*tee*·nee	**Quarantine**
Udhibiti wa	oo·dhee·*bee*·tee wa	**Passport Control**
Pasipoti	pa·see·*poh*·tee	
Uhamiaji	oo·ha·mee·*a*·jee	**Immigration**

Where's (the market)?
(Soko) iko wapi? (soh·koh) ee·koh wa·pee

What's the address?
Anwani ni nini? an·wa·nee nee nee·nee

How do I get there?
Nifikaje? nee·fee·ka·jay

How far is it?
Ni umbali gani? nee oom·ba·lee ga·nee

Can you show me (on the map)?
Unaweza kunionyesha oo·na·way·za koo·nee·oh·nyay·sha
(katika ramani)? (ka·tee·ka ra·ma·nee)

It's ...	Iko ...	ee·koh ...
behind ...	*nyuma ya ...*	nyoo·ma ya ...
close	*karibu*	ka·ree·boo
here	*hapa*	ha·pa
in front of ...	*mbele ya ...*	m·bay·lay ya ...
near ...	*karibu na ...*	ka·ree·boo na ...
next to ...	*jirani ya ...*	jee·ra·nee ya ...
on the corner	*pembeni*	paym·bay·nee
opposite ...	*ng'ambo ya ...*	ng·am·boh ya ...
straight ahead	*moja kwa moja*	moh·ja kwa moh·ja
there	*hapo*	ha·poh

Turn ...	Geuza ...	gay·oo·za ...
at the corner	*kwenye kona*	kway·nyay koh·na
at the traffic	*kwenye taa za*	kway·nyay ta za
** lights**	*barabarani*	ba·ra·ba·ra·nee
left	*kushoto*	koo·shoh·toh
right	*kulia*	koo·lee·a

... *dakika*	... da·*kee*·ka	... minutes
... *kilomita*	... kee·loh·*mee*·ta	... kilometres
... *mita*	... *mee*·ta	... metres

north	*kaskazini*	kas·ka·*zee*·nee
south	*kusini*	koo·*see*·nee
east	*mashariki*	ma·sha·*ree*·kee
west	*magharibi*	ma·ga·*ree*·bee

by ...	*kwa* ...	kwa ...
bus	*basi*	*ba*·see
foot	*miguu*	mee·*goo*
taxi	*teksi*	*tayk*·see
train	*treni*	*tray*·nee

What ... is this?	*Hapa ni ... gani?*	*ha*·pa nee ... *ga*·nee
neighbourhood	*mtaa*	m·*ta*
street	*njia*	n·*jee*·a
village	*kijiji*	kee·*jee*·jee

traffic lights
taa za barabarani
ta za ba·ra·ba·*ra*·nee

shop
duka
doo·ka

pedestrian crossing
kivuko cha wanaotembea
kee·*voo*·koh cha wa·na·oh·taym·*bay*·a

bus
basi
ba·see

intersection
njiapanda
n·jee·a·*pan*·da

corner
pembe
paym·bay

taxi
teksi
tayk·see

finding accommodation

kugundua malazi

Where's a ...?	*... iko wapi?*	*... ee·koh wa·pee*
camping ground	*Uwanja wa kambi*	*oo·wan·ja wa kam·bee*
guesthouse	*Gesti*	*gay·stee*
hotel	*Hoteli*	*hoh·tay·lee*
restaurant	*Hoteli*	*hoh·tay·lee*
youth hostel	*Hosteli ya vijana*	*hoh·stay·lee ya vee·ja·na*
Can you recommend somewhere ...?	*Unaweza kunipendekeza malazi ...?*	*oo·na·way·za koo·nee·payn·day·kay zay·a ma·la·zee ...*
cheap	*rahisi*	*ra·hee·see*
good	*nzuri*	*n·zoo·ree*
luxurious	*ya anasa*	*ya a·na·sa*
nearby	*hapo karibuni*	*ha·poh ka·ree·boo·nee*
romantic	*kwa wapenzi*	*kwa wa·payn·zee*

What's the address?
Anwani ni nini?   *an·wa·nee nee nee·nee*

For responses, see **directions**, page 65.

local talk		
dive	*mahali pabaya*	*ma·ha·lee pa·ba·ya*
rat-infested	*yenye panya*	*yay·nyay pa·nya*
top spot	*safi kabisa*	*sa·fee ka·bee·sa*

booking ahead & checking in

I'd like to book a room, please.
Nataka kufanya   na·*ta*·ka koo·*fa*·nya
buking, tafadhali.   boo·keeng ta·fa·*dha*·lee

I have a reservation.
Nina buking.   nee·na boo·keeng

My name's …
Jina langu ni …   jee·na *lan*·goo nee …

For (three) nights/weeks.
Kwa siku/wiki (tatu).   kwa see·koo/wee·kee (*ta*·too)

From (June 30) to (July 6).
Kutoka tarehe   koo·*toh*·ka ta·*ray*·hay
(thelathini mwezi   (thay·la·*thee*·nee mway·zee
wa sita) mpaka tarehe   wa see·ta) m·*pa*·ka ta·*ray*·hay
(sita mwezi wa saba).   (*see*·ta mway·zee wa *sa*·ba)

Do you have a	*Kuna chumba*	koo·na *choom*·ba
… room?	*kwa …?*	kwa …
double	*watu wawili,*	wa·too wa·*wee*·lee
(one bed)	*kitanda kimoja*	kee·*tan*·da kee·*moh*·ja
single	*mtu mmoja*	m·too m·*moh*·ja
twin	*watu wawili,*	wa·too wa·*wee*·lee
(two beds)	*vitanda viwili*	vee·*tan*·da vee·*wee*·lee

Do you have a suite?
Kuna chumba   koo·na *choom*·ba
chenye sebule?   *chay*·nyay say·*boo*·lay

Can I see the room?
Naomba nione chumba.   na·*ohm*·ba nee·*oh*·nay *choom*·ba

Imejaa.	ee·may·ja	**It's full.**
mapokezi	ma·poh·*kay*·zee	**reception**
pasipoti	pa·see·*poh*·tee	**passport**
Siku ngapi?	see·koo n·*ga*·pee	**How many nights?**
ufunguo	oo·foon·*goo*·oh	**key**

How much is	*Ni bei gani*	nee bay *ga*·ne
it per ...?	*kwa ...?*	kwa ...
day	*siku*	see·koo
person	*mtu*	m·too
week	*wiki*	wee·kee

That's too expensive.
  Ni ghali mno.   nee *ga*·lee m·noh

Can you lower the price?
  Naomba upunguze   na·*ohm*·ba oo·poon·*goo*·zay
  bei?   bay

I'll take it.
  Nataka.   na·*ta*·ka

Do I need to pay upfront?
  Ni lazima nilipe   nee *la*·zee·ma nee·*lee*·pay
  kwanza?   kwan·za

Can I pay	*Naweza kulipa*	na·*way*·za koo·*lee*·pa
by ...?	*kwenye ...?*	*kway*·nyay ...
credit card	*kadi ya benki*	*ka*·dee ya *bayn*·kee
travellers	*hundi ya*	*hoon*·dee ya
cheque	*msafiri*	m·sa·*fee*·ree

For other methods of payment, see **shopping**, page 77, and
money, page 45.

Hakuna Nafasi	ha·*koo*·na na·*fa*·see	**no vacancy**
Nafasi Ipo	na·*fa*·see ee·po	**vacancy**

requests & queries

When/Where is breakfast served?
Chai ya asubuhi — *cha·ee ya a·soo·boo·hee*
inapatikana lini/wapi? — *ee·na·pa·tee·ka·na lee·nee/wa·pee*

Please wake me at (seven).
Tafadhali niamshe — *ta·fa·dha·lee nee·am·shay*
saa (moja). — *sa (moh·ja)*

Do you arrange tours here?
Mnapanga safari hapa? — *m·na·pan·ga sa·fa·ree ha·pa*

Do you change money here?
Mnabadilisha hela hapa? — *m·na·ba·dee·lee·sha hay·la ha·pa*

Can I use the ...?	*Je, naweza kutumia ...?*	*jay na·way·za koo·too·mee·a ...*
kitchen	*jiko*	*jee·ko*
laundry	*udobi*	*oo·doh·bee*
telephone	*simu*	*see·mu*

Do you have a/an ...?	*Kuna ...?*	*koo·na ...*
elevator	*lifti*	*leef·tee*
laundry service	*dobi*	*doh·bee*
message board	*kibao cha ujumbe*	*kee·ba·oh cha oo·joom·bay*
safe	*kasha la fedha*	*ka·sha la fay·dha*
swimming pool	*bwawa la kuogelea*	*bwa·wa la koo·oh·gay·lay·a*

a knock at the door ...

Who is it?	*Ni nani?*	*nee na·nee*
Just a moment.	*Subiri kidogo.*	*soo·bee·ree kee·doh·goh*
Come in.	*Ingia.*	*een·gee·a*
Come back later, please.	*Rudi baadaye, tafadhali.*	*roo·dee ba·a·da·yay, ta·fa·dha·lee*

Could I have …, please?	Naomba …, afadhali.	na·*ohm*·ba … ta·fa·*dha*·li
a mosquito net	chandarua	chan·da·*roo*·a
a receipt	risiti	ree·*see*·tee
an extra blankt	blanketi nyingine	blan·*kay*·tee nyeen·*gee*·nay
my key	ufunguo wangu	oo·foon·*goo*·oh *wan*·goo
toilet paper	karatasi ya choo	ka·ra·*ta*·see ya choh

Can you wash these clothes?

Mnaweza kufua nguo hizi?
m·na·*way*·za koo·*foo*·a n·*goo*·oh *hee*·zee

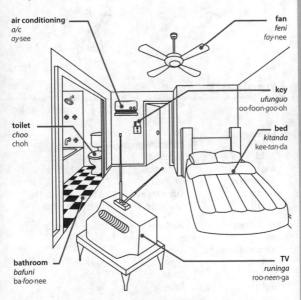

air conditioning
a/c
ay·see

fan
feni
fay·nee

key
ufunguo
oo·foon·*goo*·oh

toilet
choo
choh

bed
kitanda
kee·*tan*·da

bathroom
bafuni
ba·*foo*·nee

TV
runinga
roo·*neen*·ga

washerman/ -woman	*dobi*	*doh*·bee
wash clothes	*fua nguo*	*foo*·a n·*goo*·oh
with starch	*weka stachi*	*way*·ka *sta*·chee
without starch	*usiweke stachi*	oo·see·*way*·kay *sta*·chee

Is there a message for me?
  Kuna ujumbe wangu?   koo·na oo·*joom*·bay *wan*·goo

Can I leave a message for someone?
  Naweza kumwachia   na·*way*·za koom·wa·*chee*·a
  mtu ujumbe?   m·too oo·*joom*·bay

I'm locked out of my room.
  Nimefungwa nje ya   nee·may·*foon*·gwa n·jay ya
  chumba changu.   *choom*·ba *chan*·goo

complaints

It's too ...	... *mno.*	... m·noh
bright	*Kuna mwanga*	koo·na *mwan*·ga
cold	*Ni baridi*	nee ba·*ree*·dee
dark	*Kuna giza*	koo·na *gee*·za
expensive	*Ni ghali*	nee *ga*·lee
noisy	*Kuna kelele*	koo·na kay·*lay*·lay
small	*Ni ndogo*	nee n·*doh*·goh

The ... doesn't work.	... *haifanyi kazi.*	... ha·ee·*fa*·nyee ka·zee
air conditioning	*A/c*	ay·*see*
fan	*Feni*	*fay*·nee
toilet	*Choo*	choh
light	*Taa*	ta

Can I get another (blanket)?
    Inawezekana   ee·na·way·zay·*ka*·na
    nipate (blanketi)   nee·*pa*·tay (blan·*kay*·tee)
    nyingine?   nyeen·*gee*·nay

Can you clean the room?
    Inawezekana   ee·na·way·zay·*ka*·na
    kusafisha chumba?   koo·sa·*fee*·sha *choom*·ba

This (pillow) isn't clean.
    (Mto) huu si safi.   (*m*·toh) hoo see *sa*·fee

There's no ...   *Hakuna ...*   ha·*koo*·na ...
    electricity   *umeme*   oo·*may*·may
    hot water   *maji ya moto*   *ma*·jee ya *moh*·toh

checking out

kuachia chumba

What time is checkout?
    Muda wa kuachia   *moo*·da wa koo·ach·*ee*·a
    chumba ni saa ngapi?   *choom*·ba nee sa n·*ga*·pee

Can I have a late checkout?
    Naweza kuchelewa   na·*way*·za koo·chay·*lay*·wa
    kuachia chumba?   koo·ach·*ee*·a *choom*·ba

Can you call a taxi for me (for 11 o'clock)?
    Naomba teksi   na·*ohm*·ba *tayk*·si
    kwa saa (tano).   kwa sa (*ta*·noh)

I'm leaving now.
    Naondoka sasa.   na·ohn·*doh*·ka *sa*·sa

Can I leave my bags here?
    Naweza kuacha   na·*way*·za koo·*ach*·a
    mizigo yangu hapa?   mee·*zee*·goh yan·goo *ha*·pa

There's a mistake in the bill.
    Mmekosa kwenye   m·*may*·koh·sa *kway*·nyay
    bili yangu.   *bee*·lee yan·goo

Can I have my ...?	Naomba ...yangu.	na·ohm·ba ...yan·goo
deposit	maweko	ma·way·koh
passport	pasipoti	pa·see·poh·tee
valuables	vitu vya	vee·too vya
	thamani	tha·ma·nee

I'll be back ...	Nitarudi ...	nee·ta·roo·dee ...
in (three)	baada ya	ba·a·da ya
days	siku (tatu)	see·koo (ta·too)
on (Tuesday)	(Jumanne)	(joo·ma·n·nay)

I've been very happy here, thank you.
| Nimefurahi sana | nee·may·foo·ra·hee sa·na |
| hapa, asante. | ha·pa a·san·tay |

I'll recommend it to my friends.
| Nitawapendekezea | nee·ta·wa·payn·day·kay·zay·a |
| rafiki zangu. | ra·fee·kee zan·goo |

camping

Do you have ...?	Kuna ...?	koo·na ...
a laundry	udobi	oo·doh·bee
a tent site	nafasi kupiga	na·fa·see koo·pee·ga
	hema	hay·ma
a car site	nafasi	na·fa·see
	kuegesha gari	koo·ay·gay·sha ga·ree
electricity	umeme	oo·may·may
hot water	maji ya moto	ma·jee ya moh·toh
shower facilities	bafuni	ba·foo·nee
tents for hire	hema	hay·ma
	kukodisha	koo·koh·dee·sha

How much is it per ...?	Ni bei gani kila ...?	nee bay ga·nee kee·la ...
caravan	lori	loh·ree
person	mtu	m·too
tent	hema	hay·ma
vehicle	gari	ga·ree

Can I ...?	Naweza ...?	na·*way*·za ...
camp here	kuwa hapa	*koo*·wa *ha*·pa
	kwa usiku	kwa oo·*see*·koo
park next to	kuegesha gari	koo·ay·*gay*·sha *ga*·ree
my tent	jirani ya hema	jee·*ra*·nee ya *hay*·ma

Is the water drinkable?
Je, maji ni safi   jay *ma*·jee nee *sa*·fee
kunywa?   *koony*·wa

Who do I ask to stay here?
Niongee na nani   nee·ohn·*gay*·ay na *na*·nee
nikitaka kukaa hapa?   nee·kee·*ta*·ka koo·*ka ha*·pa

Could I borrow ...?
Naomba niazimie ...   na·*ohm*·ba nee·a·zee·*mee*·ay ...

renting

I'm here about	Nimekuja	nee·may·*koo*·ja
the ... for rent.	kuhusu	koo·*hoo*·soo
	kukodisha ...	koo·koh·*dee*·sha ...
Do you have	Kuna ...	*koo*·na ...
a/an ... for rent?	kukodisha?	koo·koh·*dee*·sha
apartment	fleti	*flay*·tee
cabin	kibanda	kee·*ban*·da
house	nyumba	*nyoom*·ba
room	chumba	*choom*·ba
furnished	kwenye	*kway*·nyay
	fenicha zote	*fay*·nee·cha *zoh*·tay
partly furnished	kwenye	*kway*·nyay
	fenicha kadhaa	*fay*·nee·cha ka·*dha*
unfurnished	bila fenicha	*bee*·la *fay*·nee·cha

staying with locals

Can I stay at your place?
Naweza kukaa   na·*way*·za koo·*ka*
nyumbani kwako?   nyoom·*ba*·nee *kwa*·koh

Is there anything I can do to help?
Nisaidie namna gani?   nee·sa·ee·*dee*·ay *nam*·na *ga*·nee

I have my own ...	Nina ...	nee·na ...
mattress	godolo langu	goh·*doh*·loh *lan*·goo
sleeping bag	mfuko wa	m·*foo*·koh wa
	kulalia wangu	koo·la·*lee*·a *wan*·goo

Can I ...?	Naweza ...?	na·*way*·za ...
bring anything	kuchangia	koo·chan·*gee*·a
for the meal	lisho	*lee*·shoh
do the dishes	safisha vyombo	sa·*fee*·sha *vyohm*·boh
set/clear	kutayarisha/	koo·ta·ya·*ree*·sha/
the table	kuondoa meza	koo·ohn·*doh*·a *may*·za
take out	kufuta	koo·*foo*·ta
the rubbish	takataka	ta·ka·*ta*·ka

Thanks for your hospitality.
Asante sana kwa   a·*san*·tay *sa*·na kwa
wema wako.   *way*·ma *wa*·koh

For dining-related expressions, see **food**, page 153.

---

address: unknown

Other than downtown in some cities, exact street addresses –
or even street names – are not common. The best way to find
a specific person or place is often to go to the centre of a
neighbourhood, eg the local bus stop, and ask for a particular
landmark or a person who can lead you to your destination.

What's the	Ni anwani	nee an·*wa*·nee
address?	gani?	*ga*·nee
road	barabara	ba·ra·*ba*·ra
street	njia	n·*jee*·a

looking for ...

kutafutia

Where's a ...?	... iko wapi?	... ee·koh wa·pee
department store	Duka lenye vitu vingi	doo·ka lay·nyay vee·too veen·gee
general store	Duka lenye vitu mbalimbali	doo·ka lay·nyay vee·too m·ba·lee·m·ba·lee
market	Soko	soh·koh

Where can I buy (a padlock)?
Naweza kununua (kufuli) wapi?
na·way·za koo·noo·noo·a (koo·foo·lee) wa·pee

For phrases on directions, see **directions**, page 65.
For more on shops and services, see the **dictionary**.

making a purchase

wakati wa kununua

I'm just looking.
Naangalia tu.
na·an·ga·lee·a too

I'd like to buy (an adaptor plug).
Nataka kununua (adapta ya umeme).
na·ta·ka koo·noo·noo·a (a·dap·ta ya oo·may·may)

How much is it?
Ni bei gani?
ni bay ga·nee

shopping

it's not what you say, it's how you say it

Swahili speakers tend to reserve *tafadhali* ta·fa·*dha*·lee (please) for fairly formal situations, and generally don't use it in ordinary encounters such as shopping. Instead of saying 'could you' or 'I'd like' or 'please show me', a simple request such as *Nipe ... nee*·pay ... (give me ...), *Naomba ...* na·*ohm*·ba ... (I request ...) or *Nataka ...* na·*ta*·ka ... (I want ...), when spoken with a pleasant tone of voice, will usually convey all the necessary politeness of casual interactions.

Can you write down the price?		
Andika bei.	an·*dee*·ka bay	
Do you have any others?		
Kuna nyingine?	koo·na nyeen·*gee*·nay	
Can I look at it?		
Naomba nione.	na·*ohm*·ba nee·*oh*·nay	
I don't like it.		
Sipendi.	see·*payn*·dee	
I'll take it.		
Nataka.	na·*ta*·ka	
Could I have it wrapped?		
Funga, tafadhali.	*foon*·ga ta·fa·*dha*·lee	
Does it have a guarantee?		
Kuna dhamana?	koo·na dha·*ma*·na	
Can I have it sent overseas?		
Naweza kuipostia	na·*way*·za koo·ee·poh·*stee*·a	
kwenye nchi za nje?	*kway*·nyay n·chee za n·jay	
Can you order it for me?		
Unaweza kuniagizia?	oo·na·*way*·za koo·nee·a·gee·*zee*·a	
Can I pick it up later?		
Naweza kuichukua	na·*way*·za koo·ee·choo·*koo*·a	
baadaye?	ba·a·*da*·yay	
It's faulty.		
Haifanyi kazi.	ha·ee·*fa*·nyee *ka*·zee	

PRACTICAL

78

bargain	*bei nafuu*	bay na·*foo*
bottom price	*bei ya mwisho*	bay ya m·*wee*·shoh
cheap	*rahisi*	ra·*hee*·see
rip-off	*feki*	*fay*·kee
sale	*seli*	*say*·lee
specials	*maalum*	ma·*loom*

Do you accept ...?	*Mnakubali ...*	m·na·koo·*ba*·lee ...
credit cards	*kadi ya benki*	*ka*·dee ya *bayn*·kee
travellers	*hundi ya*	*hoon*·dee ya
cheques	*msafiri*	m·sa·*fee*·ree

I'd like ..., please.	*Nataka ...,*	na·*ta*·ka ...
	tafadhali.	ta·fa·*dha*·lee
my change	*chenji yangu*	*chayn*·jee *yan*·goo
a refund	*unirudishie*	oo·nee·roo·dee·*shee*·ay
	hela	*hay*·la
to return this	*kurudisha*	koo·roo·*dee*·sha
	kitu hiki	*kee*·too *hee*·kee

Could I have	*Naomba ...*	na·*ohm*·ba ...
a ..., please?		
bag	*mfuko*	m·*foo*·koh
receipt	*risiti*	ree·*see*·tee

bargaining

kubishana bei

How much is it?
Ni bei gani?
ni bay *ga*·nee

That's too expensive.
Ni ghali mno.
nee *ga*·lee m·noh

Please lower the price.
Punguza bei.
poon·*goo*·za bay

It's not a fair price.
Siyo bei nafuu.
see·yoh bay na·*foo*

Do you have something cheaper?
Kuna rahisi zaidi?   koo·na ra·*hee*·see za·*ee*·dee

I'll give you (500 shillings).
Nitakupa   nee·ta·*koo*·pa
(shilingi mia tano).   (shee·*leen*·gee *mee*·a ta·noh)

clothes

nguo

My size is ...	*Saizi yangu ni ...*	sa·ee·zee *yan*·goo nee ...
(40)	*(arobaini)*	(a·roh·ba·*ee*·nee)
small	*ndogo*	n·*doh*·goh
medium	*wastani*	wa·sta·nee
large	*kubwa*	*koob*·wa

Can I try it on?
Je, naweza kujaribu   jay na·*way*·za koo·ja·*ree*·boo
kuvaa?   koo·*va*

It doesn't fit.
Haifai.   ha·ee·*fa*·ee

Can you recommend a seamstress/tailor?
Unaweza kupendekeza   oo·na·*way*·za koo·payn·day·*kay*·za
mshonaji?   m·shoh·*na*·jee

Could you alter/mend this?
Unaweza kubadilisha/   oo·na·*way*·za koo·ba·dee·*lee*·sha/
kushona hii?   koo·*sho*·na hee

Could you make me a (dress)?
Unaweza kunishonea   oo·na·*way*·za koo·nee·shoh·*nay*·a
(gauni)?   (ga·*oo*·nee)

For clothing items, see the **dictionary**.

repairs

matengenezo

Can I have my	*Mnaweza*	m·na·*way*·za
... repaired	*kutengeneza* ...	koo·tayn·gay·*nay*·za ...
here?	*yangu hapa?*	*yan*·goo *ha*·pa
When will my	... *yangu*	... *yan*·goo
... be ready?	*itakuwa*	ee·ta·*koo*·wa
	tayari lini?	ta·*ya*·ree *lee*·nee
backpack	*shanta*	*shan*·ta
camera	*kemra*	*kaym*·ra
(sun)glasses	*miwani (ya jua)*	mee·*wa*·nee (ya *joo*·a)
shoes	*viatu*	vee·*a*·too

hairdressing

I'd like (a) ...	Nataka ...	na·ta·ka ...
colour	kuweka rangi	koo·way·ka ran·gee
haircut	kukata nywele	koo·ka·ta nyway·lay
my hair	kusuka	koo·soo·ka
braided	nywele	nyway·lay
my hair	kuosha	koo·oh·sha
washed	nywele	nyway·lay
shave	kunyoa ndevu	koo·nyoh·a n·day·voo
trim	kupunguza	koo·poon·goo·za
	nywele kidogo	nyway·lay kee·doh·goh

Don't cut it too short.
Usipunguze mno.   oo·see·poon·goo·zay m·noh

Please use a new blade.
Tumia wembe mpya.   too·mee·a waym·bay m·pya

Please use hot water.
Tumia maji ya moto.   too·mee·a ma·jee ya moh·toh

Shave it all off!
Nyoa zote!   nyoh·a zoh·tay

I should never have let you near me!
Nilikosa hata   nee·lee·koh·sa ha·ta
uliponikaribia!   oo·lee·poh·nee·ka·ree·bee·a

barber	kinyozi	kee·nyoh·zee
hairdresser for braiding	msusi	m·soo·see
hairdresser for cutting	mtengenezaji wa nywele	m·tayn·gay·nay·za·jee wa nyway·lay

For colours, see the **dictionary**.

books & reading

Do you have a book by (Ngugi wa Thiong'o)?
Kuna kitabu   koo·na kee·*ta*·boo
kuandikwa na   koo·an·*deek*·wa na
(Ngugi wa Thiong'o)?   (n·*goo*·gee wa thee·*ohng*·oh)

Is there an English-language bookshop?
Kuna duka la vitabu   koo·na *doo*·ka la vee·*ta*·boo
vya Kiingereza?   vya kee·een·gay·*ray*·za

Can you recommend a book for me?
Unaweza   oo·na·*way*·za
kunipendekezea   koo·nee·payn·day·kay·*zay*·a
kitabu?   kee·*ta*·boo

Do you have Lonely Planet guidebooks?
Mna vitabu vya   m·na vee·*ta*·boo vya
Lonely Planet?   *lohn*·lee *pla*·nayt

I'd like a ...	*Nataka ...*	na·*ta*·ka ...
dictionary	*kamusi*	ka·*moo*·see
newspaper	*gazeti (kwa*	ga·*zay*·tee (kwa
(in English)	*Kiingereza)*	kee·een·gay·*ray*·za)
notepad	*daftari*	daf·*ta*·ree

electronic goods

Where can I buy duty-free electronic goods?
Duty-free kununua   doo·tee·*free* koo·noo·*noo*·a
bidhaa za umeme iko   bee·*dha* za oo·*may*·may ee·koh
wapi?   *wa*·pee

Will this work on any DVD player?
Itafanya kazi katika   ee·ta·*fa*·nya *ka*·zee ka·*tee*·ka
DVD zote?   dee·vee·*dee* zoh·tay

shopping

Is this a (PAL/NTSC) system?
Ni mfumo wa (PAL/NTSC)?
nee m·*foo*·moh wa (pal/ayn·tee·*ays*·see)

Is this the latest model?
Ni aina mpya kabisa?
nee a·*ee*·na m·pya ka·*bee*·sa

Is this (240) volts?
Ni volti (mia mbili arobaini)?
nee *vol*·tee (*mee*·a m·*bee*·lee a·roh·ba·*ee*·nee)

music

muziki

I'd like a ...	*Nataka ...*	na·*ta*·ka ...
blank tape	*kanda tupo*	*kan*·da *too*·poh
CD	*CD*	see·*dee*
drum	*ngoma*	n·*goh*·ma
xylophone	*marimba*	ma·*reem*·ba

I'm looking for something by (Remi Ongala).
Natafuta muziki ya (Remi Ongala).
na·ta·*foo*·ta moo·*zee*·kee ya (*ray*·mee ohn·*ga*·la)

What's their best recording?
Kanda gani yao inazidi?
kan·da *ga*·nee *ya*·oh ee·na·*zee*·dee

Can I listen to this?
Naomba tusikilize.
na·*ohm*·ba too·see·kee·*lee*·zay

> ### listen for ...
>
> *Unataka msaada?*
> oo·na·*ta*·ka m·*sa*·da
> **Do you want help?**
>
> *Nyingine?*
> nyeen·*gee*·nay
> **Anything else?**
>
> *Hamna/Hakuna.*
> *ham*·na/ha·*koo*·na
> **No, we don't have any.**

photography

I need ... film	Nahitaji	na·hee·ta·jee
for this camera.	filamu ... kwa	fee·la·moo ... kwa
	kemra hii.	kaym·ra hee
APS	APS	a·pee·ays
B&W	nyeusi na	nya·oo·see na
	nyeupe	nyay·oo·pay
colour	ya rangi	ya ran·gee
slide	ya slaidi	ya sla·ee·dee
(400) speed	ya spidi	ya spee·dee
	(mia nne)	(mee·a n·nay)

Can you ...?	Mnaweza ...?	m·na·way·za ...
develop this	kusafishu	koo·sa·fee·sha
film	mkanda huu	m·kan·da hoo
develop	kusafisha	koo·sa·fee·sha
digital	picha za	pee·cha za
photos	tarakimu	ta·ra·kee·moo
load my	kuweka mkanda	koo·way·ka m·kan·da
film	katika kemra	ka·tee·ka kaym·ra
recharge the	kuchajisha	koo·cha·jee·sha
battery for	betri kwa	bay·tree kwa
my digital	kemra yangu	kaym·ra yan·goo
camera	ya tarakimu	ya ta·ra·kee·moo
transfer photos	kuhamisha	koo·ha·mee·sha
from my	picha kutoka	pee·cha koo·toh·ka
camera to CD	kemra	kaym·ra
	kwenye CD	kway·nyay see·dee

Please don't use a red tint.
Usitumie rangi oo·see·*too·mee*·ay ran·gee
nyekundu nyekundu. nyay·*koon*·doo nyay·*koon*·doo

When will it be ready?
Itakuwa tayari lini? ee·ta·*koo*·wa ta·*ya*·ree *lee*·nee

How much is it?
Ni bei gani? ni bay *ga*·nee

I need a passport photo taken.
Nahitaji picha ya na·hee·*ta*·jee *pee*·cha ya
pasipoti. pa·see·*poh*·tee

I'm not happy with these photos.
Sifurahi na picha hizi. see·foo·*ra*·hee na *pee*·cha *hee*·zee

souvenirs

basket	*kikapu*	kee·*ka*·poo
batik	*batiki*	ba·*tee*·kee
bowl	*bakuli*	ba·*koo*·lee
candlestick holder	*mshumaa*	m·shoo·*ma*
ceramic pot	*chungu*	*choo*·ngoo
copper tray	*sinia ya shaba*	see·*nee*·a ya *sha*·ba
(folding safari) chair	*kiti*	*kee*·tee
jewellery	*vipuli*	vee·*poo*·lee
leather shield	*ngao ya ngazi*	n·*ga*·oh ya n·*ga*·zee
mask	*kinyago*	kee·*nya*·goh
plaited mat	*mkeka*	m·*kay*·ka
spear	*mkuki*	m·*koo*·kee
textiles	*vitambaa*	vee·tam·*ba*
three-legged stool	*kigoda*	kee·*goh*·da
woodcarving	*uchongaji*	oo·chohn·*ga*·jee

post office

posta

I want to send a/an ...	Nataka kupeleka ...	na·ta·ka koo·pay·lay·ka ...
fax	faksi	fak·see
letter	barua	ba·roo·a
parcel	kifurushi	kee·foo·roo·shee
postcard	postkadi	pohst·ka·dee
trunk (tea chest)	sanduku	san·doo·koo

I want to buy a/an ...	Nataka kununua ...	na·ta·ka koo·noo·noo·a ...
aerogram	aerogramu	a·ay·roh·gra·moo
envelope	bahasha	ba·ha·sha
stamp	stempu	staym·poo

customs declaration	azimio la forodha	a·zee·mee·oh la foh·roh·dha
domestic	ndani ya nchi	n·da·nee ya n·chee
fragile	dhaifu	dha·ee·foo
international	nje ya nchi	n·jay ya n·chee
mail	barua	ba·roo·a
mailbox	sanduku la posta	san·doo·koo la poh·sta
PO Box	Sanduku la Posta	san·doo·koo la poh·sta
postcode	simbo ya posta	seem·boh ya poh·sta

snail mail

air	kwa ndege	kwa n·day·gay
express	ekspres	ayk·sprays
registered	barua ya rejesta	ba·roo·a ya ray·jay·sta
sea	kwa meli	kwa may·lee
surface (land)	kwa lori	kwa loh·ree

Please send it by air/surface mail to (Australia).

Peleka kwa ndege/	pay·*lay*·ka kwa n·*day*·gay/
meli kwenda	*may*·lee *kwayn*·da
(Australia).	(a·oo·*stra*·lee·a)

It contains (souvenirs).

Kuna (kumbukumbu)	*koo*·na (koom·boo·*koom*·boo)
ndani.	n·*da*·nee

Where's the poste restante section?

Posta restante	*poh*·sta ray·*stan*·tay
iko wapi?	*ee*·koh *wa*·pee

Is there any mail for me?

Kuna barua zozote	*koo*·na ba·*roo*·a zoh·*zoh*·tay
zangu?	*zan*·goo

phone

What's your phone number?

Nipe simu yako?	nee·pay *see*·moo *ya*·koh

Where's the nearest public phone?

Kuna simu ya kadi	*koo*·na *see*·moo ya *ka*·dee
wapi jirani?	*wa*·pee jee·*ra*·nee

Where's the nearest telecom centre?

Telekom iko wapi?	tay·lay·*kohm ee*·ko *wa*·pee

Can I look at a phone book?

Nionyeshe kitabu	nee·oh·*nyay*·shay kee·*ta*·boo
cha namba za simu?	cha *nam*·ba za *see*·moo

The number is ...

Namba ni ...	*nam*·ba ni ...

What's the area/country code for (New Zealand)?

Namba ya miito/	*nam*·ba ya mee·*ee*·toh/
kimataifa kwa	kee·ma·ta·*ee*·fa kwa
(New Zealand) ni nini?	(noo *zee*·land) nee *nee*·nee

I want to …	*Nataka …*	na·*ta*·ka …
buy a	*kununua*	koo·noo·*noo*·a
phonecard	*kadi ya simu*	*ka*·dee ya *see*·moo
call (Singapore)	*kupiga simu*	koo·*pee*·ga *see*·moo
	kwa (Singapore)	kwa (seen·ga·*pohr*)
make a (local)	*kupiga simu*	koo·*pee*·ga *see*·moo
call	*(jirani)*	(jee·*ra*·nee)
reverse the	*kugeuza*	koo·gay·*oo*·za
charges	*gharama*	ga·*ra*·ma
speak for	*kuongea kwa*	koo·ohn·*gay*·a kwa
(three) minutes	*dakika (tatu)*	da·*kee*·ka (*ta*·too)
How much for …?	*… ni bei gani?*	… nee bay *ga*·nee
a (three)-	*Kupiga*	koo·*pee*·ga
minute call	*simu kwa*	*see*·moo kwa
	dakika (tatu)	da·*kee*·ka (*ta*·too)
each extra	*Kila dakika*	*kee*·la da·*kee*·ka
minute	*nyingine*	nyeen·*gee*·nay

---

listen for …

Umekosa namba. oo·may·*koh*·sa *nam*·ba	**Wrong number.**
Ni nani? nee *na*·nee	**Who's calling?**
Unataka (kuongea na) nani? oo·na·*ta*·ka (koo·ohn·*gay*·a na) *na*·nee	**Who do you want (to speak to)?**
Dakika moja. da·*kee*·ka *moh*·ja	**One moment.**
Hayupo. ha·*yoo*·poh	**He/She is not here.**

It's engaged.
Inatumika. ee·na·too·*mee*·ka

I've been cut off.
Imekatika. ee·may·ka·*tee*·ka

The connection's bad.
Kiungo ni kibaya. kee·*oon*·goh nee kee·*ba*·ya

Hello.
Halo. ha·*loh*

It's ...
Ni ... nee ...

Is ... there?
... yuko? ... *yoo*·koh

Can I speak to ...?
Nataka kuongea na ... na·*ta*·ka koo·ohn·*gay*·a na ...

Who am I speaking to?
Naongea na nani? na·ohn·*gay*·a na *na*·nee

Please tell him/her I called.
Mwambie nilipiga m·wam·*bee*·ay nee·lee·*pee*·ga
simu. *see*·moo

Can I leave a message?
Naomba niache na·*ohm*·ba nee·*a*·chay
ujumbe? oo·*joom*·bay

My number is ...
Simu yangu ni ... *see*·moo *yan*·goo nee ...

I don't have a contact number.
Sina simu. *see*·na *see*·moo

I'll call back later.
Nitajaribu tena nee·ta·ja·*ree*·boo *tay*·na
baadaye. ba·a·*da*·yay

---

just hang up

Swahili speakers often don't make a ceremony of saying 'goodbye' at the end of a phone call. Instead, phone conversations often end with *haya/sawa ha*·ya/*sa*·wa (OK), after which both parties hang up.

PRACTICAL

mobile/cell phone

I'd like a ...	*Nataka ...*	na·*ta*·ka ...
charger for	*chaja kwa*	*cha*·ja kwa
my phone	*simu yangu*	*see*·moo *yan*·goo
mobile/cell	*kukodisha*	koo·koh·*dee*·sha
phone for hire	*simu ya*	*see*·moo ya
	mkononi	m·koh·*noh*·nee
prepaid mobile/	*kadi ya simu*	*ka*·dee ya *see*·moo
cell phone	*ya mkononi*	ya m·koh·*noh*·nee
SIM card	*kadi ya sim*	*ka*·dee ya seem

What are the rates?
Ni bei gani?   nee bay *ga*·nee

(500 shillings) per (30) seconds.
(Shilingi mia tano)   (shee·*leen*·gee *mee*·a *ta*·noh)
kwa sekundi   kwa say·*koon*·dee
(thelathini).   (thay·la·*thee*·nee)

the internet

Where's the local Internet cafe?
Intanet Kafe iko wapi?   een·*ta*·nayt ka·*fay* ee·koh *wa*·pee

I'd like to ...	*Nataka ...*	na·*ta*·ka ...
check my	*kusoma barua*	koo·*soh*·ma ba·*roo*·a
email	*pepe yangu*	*pay*·pay *yan*·goo
get Internet	*kutumia*	koo·too·*mee*·a
access	*intaneti*	een·ta·*nay*·tee
use a printer	*kutumia*	koo·too·*mee*·a
	printa	*preen*·ta
use a scanner	*kutumia*	koo·too·*mee*·a
	skana	*ska*·na

Do you have ...?	Kuna ...?	koo·na ...
Macs	Mac	mak
PCs	PC	pee·see
a Zip drive	draivu ya zip	dra·ee·voo ya zeep

How much per ...?	Ni bei gani kwa ...?	nee bay ga·nee kwa ...
hour	saa	sa
(five) minutes	dakika (tano)	da·kee·ka (ta·noh)
page	ukurasa	oo·koo·ra·sa

How do I log on?

Nianziaje?   nee·an·zee·a·jay

Please change it to the English-language setting.

Tafadhali badilisha   ta·fa·dha·lee ba·dee·lee·sha
kutumia Kiingereza.   koo·too·mee·a kee·een·gay·ray·za

The connection is too slow.

Kiungo ni   kee·oon·goh nee
polepole mno.   poh·lay·poh·lay m·noh

It's crashed.

Imekwama.   ee·may·kwa·ma

I've finished.

Nimemaliza.   nee·may·ma·lee·za

In major urban areas you'll be able to use your overseas ATM card, make purchases at upscale locations with your credit card, and change cash or travellers cheques in foreign exchange offices.

Where's ...? ... *iko wapi?* ... *ee*·koh *wa*·pee
an automated *Mashine ya* ma·*shee*·nay ya
teller machine *kutolea pesa* koo·toh·*lay*·a *pay*·sa
a foreign *Foreks* *foh*·rayks
exchange office

What time does the bank open?
Benki inafungua *bayn*·kee ee·na·foon·*goo*·a
saa ngapi? sa n·*ga*·pee

Can I use my credit card to withdraw money?
Naweza kutumia kadi ya na·*way*·za koo·too·*mee*·a *ka*·dee ya
benki kuondoa hela? *bayn*·kee koo·ohn·*doh*·a *hay*·la

---

listen for ...

kitambulisho	kee·tam·boo·*lee*·shoh	**identification**
pasipoti	pa·see·*poh*·tee	**passport**
Hatuwezi.		
ha·too·*way*·zee		**We can't do that.**
Kiungo kimekwisha.		
kee·*oon*·goh		**The connection's down.**
kee·may·*kwee*·sha		
Kuna shida.		
koo·na *shee*·da		**There's a problem.**
Pesa zako zimekwisha.		
pay·sa za·koh		**You have no funds left.**
zee·may·*kwee*·sha		
Saini hapa.		
sa·*ee*·nee *ha*·pa		**Sign here.**

I'd like to …	*Nataka* …	na·*ta*·ka …
cash a cheque	*kulipwa fedha*	koo·*leep*·wa *fay*·dha
	kutokana na hundi	koo·toh·*ka*·na na *hoon*·dee
change a travellers cheque	*kubadilisha hundi ya msafiri*	koo·ba·dee·*lee*·sha *hoon*·dee ya m·sa·*fee*·ree
change money	*kubadilisha hela*	koo·ba·dee·*lee*·sha *hay*·la
get a cash advance	*kupata hela ya awali*	koo·*pa*·ta *hay*·la ya *a*·wa·lee
withdraw money	*kuondoa hela*	koo·ohn·*doh*·a *hay*·la

What's the …?	… *ni nini?*	… nee *nee*·nee
charge for that	*Gharama yake*	ga·*ra*·ma *ya*·kay
exchange rate	*Kiwango cha kubadilisha hela*	kee·*wan*·goh cha koo·ba·dee·*lee*·sha *hay*·la
large bill exchange rate	*Kiwango cha kubadilisha noti kubwa*	kee·*wan*·goh cha koo·ba·dee·*lee*·sha *noh*·tee *koob*·wa
small bill exchange rate	*Kiwango cha kubadilisha noti ndogo*	kee·*wan*·goh cha koo·ba·dee·*lee*·sha *noh*·tee n·*doh*·goh

The automated teller machine took my card.

Mashine ya kutolea pesa ilichukua kadi yangu.

ma·*shee*·nay ya koo·toh·*lay*·a *pay*·sa ee·lee·choo·*koo*·a *ka*·dee *yan*·goo

I've forgotten my PIN.

Nimesahau pin namba siri.

nee·may·sa·*ha*·oo peen *nam*·ba *see*·ree

Has my money arrived yet?

Je, hela yangu imeshafika?

jay *hay*·la *yan*·goo ee·may·sha·*fee*·ka

How long will it take to arrive?

Je, itachukua muda gani kufika?

jay ee·ta·choo·*koo*·a *moo*·da *ga*·nee koo·*fee*·ka

sightseeing

matembezi ya kuangalia mandhari

I'd like a ...	*Nataka ...*	na·*ta*·ka ...
guide	*kiongozi*	kee·ohn·*goh*·zee
guidebook in	*kitabu cha*	kee·*ta*·boo cha
English	*kuongoza kwa*	koo·ohn·*goh*·za kwa
	Kiingereza	kee·een·gay·*ray*·za
(local) map	*ramani*	ra·*ma*·nee
	(ya eneo hili)	(ya ay·*nay*·oh hee·lee)

Do you have	*Mna maarifa*	m·na ma·*ree*·fa
information	*kuhusu*	koo·*hoo*·soo
on ... sights?	*sehemu za ...?*	say·*hay*·moo za ...
cultural	*utamaduni*	oo·ta·ma·*doo*·nee
historical	*historia*	hee·stoh·*ree*·a
religious	*dini*	*dee*·nee
wildlife	*wanyama pori*	wa·*nya*·ma *poh*·ree

I'd like to see ...
Nataka kuona ...   na·*ta*·ka koo·*oh*·na ...

What's that?
Hiyo ni nini?   *hee*·yoh nee *nee*·nee

Who made it?
Ilitengenezwa na nani?   ee·lee·tayn·gay·*nayz*·wa na *na*·nee

How old is it?
Ina umri gani?   ee·na *oom*·ree *ga*·nee

Can I take a photograph (of you)?
Ni sawa nikipiga   nee *sa*·wa nee·kee·*pee*·ga
picha (ya wewe)?   *pee*·cha (ya *way*·way)

Polite requests, which in English have the form of questions, are usually statements in Swahili. If you'd ask 'Can you take my picture?' the answer in Swahili is likely to be a factual 'yes' (I know how to use a camera) or 'no' (I'm not a photographer). If you actually want your picture taken, a request, such as, 'I ask that you take my picture', is more likely to yield the answer 'Sure, I'll do it', or 'Sorry, I can't'.

I ask that you take my picture.

Naomba upige	na·ohm·ba oo·pee·gay
picha yangu.	pee·cha yan·goo

I'll send you the photograph.

Nitakutumia picha hii.　　　nee·ta·koo·too·mee·a pee·cha hee

Can you write down your address so I can send you the picture?

Andika anwani ili	an·dee·ka an·wa·nee ee·lee
nikutumie picha.	nee·koo·too·mee·ay pee·cha

I didn't realise I'd have to pay you.

Sikuelewa inabidi	see·koo·ay·lay·wa ee·na·bee·dee
nikulipe.	nee·koo·lee·pay

getting in

kuingia

What time does it open/close?

Inafungua/Inafunga	ee·na·foon·goo·a/ee·na·foon·ga
saa ngapi?	sa n·ga·pee

What's the admission charge?

Ni bei gani kuingia?　　　nee bay ga·nee koo·een·gee·a

Can I enter this building?

Inaruhusiwa kuingia	ee·na·roo·hoo·see·wa koo·een·gee·a
jengo hili?	jayn·goh hee·lee

Are women allowed in this mosque?

Wanawake huruhusiwa	wa·na·*wa*·kay hoo·roo·hoo·*see*·wa	
kuingia msikiti huu?	koo·een·*gee*·a m·see·*kee*·tee hoo	

Is there a	*Kuna upungufu*	koo·na oo·poon·*goo*·foo
discount for …?	*wa bei kwa …?*	wa bay kwa …
children	*watoto*	wa·*toh*·toh
families	*familia*	fa·mee·*lee*·a
groups	*vikundi*	vee·*koon*·dee
older people	*wazee*	wa·*zay*
students	*wanafunzi*	wa·na·*foon*·zee

tours/safaris

safari

Safari is the Swahili word for 'trip'. It has come into English to mean 'wildlife spotting' or 'adventure travel', and is of course used so along the African safari circuit. However, it also retains its original meaning in Swahili – so don't be surprised if people use it to refer to any sort of travel, no matter how mundane.

Can you	*Unajua …*	oo·na·*joo*·a …
recommend a …?	*nzuri?*	n·*zoo*·ree
boat trip	*safari ya boti*	sa·*fa*·ree ya *boh*·tee
camel safari	*safari ya*	sa·*fa*·ree ya
	ngamia	n·ga·*mee*·a
day trip	*safari ya*	sa·*fa*·ree ya
	siku moja	*see*·koo *moh*·ja
safari/tour	*safari*	sa·*fa*·ree
walking safari	*safari ya*	sa·*fa*·ree ya
	kutembea	koo·taym·*bay*·a

When's the next (safari)?

(Safari) ijayo itakuwa	(sa·*fa*·ree) ee·*ja*·yoh ee·ta·*koo*·wa	
lini?	*lee*·nee	

What time should we be back?

Turudi saa ngapi?	too·*roo*·dee sa n·*ga*·pee

Is/Are ... included?	*Inazingatia ...?*	ee·na·zeen·ga·*tee*·a ...
accommodation	*malazi*	ma·*la*·zee
(before/after)	*(kabla/*	*(ka*·bla/
	baadaye)	ba·a·*da*·yay)
airport transfers	*usafiri*	oo·sa·*fee*·ree
	kwenda na	*kwayn*·da na
	kutoka uwanja	koo·*toh*·ka oo·*wan*·ja
	wa ndege	wa n·*day*·gay
equipment	*kukodisha*	koo·koh·*dee*·sha
rental	*vifaa*	vee·*fa*
fuel	*mafuta*	ma·*foo*·ta
food	*chakula*	cha·*koo*·la
park entrance fees	*ada za hifadhi*	*a*·da za hee·*fa*·dhee
tent rental	*kukodisha*	koo·koh·*dee*·sha
	hema	*hay*·ma
transport	*usafiri*	oo·sa·*fee*·ree

The guide has paid.
Kiongozi amelipa.   kee·ohn·*goh*·zee a·may·*lee*·pa

How large a tip should I pay?
Nilipe bakshishi   nee·*lee*·pay bak·*shee*·shee
kiasi gani?   kee·*a*·see ga·nee

How long is the tour?
Safari itachukua   sa·*fa*·ree ee·ta·choo·*koo*·a
muda gani?   *moo*·da ga·nee

How many people will be in the group?
Kundi itakuwa na   *koon*·dee ee·ta·*koo*·wa na
watu wangapi?   *wa*·too wan·*ga*·pee

What animals are we likely to see?
Tutegemee kuona   too·tay·gay·*may* koo·*oh*·na
wanyama gani?   wa·*nya*·ma ga·nee

We're very keen to see (elephants).
Tunataka sana   too·na·*ta*·ka *sa*·na
kuona (tembo).   koo·*oh*·na (*taym*·bo)

I've lost my group.
Nimepotea   nee·may·poh·*tay*·a
kundi yangu.   *koon*·dee *yan*·goo

For animals that you might see on safari, see the **dictionary**.

I'm attending a ...	*Nahudhuria ...*	na·hoo·dhoo·*ree*·a ...
conference	*mikutano*	mee·koo·*ta*·noh
course	*mafunzo*	ma·*foon*·zoh
meeting	*mkutano*	m·koo·*ta*·noh
trade fair	*maonyesho ya*	ma·oh·*nyay*·shoh ya
	biashara	bee·a·*sha*·ra

I'm with ...	*Nipo na ...*	*nee*·poh na ...
(Tanzania	*(Tanzania*	(tan·za·*nee*·a
Breweries)	*Breweries)*	broo·ay·rees)
my colleague	*mwenzi*	mwayn·zee
my colleagues	*wenzi wangu*	wayn·zee *wan*·goo
(two) others	*(wawili)*	(wa·*wee*·lee)
	wengine	wayn·*gee*·nay

I'm alone.
Nipo peke yangu.   *nee*·poh *pay*·kay yan·goo

I have an appointment with ...
Nina mkutano na ...   *nee*·na m·koo·*ta*·noh na ...

I'm staying at ..., room ...
Ninakaa ..., chumba ...   nee·na·*ka* ... *choom*·ba ...

I'm here for (two) days/weeks.
Nipo kwa siku/   *nee*·poh kwa *see*·koo/
wiki (mbili).   *wee*·kee (m·*bee*·lee)

What's your ...?	*... yako ni nini?*	... *ya*·koh nee *nee*·nee
(email) address	*Anwani (ya*	an·*wa*·nee (ya
	barua pepe)	ba·*roo*·a *pay*·pay)
fax number	*Namba ya faksi*	*nam*·ba ya *fak*·see
mobile number	*Simu ya*	*see*·moo ya
	mkononi	m·koh·*noh*·ni
pager number	*Namba ya bipa*	*nam*·ba ya *bee*·pa
work number	*Simu ya kazi*	*see*·moo ya *ka*·zee

Here's my …	*Hii ni … yangu.*	hee nee … *yan·*goo
business card	*kadi ya*	*ka·*dee ya
	biashara	bee·a·*sha·*ra
(email) address	*anwani (ya*	an·*wa·*nee (ya
	barua pepe)	ba·*roo·*a *pay·*pay)
fax number	*namba ya faksi*	*nam·*ba ya *fak·*see
mobile number	*simu ya*	*see·*moo ya
	mkononi	m·koh·*noh·*ni
pager number	*namba ya bipa*	*nam·*ba ya *bee·*pa
work number	*simu ya kazi*	*see·*moo ya *ka·*zee

Where's the …?	*… iko wapi?*	… ee·koh *wa·*pee
business centre	*Kituo ya*	kee·*too·*oh ya
(eg in hotel)	*biashara*	bee·a·*sha·*ra
conference	*Mikutano*	mee·koo·*ta·*noh
meeting	*Mkutano*	m·koo·*ta·*noh

I need …	*Nahitaji …*	na·hee·*ta·*jee …
a computer	*kompyuta*	kohm·*pyoo·*ta
the Internet	*intaneti*	een·ta·*nay·*tee
an interpreter	*mkalimani*	m·ka·lee·*ma·*nee
more business	*kadi zaidi*	*ka·*dee za·ee·dee
cards	*za biashara*	za bee·a·*sha·*ra
some space to	*mahali pa*	ma·*ha·*lee pa
set up	*kuandaa*	koo·an·*da*
to send a fax	*kupeleka faksi*	koo·pay·*lay·*ka *fak·*see

That went very well.
Ilikwenda vizuri.　　　　ee·lee·*kwayn·*da vee·*zoo·*ree

Thank you for your time.
Asante kwa muda wako.　　a·*san·*tay kwa *moo·*da *wa·*koh

Thank you all for your time.
Asanteni kwa muda wenu.　a·san·*tay·*nee kwa *moo·*da *way·*noo

Shall we go for a drink/meal?
Twende kwa vinywaji/　　　twayn·day kwa vee·*nywa·*jee/
chakula?　　　　　　　　　cha·*koo·*la

It's on me.
Ofa yangu.　　　　　　　　oh·fa yan·goo

senior & disabled travellers
watalii wazee na wasioweza

In East Africa you're very unlikely to encounter special facilities such as modified toilets or bathroom rails, accessible parking spaces, or special taxis.

I have a disability.
Nina ulemavu. nee·na oo·lay·*ma*·voo

I need assistance.
Nahitaji msaada. na·hee·*ta*·jee m·*sa*·da

What services do you have for people with a disability?
Kuna huduma koo·na hoo·*doo*·ma
gani kwa watu ga·nee kwa *wa*·too
wenye ulemavu? way·nyay oo·lay·*ma*·voo

Is there wheelchair access?
Kuna njia ya kuingia koo·na n·*jee*·a ya koo·een·*gee*·a
kwa kiti cha kwa *kee*·tee cha
magurudumu? ma·goo·roo·*doo*·moo

How wide is the entrance?
Mlango ni upana gani? m·*lan*·goh nee oo·*pa*·na *ga*·nee

How many steps are there?
Kuna ngazi ngapi? koo·na n·*ga*·zee n·*ga*·pee

Is there a lift?
Kuna lifti? koo·na *leef*·tee

I'm deaf.
Mimi ni kiziwi. mee·mee nee kee·*zee*·wee

I have a hearing aid.
Nina chombo cha nee·na *chohm*·boh cha
kusaidia kusikia. koo·sa·ee·*dee*·a koo·see·*kee*·a

Where can I buy a hearing aid battery?
Naweza kununua wapi na·*way*·za koo·noo·*noo*·a *wa*·pee
kibetri cha chombo cha kee·*bay*·tree cha *chohm*·boh cha
kusaidia kusikia? koo·sa·ee·*dee*·a koo·see·*kee*·a

I can't see well.
Siwezi kuona vizuri.   see·*way*·zee koo·*oh*·na vee·*zoo*·ree

I'm blind.
Mimi ni kipofu.   *mee*·mee nee kee·*poh*·foo

Are guide dogs permitted?
Mbwa wa kuongoza   m·bwa wa koo·ohn·*goh*·za
kipofu huruhusiwa   kee·*poh*·foo hoo·roo·hoo·*see*·wa
hapa?   *ha*·pa

Could you help me cross the street safely?
Naomba unisaidie   na·*ohm*·ba oo·nee·sa·ee·*dee*·ay
kuvuka barabara   koo·*voo*·ka ba·ra·*ba*·ra
kwa usalama.   kwa oo·sa·*la*·ma

Is there somewhere I can sit down?
Kuna kiti?   *koo*·na *kee*·tee

guide dog	mbwa wa kuongoza	m·bwa wa koo·ohn·*goh*·za
older person	mzee	m·*zay*
person with a disability	mtu mwenye ulemavu	m·too *mway*·nyay oo·lay·*ma*·voo
ramp	mbao wa kushukia	m·*ba*·oh wa ku·shoo·*kee*·a
walking frame	magongo ya kutembelea	ma·*gohn*·goh ya koo·taym·bay·*lay*·a
walking stick	fimbo	*feem*·boh
wheelchair	kiti cha magurudumu	*kee*·tee cha ma·goo·roo·*doo*·moo

travelling with children

Is there a …?	Kuna …?	koo·na …
baby change room	chumba cha kuvalia mtoto	choom·ba cha koo·va·lee·a m·toh·toh
child-minding service	anayeweza kumlea mtoto	a·na·yay·way·za koom·lay·a m·toh·toh
child-sized portion	kiasi kwa mtoto	kee·a·see kwa m·toh·toh
children's menu	menyu kwa watoto	may·nyoo kwa wa·toh·toh
crèche	wanapolea watoto wadogo	wa·na·poh·lay·a wa·toh·toh wa·doh·goh
discount for children	punguzo la bei kwa watoto	poon·goo·zoh la bay kwa wa·toh·toh
family ticket	tiketi kwa familia	tee·kay·tee kwa fa·mee·lee·a

Do you sell …?	Mnauza …?	m·na·oo·za …
baby wipes	vitambaa kupangusa watoto	vee·tam·ba koo·pan·goo·sa wa·toh·toh
disposable nappies/diapers	nepi	nay·pee
painkillers for infants	dawa la kutuliza maumivu kwa watoto	da·wa la koo·too·lee·za ma·oo·mee·voo kwa wa·toh·toh

I need a/an …	Nahitaji …	na·hee·ta·jee …
baby seat	kiti cha kitoto	kee·tee cha kee·toh·toh
(English-speaking) babysitter	yaya (anayesema Kiingereza)	ya·ya (a·na·yay·say·ma kee·een·gay·ray·za)
booster seat	kiti kumpandisha mtoto juu	kee·tee koom·pan·dee·sha m·toh·toh joo
cot/crib	kitanda cha mtoto mchanga	kee·tan·da cha m·toh·toh m·chan·ga
highchair	kiti juu cha mtoto	kee·tee juu cha m·toh·toh
plastic bag	mfuko wa plastiki	m·foo·koh wa pla·stee·kee
potty	choo cha mtoto	choh cha m·toh·toh
pram/stroller	kigari cha mtoto	kee·ga·ree cha m·toh·toh

Do you hire prams/strollers?
Mnakodisha vigari vya watoto? — m·na·koh·dee·sha vee·ga·ree vya wa·toh·toh

Where can I change a nappy?
Nibadilishe nepi wapi? — nee·ba·dee·lee·shay nay·pee wa·pee

Where's a water tap?
Kuna bomba la maji wapi? — koo·na bohm·ba la ma·jee wa·pee

Are there any good places to take children around here?
Kuna mahali pazuri kwa watoto hapa eneo hili? — koo·na ma·ha·lee pa·zoo·ree kwa wa·toh·toh ha·pa ay·nay·oh hee·lee

Are children under (12) allowed?
Watoto chini ya miaka (kumi na miwili) huruhusiwa? — wa·toh·toh chee·nee ya mee·a·ka (koo·mee na mee·wee·lee) hoo·roo·hoo·see·wa

Is this suitable for (three)-year old children?
Inafaa kwa watoto wa miaka (mitatu)? — ee·na·fa kwa wa·toh·toh wa mee·a·ka (mee·ta·too)

Do you know a doctor who is good with children?

Unajua daktari ambaye   oo·na·*joo*·a dak·*ta*·ree am·*ba*·yay
watoto wanapenda?   wa·*toh*·toh wa·na·*payn*·da

If your child is sick, see **health**, page 183.

talking with children

kuongea na watoto

What's your name?
Jina lako nani?   *jee*·na *la*·koh *na*·nee

How old are you?
Una miaka mingapi?   oo·na mee·*a*·ka meen·*ga*·pee

When's your birthday?
Siku yako ya kuzaliwa   *see*·koo *ya*·koh ya koo·za·*lee*·wa
ni lini?   nee *lee*·nee

Do you go to school?
Unahudhuria shule?   oo·na·hoo·dhoo·*ree*·a *shoo*·lay?

What grade are you in?
Unasoma darasa gani?   oo·na·*soh*·ma da·*ra*·sa *ga*·nee

Do you learn English?
Unajifunza Kiingereza?   oo·na·jee·*foon*·za kee·een·gay·*ray*·za

Do you like sport?
Unapenda michezo?   oo·na·*payn*·da mee·*chay*·zoh

kids' talk

Children will often greet adult strangers by calling out *shikamoo* shee·ka·*moh* (lit: respectful greetings), and will be delighted if you reply with a warm *marahaba* ma·ra·*ha*·ba (lit: thank you for your respectful greetings). In many areas they'll run towards you with both hands raised above their heads. You can kneel or squat for them to place their hands on your forehead while they greet you. After this initial respectful greeting you'll usually continue by exchanging one or many of the standard greetings (see page 107).

talking about children

Is this your first child?
Huyu ni mtoto wako
wa kwanza?
hoo·yoo nee m·*toh*·toh wa·koh
wa *kwan*·za

How many children do you have?
Una watoto wangapi?
oo·na wa·*toh*·toh wan·*ga*·pee

What a beautiful child!
Kumbe, huyu ni mtoto
anayependeza!
koom·bay hoo·yoo nee m·*toh*·toh
a·na·yay·payn·*day*·za

Is it a boy or a girl?
Je, huyu ni mvulana
au msichana?
jay hoo·yoo nee m·voo·*la*·na
a·oo m·see·*cha*·na

How old is he/she?
Ana umri gani?
a·na oom·ree *ga*·nee

What's his/her name?
Anaitwa nani?
a·na·*eet*·wa na·nee

He/She looks like you.
Anakufanana.
a·na·koo·fa·*na*·na

Does he/she go to school?
Anahudhuria shule?
a·na·hoo·dhoo·*ree*·a shoo·lay

Is he/she well behaved?
Ana tabia nzuri?
a·na ta·*bee*·a n·*zoo*·ree

baby talk

Attitude towards pregnancy and motherhood in East Africa
can be surprising for a Western visitor. For example, breast-
feeding in public is always acceptable and a permission
would never be asked for in Swahili.

On the other hand, two questions you shouldn't ask
expectant mothers are: 'When's the baby due?' and 'What
are you going to call the baby?' With events like childbirth,
many Swahili speakers prefer not to count their chickens
before they hatch.

basics

Yes.	*Ndiyo.*	n·*dee*·yoh
No.	*Hapana.*	ha·*pa*·na
Please.	*Tafadhali.*	ta·fa·*dha*·lee
Thank you (very much).	*Asante (sana).*	a·*san*·tay (*sa*·na)
Thank you all (very much).	*Asanteni (sana).*	a·san·*tay*·nee (*sa*·na)
You're welcome.	*Karibu.*	ka·*ree*·boo
You're all welcome.	*Karibuni.*	ka·ree·*boo*·nee
Excuse me.	*Samahani.*	sa·ma·*ha*·nee
Forgive me.	*Nisamele.*	nee·sa·*may*·lay
Sorry.	*Pole.*	*poh*·lay

greetings & goodbyes

You can never spend too long exchanging greetings in East Africa. They vary depending on whether you're speaking to one person or several, or to an older or younger person. People often spend a few minutes with hands clasped, catching up on all the latest news.

You may notice many gestures that accompany greetings – respectful curtsies, grasped upper forearms, hand kisses or cool handshakes. Expect to shake hands often in East Africa. If your right hand is full or dirty, offer your wrist instead.

hi there

The most common greeting is *habari* ha·*ba*·ree (lit: news). The variations on this greeting are many. Common ones include *salama* sa·*la*·ma (lit: safe) instead of *habari*, which may be dropped from the greeting altogether: *(Habari) Za leo?* (ha·*ba*·ree) za *lay*·oh (lit: news of today). You can use *salama* to greet anybody you pass or to reply to any greeting.

Hello./How are you?
Habari?   ha·*ba*·ree

What's the news?
Habari gani?   ha·*ba*·ree *ga*·nee

How are you all?
Habari zenu?   ha·*ba*·ree *zay*·noo

How's everyone at home?
Habari za nyumbani?   ha·*ba*·ree za nyoom·*ba*·nee

How's work?
Habari za kazi?   ha·*ba*·ree za *ka*·zee

Good ...	*Habari za ...?*	ha·*ba*·ree za ...
day	*leo*	*lay*·oh
morning	*asubuhi*	a·soo·*boo*·hee
afternoon	*mchana*	m·*cha*·na
evening	*jioni*	jee·*oh*·nee

You can reply to almost any *habari* greeting using *nzuri* n·*zoo*·ree, *salama* sa·*la*·ma or *safi* sa·*fee* (fine). If things are just OK, add *tu* too (only) after any of these replies. Even if things are really bad, most people will reply to greetings with *nzuri tu* (lit: only fine), rather than *mbaya* m·*ba*·ya (bad). If things are really good, you can add *sana* sa·na (very), or *kabisa* ka·*bee*·sa (totally) instead of *tu*.

What's your name?
Jina lako nani?   *jee*·na *la*·koh *na*·nee

My name is ...
Jina langu ni ...   *jee*·na *lan*·goo nee ...

I'd like to introduce you to ...
Huyu ni ...   *hoo*·yoo nee ...

This is my ...	Huyu ni ...	hoo·yoo nee ...
child	mtoto wangu	m·toh·toh wan·goo
colleague	mwenzi	mwayn·zee
	wangu	wan·goo
friend	rafiki yangu	ra·fee·kee yan·goo
husband	mume wangu	moo·may wan·goo
partner	mpenzi	m·payn·zee
(intimate)	wangu	wan·goo
wife	mke wangu	m·kay wan·goo

For more kinship terms, see also **family**, page 115 and the dictionary.

I'm pleased to	Nafurahi	na·foo·ra·hee
meet you.	kukufahamu.	koo·koo·fa·ha·moo
See you later.	Baadaye.	ba·a·da·yay
Goodbye.	Tutaonana.	too·ta·oh·na·na
Bye.	Kwa heri.	kwa hay·ree
Good night.	Usiku mwema.	oo·see·koo mway·ma
Bon voyage!	Safari njema!	sa·fa·ree n·jay·ma

addressing people

There are two forms of addressing women, different in the level of formality. The word *bibi bee·bee* is more informal than *bi bee*, and can be used by anyone to refer to their grandmother, and by a husband to refer to his wife. The general term *bwana bwa·na* is used for addressing men both in formal and informal situations.

Mr/Sir	Bwana	bwa·na
Mrs/Madam	Bi	bee
Ms/Miss	Bibi	bee·bee

When addressing an older person or an authority figure, the usual exchange of greetings is:

Respectful greetings.
   Shikamoo.   shee·ka·*moh*

Thank you for your respectful greetings.
(an older person to a younger person)
   Marahaba.   ma·ra·*ha*·ba

Thank you for your respectful greetings.
(a younger person to an older person)
   Asante.   a·*san*·tay

It's common to address people by their likely position within a family. You can call an elder man 'grandfather', a middle-aged man 'father', and a youthful man 'brother'. In addition, parents are often addressed as the mother or father of one of their children (not necessarily the first born), rather than using the parent's own name, eg *mama Amina* ma·ma a·*mee*·na (Amina's mother), *baba Flora* ba·ba *floh*·ra (Flora's father).

auntie (any elder woman)	*shangazi*	shan·*ga*·zee
brother	*kaka*	*ka*·ka
father	*baba*	*ba*·ba
grandmother	*bibi*	*bee*·bee
grandfather	*babu*	*ba*·boo
mother	*mama*	*ma*·ma
respected elder	*mzee*	m·*zay*
sister	*dada*	*da*·da
sibling/friend	*ndugu*	n·*doo*·goo
uncle (any elder man)	*mjomba*	m·*johm*·ba

For information on addressing children, see **talking with children**, page 105.

making conversation

kuzungumza

What a beautiful day!
Ni siku nzuri sana!
nee see·koo n·zoo·ree sa·na

Nice/Awful weather, isn't it?
Hali ya hewa ni nzuri/mbaya, sivyo?
ha·lee ya hay·wa nee n·zoo·ree/m·ba·ya seev·yoh

Do you live here?
Unakaa hapa?
oo·na·ka ha·pa

Where are you going?
Unaenda wapi?
oo·na·ayn·da wa·pee

What are you doing?
Unafanya nini?
oo·na·fa·nya nee·nee

Do you like it here?
Unapapenda hapa?
oo·na·pa·payn·da ha·pa

I love it here.
Napapenda hapa.
na·pa·payn·da ha·pa

What's this called?
Hii inaitwa nini?
hee ee·na·eet·wa nee·nee

That's beautiful, isn't it?
Inapendeza sana, sivyo?
ee·na·payn·day·za sa·na seev·yo

meeting people

111

Where are you coming from?	*Umetoka wapi?*	oo·may·*toh*·ka *wa*·pee
I'm coming from ...	*Nimetoka ...*	nee·may·*toh*·ka ...
home	*nyumbani*	nyoom·*ba*·nee
the market	*sokoni*	soh·*koh*·nee
town	*mjini*	m·*jee*·nee
Are you here on holiday?	*Uko hapa kwa likizo?*	oo·koh *ha*·pa kwa lee·*kee*·zoh
I'm here ...	*Nipo kwa ...*	nee·poh kwa ...
for a holiday	*likizo*	lee·*kee*·zoh
on business	*biashara*	bee·a·*sha*·ra
to study	*masomo*	ma·*soh*·moh

How long are you here for?

Upo kwa muda gani?   oo·poh kwa *moo*·da *ga*·nee

I'm here for (four) weeks/days.

Nipo kwa wiki/siku (nne).   nee·poh kwa *wee*·kee/*see*·koo (*n*·nay)

---

local talk

Cool.	*Poa.*	*poh*·a
Great!	*Safi!*	*sa*·fee
Hey!	*We!*	way
How are things?	*Mambo?*	*mam*·boh
It's OK.	*Ni sawa.*	nee *sa*·wa
Just a minute.	*Subiri kidogo.*	soo·*bee*·ree kee·*doh*·goh
Just joking.	*Natania tu.*	na·ta·*nee*·a too
Maybe.	*Labda.*	*lab*·da
No problem.	*Hamna shida.*	*ham*·na *shee*·da
No way!	*Haiwezekani!*	ha·ee·way·zee·*ka*·nee
Sure.	*Sawa.*	*sa*·wa
What's the news?	*Lete habari.*	*lay*·tay ha·*ba*·ree
What's up?	*Vipi?*	*vee*·pee

The following tips on East African etiquette should help you wherever you travel in the region.

● Men and women maintain a formal distance in many social situations. Public displays of affection between sexes don't happen, but friends of the same sex often hold hands when walking around town. Feel honoured if someone of your gender makes such a display of friendship.

● It's fine to wear shorts in tourist areas. However, long pants or skirts, as well as tops with sleeves, are essential when visiting government offices or people's homes, and are preferable at most other times, especially along the Muslim-dominated coast and in rural areas.

● If you accept a gift or treat from someone, they'll often anticipate some reciprocal gesture of friendship, often a meal or gift of equivalent value. Spoken thanks are not so common in East Africa, so don't be surprised if the appreciation isn't expressed verbally.

nationalities

uraia

Where are you from?
Unatoka wapi?   oo·na·*toh*·ka *wa*·pee

I'm from …	*Natoka …*	na·*toh*·ka …
America	*Marekani*	ma·ray·*ka*·nee
Australia	*Australia*	a·oo·*stra*·lee·a
Canada	*Kanada*	*ka*·na·da
England	*Uingereza*	oo·een·gay·*ray*·za

age

How old are you?
Una miaka mingapi?   oo·na mee·*a*·ka meen·*ga*·pee

How old is your child?
Mtoto wako ana   m·*toh*·toh *wa*·koh *a*·na
miaka mingapi?   mee·*a*·ka meen·*ga*·pee

I'm ... years old.
Nina miaka ...   *nee*·na mee·*a*·ka ...

He/She is ... years old.
Ana miaka ...   *a*·na mee·*a*·ka ...

Too old!
Mzee mno!   m·*zay* m·noh

For your age, see **numbers & amounts**, page 37.

occupations & studies

What's your occupation?
Unafanya kazi gani?   oo·na·*fa*·nya *ka*·zee *ga*·nee

I'm a ...	*Mimi ni ...*	*mee*·mee nee ...
business person	*mfanyabiashara*	m·fa·nya·bee·a·*sha*·ra
chef	*mpishi*	m·*pee*·shee
driver	*dereva*	day·*ray*·va
farmer	*mkulima*	m·koo·*lee*·ma
fisher	*mvuvi*	m·*voo*·vee
journalist	*ripota*	ree·*poh*·ta
soldier	*askari*	as·*ka*·ree
teacher	*mwalimu*	mwa·*lee*·moo

I work in ...	Nafanya kazi kwenye ...	na·fa·nya ka·zee kway·nyay ...
administration	usimamizi	oo·see·ma·mee·zee
health	afya	af·ya
sales & marketing	uuzaji	oo·oo·za·jee

I'm ...		
retired	Nimestaafu.	nee·may·sta·foo
self-employed	Najiajiri.	na·jee·a·jee·ree
unemployed	Sina kazi sasa.	see·na ka·zee sa·sa

What are you studying?	Unasoma masomo gani?	oo·na·soh·ma ma·soh·mo ga·nee

I'm studying ...	Nasoma ...	na·soh·ma ...
African music/ dance	densi/muziki ya kiafrika	dayn·see/moo·zee·kee ya kee·af·ree·ka
humanities	sayansi za jurnll	sa·yan·see za ja·mee
Swahili	Kiswahili	kee·swa·hee·lee
science	sayansi	sa·yan·see

family

Do you have a ...?	Una ...?	oo·na ...
I have/don't have a ...	Nina/Sina ...	nee·na/see·na ...
boyfriend	mpenzi	m·payn·zee
brother	kaka	ka·ka
daughter	binti	been·tee
girlfriend	mpenzi	m·payn·zee
grandchild	mjukuu	m·joo·koo
husband	mume	moo·may
partner/fiancé(e)	mchumba	m·choom·ba
sister	dada	da·da
son	mwana	mwa·na
wife	mke	m·kay

For more kinship terms, see the **dictionary**.

Swahili kinship connections through your father's brothers and your mother's sisters are regarded very highly. Rather than being 'uncles' and 'aunts', they're considered your parents too. If they're older than your birth parents they're *mkubwa* m·*koob*·wa ('big'), if they're younger they're *mdogo* m·*doh*·goh ('little'). However, mother's brothers and father's sisters don't get distinguished by age. Many families in East Africa consist of one husband and two or more wives. Children of co-wives generally consider themselves brothers and sisters.

aunt	*shangazi*	shan·*ga*·zee
(father's sister)		
aunt	*mama mkubwa*	ma·ma m·*koob*·wa
(mother's older sister)		
aunt	*mama mdogo*	ma·ma m·*doh*·goh
(mother's younger sister)		
uncle	*mjomba*	m·*johm*·ba
(mother's brother)		
uncle	*baba mkubwa*	ba·ba m·*koob*·wa
(father's older brother)		
uncle	*baba mdogo*	ba·ba m·*doh*·goh
(father's younger brother)		
big mother	*mama mkubwa*	ma·ma m·*koob*·wa
(father's wife senior to your mother – the one he married before)		
little mother	*mama mdogo*	ma·ma m·*doh*·goh
(father's wife junior to your mother – the one he married after)		

Do you have children?
Una watoto? oo·na wa·*toh*·toh

How many children do you have?
Una watoto wangapi? oo·na wa·*toh*·toh wan·*ga*·pee

Are you married?
Umeoa?/Umeolewa? m/f oo·may·*oh*·a/oo·may·oh·*lay*·wa

I live with someone.
Naishi na mchumba. na·*ee*·shee na m·*choom*·ba

I'm ...

divorced	*Tumeachana.*	too·may·a·*cha*·na
married	*Nimeoa/*	nee·may·oh·a/
	Nimeolewa. m/f	nee·may·oh·*lay*·wa
not married	*Sijaoa/*	see·ja·oh·a/
yet	*Sijaolewa bado.* m/f	see·ja·oh·*lay*·wa ba·doh
separated	*Tumetengana.*	too·may·tayn·*ga*·na
single	*Mimi sina*	mee·mee *see*·na
	mpenzi.	m·*payn*·zee

farewells

kuagana

In contrast to the amount of time East Africans spend greeting each other, they put relatively little energy into saying goodbye. Often farewells simply involve confirming when you'll next meet, then walking away with a simple *haya* ha·ya (OK). Saying goodbyes before a long trip is more involved: hands clasped, the traveller is wished well and told to greet everybody at their destination.

Tomorrow is my last day here.

Kesho ni siku yangu
ya mwisho hapa.

kay·shoh nee *see*·koo *yan*·goo
ya *mwee*·shoh ha·pa

It's been great meeting you.

Nimefurahi
kukufahamu.

nee·may·foo·*ra*·hee
koo·koo·fa·*ha*·moo

---

well-wishing

Bless you!	*Heri zote!*	hay·ree zoh·tay
Bon voyage!	*Safari njema!*	sa·fa·ree n·*jay*·ma
Congratulations!	*Hongera!*	hohn·*gay*·ra
Good luck!	*Bahati njema!*	ba·*ha*·tee n·*jay*·ma
Happy birthday!	*Heri za siku kuu*	hay·ree za *see*·koo koo
	ya kuzaliwa!	ya koo·za·*lee*·wa
Merry Christmas!	*Heri za*	hay·ree za
	Krismasi!	krees·*ma*·see

If you come to (Scotland) you can stay with me.

Ukija (Skotland), karibu		oo·kee·ja (skoht·land) ka·ree·boo
sana kukaa kwetu.		sa·na koo·ka kway·too

Keep in touch!

Niwasiliane!		nee·wa·see·lee·a·nay

Here's my ...	Hii ni ... yangu.	hee nee ... yan·goo
address	anwani	an·wa·nee
email address	anwani ya	an·wa·nee ya
	barua pepe	ba·roo·a pay·pay
phone number	simu	see·moo
What's your ...?	... yako ni nini?	... ya·koh nee nee·nee
address	Anwani	an·wa·nee
email address	Anwani ya	an·wa·nee ya
	barua pepe	ba·roo·a pay·pay

common interests

shauku za pamoja

What do you do in your spare time?
Unafanya nini kwa   oo·na·*fa*·nya *nee*·nee kwa
starehe?   sta·*ray*·hay

Do you like ...?	*Unapenda ...?*	oo·na·*payn*·da ...
I like ...	*Ninapenda ...*	nee·na·*payn*·da ...
I don't like ...	*Sipendi ...*	see·*payn*·dee ...
bao (board game)	*bao*	*ba*·oh
cooking	*kupika*	koo·*pee*·ka
dancing	*kucheza densi*	koo·*chay*·za *dayn*·see
films	*filamu*	fee·*la*·moo
gardening	*kulima bustani*	koo·*lee*·ma boo·*sta*·nee
hiking	*kutembea*	koo·taym·*bay*·a
	porini	poh·*ree*·nee
music	*muziki*	moo·*zee*·kee
painting	*sanaa*	sa·*na*
photography	*kupiga picha*	koo·*pee*·ga *pee*·cha
reading	*kusoma*	koo·*soh*·ma
shopping	*ununuzi*	oo·noo·*noo*·zee
socialising	*kuchanganyika*	koo·chan·ga·*nyee*·ka
	na wengine	na wayn·*gee*·nay
sport	*michezo*	mee·*chay*·zoh
surfing the Internet	*kutumia*	koo·too·*mee*·a
	intaneti	een·ta·*nay*·tee
travelling	*kusafiri*	koo·sa·*fee*·ree
watching TV	*kutazama*	koo·ta·*za*·ma
	televisheni	tay·lay·vee·*shay*·nee

For sporting activities, see **sport**, page 141.

music

Do you ...?	Wewe ...?	way·way ...
dance	hucheza densi	hoo·chay·za dayn·see
go to concerts	huenda kuona muziki	hoo·ayn·da koo·oh·na moo·zee·kee
listen to music	husikiliza muziki	hoo·see·kee·lee·za moo·zee·kee
play an instrument	hucheza ala ya muziki	hoo·chay·za a·la ya moo·zee·kee
sing	huimba	hoo·eem·ba

Which ... do you like?	Unapenda ... gani?	oo·na·payn·da ... ga·nee
bands	vikundi	vee·koon·dee
music	muziki	moo·zee·kee
singers	waimbaji	wa·eem·ba·jee

Which African music videos do you like?

Unapenda video gani za muziki ya kiafrika?	oo·na·payn·da vee·day·oh ga·nee za moo·zee·kee ya kee·af·ree·ka

Where can I see music videos by local bands?

Niende wapi kuona video za muziki za vikundi vya hapa?	nee·ayn·day wa·pee koo·oh·na vee·day·oh za moo·zee·kee za vee·koon·dee vya ha·pa

drums	ngoma	n·goh·ma
horns	siwa	see·wa
shakers	kayamba	ka·yam·ba
tambourine	dufu	doo·foo
xylophone	marimba	ma·reem·ba

blues	*muziki ya Marekani ya kusikitisha*	moo·*zee*·kee ya ma·ray·*ka*·nee ya koo·see·kee·*tee*·sha
brass music	*muziki ya ngoma*	moo·*zee*·kee ya n·*goh*·ma
classical music	*muziki ya Ulaya ya zamani*	moo·*zee*·kee ya oo·*la*·ya ya za·*ma*·nee
electronic music	*muziki ya Ulaya ya kilabuni*	moo·*zee*·kee ya oo·*la*·ya ya kee·la·*boo*·nee
jazz	*jazi*	*ja*·zee
Kenyan dance music	*benga*	*bayn*·ga
pop	*muziki ya kisasa*	moo·*zee*·kee ya kee·*sa*·sa
rock	*roki*	*roh*·kee
popular music of Zanzibar	*taarab*	*ta*·rab
traditional music	*muziki ya mila na desturi*	moo·*zee*·kee ya *mee*·la na day·*stoo*·ree
world music	*muziki ya sehemu mbalimbali za dunia*	moo·*zee*·kee ya say·*hay*·moo m·ba·lee·m·*ba*·lee za doo·*nee*·a
Zairean jazz	*sukosi*	soo·*koh*·see

Off to a concert? See **tickets**, page 49 and **going out**, page 127.

cinema & theatre

sinema na tamthilia

I feel like going to a ...	*Nataka kwenda ...*	na·*ta*·ka *kwayn*·da ...
Did you like the ...?	*Ulipenda ...?*	oo·lee·*payn*·da ...
ballet	*densi*	*dayn*·see
film	*filamu*	fee·*la*·moo
play	*tamthilia*	tam·thee·*lee*·a

What's showing at the cinema/theatre tonight?
Kuna filamu/tamthilia   koo·na fee·*la*·moo/tam·thee·*lee*·a
gani leo?   *ga*·nee *lay*·oh

Is it in English?
Ni kwa Kiingereza?   nee kwa kee·een·gay·*ray*·za

Does it have (English) subtitles?
kuna maandishi (ya   koo·na man·*dee*·shee (ya
Kiingereza) chini?   kee·een·gay·*ray*·za) *chee*·nee

Have you seen …?
Umeona …?   oo·may·*oh*·na …

Who's in it?
Kuna waigizaji gani?   koo·na wa·ee·gee·*za*·jee *ga*·nee

It stars …
Mwigizaji mkuu ni …   mwee·gee·*za*·jee m·*koo* nee …

I like …	*Napenda …*	na·*payn*·da …
I don't like …	*Sipendi …*	see·*payn*·dee …
action movies	*filamu zenye*	fee·*la*·moo *zay*·nyay
	misisimko	mee·see·*seem*·koh
African cinema	*filamu za*	fee·*la*·moo za
	kiafrika	kee·af·*ree*·ka
animated films	*katuni hai*	ka·*too*·nee *ha*·ee
comedies	*filamu za*	fee·*la*·moo za
	kuchekesha	koo·chay·*kay*·sha
documentaries	*filamu za hali*	fee·*la*·moo za *ha*·lee
	halisi	ha·*lee*·see
drama	*hadithi kama*	ha·*dee*·thee *ka*·ma
	riwaya	ree·*wa*·ya
Hindi cinema	*filamu za*	fee·*la*·moo za
	kihindi	kee·*heen*·dee
horror movies	*filamu za*	fee·*la*·moo za
	kutisha	koo·*tee*·sha
sci-fi	*hadithi za*	ha·*d ee*·thee za
	kubuni za	koo·*boo*·nee za
	kisayansi	kee·sa·*yan*·see
short films	*filamu fupi*	fee·*la*·moo *foo*·pee
war movies	*filamu*	fee·*la*·moo
	kuhusu vita	koo·*hoo*·soo *vee*·ta

feelings

hisia

Do you feel ...?	*Unasikia ...?*	oo·na·see·*kee*·a ...
I feel ...	*Nasikia ...*	na·see·*kee*·a ...
I don't feel ...	*Sisikii ...*	see·see·*kee* ...
cold	*baridi*	ba·*ree*·dee
happy	*furaha*	foo·*ra*·ha
hot	*joto*	*joh*·toh
hungry	*njaa*	n·*ja*
sad	*masikitiko*	ma·see·kee·*tee*·koh
thirsty	*kiu*	*kee*·oo

If feeling unwell, see **health**, page 183.

mixed feelings

a little	*kidogo*	kee·*doh*·goh
I'm a little sad.	*Nasikitika kidogo.*	na·see·kee·*tee*·ka kee·*doh*·goh
extremely/very	*sana*	*sa*·na
I'm very happy.	*Nafurahi sana.*	na·foo·*ra*·hee *sa*·na
somewhat	*tu*	too
I feel just OK.	*Nasikia nzuri tu.*	na·see·*kee*·a n·*zoo*·ree too

opinions

Do you like it?
Unaipenda?   oo·na·ee·*payn*·da

What do you think of it?
Unaionaje?   oo·na·ee·oh·*na*·jay

I thought it was ...	*Nilifikiri*	nee·lee·fee·*kee*·ree
	ilikuwa ...	ee·lee·*koo*·wa ...
It's ...	*Ni ...*	nee ...
awful	*mbaya sana*	m·*ba*·ya *sa*·na
boring	*ya kuchosha*	ya koo·*choh*·sha
great	*nzuri kabisa*	n·*zoo*·ree ka·*bee*·sa
interesting	*ya kuvutia*	ya koo·voo·*tee*·a
OK	*sawa tu*	*sa*·wa too
strange	*siyo kawaida*	*see*·yoh ka·wa·*ee*·da

politics & social issues

Conversing and debating with friends is an important part of daily life in East Africa. People express strong opinions about sport, politics and the latest local gossip.

Which party do you vote for?
Unapiga kura kwa   oo·na·*pee*·ga *koo*·ra kwa
chama gani?   *cha*·ma *ga*·nee

I support the	*Mimi*	*mee*·mee
... party.	*napendelea*	na·payn·day·*lay*·a
	chama cha ...	*cha*·ma cha ...
communist	*kikomunisti*	kee·koh·moo·*nee*·stee
democratic	*demokrasia*	day·moh·kra·*see*·a
green	*kijani*	kee·*ja*·nee
socialist	*soshalisti*	soh·sha·*lee*·stee

Did you hear about …?
   Ulisikia kuhusu …?   oo·lee·see·*kee*·a koo·*hoo*·soo …

I agree/don't agree with …
   Nakubali/Sikubali na …   na·koo·*ba*·lee/see·koo·*ba*·lee na …

How do people feel about …?
   Watu wana maoni   *wa*·too *wa*·na ma·*oh*·nee
   gani kuhusu …?   *ga*·nee koo·*hoo*·soo …

abortion	*kutoa mimba*	koo·*toh*·a *meem*·ba
AIDS	*ukimwi*	oo·*keem*·wee
animal rights	*haki za wanyama*	*ha*·kee za wa·*nya*·ma
crime	*uhalifu*	oo·ha·*lee*·foo
drugs	*madawa ya*	ma·*da*·wa ya
	kulevya	koo·*lay*·vya
the economy	*uchumi*	oo·*choo*·mee
education	*elimu*	ay·*lee*·moo
euthanasia	*eutanasia*	ay·oo·ta·na·*see*·a
Christian	*mamishionari*	ma·mee·shee·oh·*na*·ree
missionaries	*wakristo*	wa·*kree*·stoh
globalisation	*utandawazi*	oo·tan·da·*wa*·zee
human rights	*haki za*	*ha*·kee za
	binadamu	bee·na·*da*·moo
indigenous issues	*mada za wenyeji*	*ma*·da za way·*nyay*·jee
religious	*imani kali ya*	ee·*ma*·nee *ka*·lee ya
fundamentalism	*kidini*	kee·*dee*·nee
racism	*ubaguzi wa*	oo·ba·*goo*·zee wa
	rangi	*ran*·gee
sexism	*ubaguzi wa*	oo·ba·*goo*·zee wa
	kijinsia	kee·jeen·*see*·a
terrorism	*ugaidi*	oo·ga·*ee*·dee
unemployment	*ukosefu wa*	oo·koh·*say*·foo wa
	kazi	*ka*·zee
the war in …	*vita katika …*	*vee*·ta ka·*tee*·ka …

the environment

Is there a ... problem here?
  Kuna shida ya ... hapa?   koo·na *shee*·da ya ... *ha*·pa

What should be done about ...?
  Ni afadhali kufanya   nee·a·fa·*dha*·lee koo·*fa*·nya
  nini kuhusu ...?   *nee*·nee koo·*hoo*·soo ...

drought	*ukame*	oo·*ka*·may
endangered	*spishi zilizo*	*spee*·shee zee·*lee*·zoh
species	*hatarini*	ha·ta·*ree*·nee
genetically	*chakula chenye*	cha·*koo*·la *chay*·nyay
modified	*jini*	*jee*·nee
food	*iliyoumbwa*	ee·lee·yoh·*oom*·bwa
hunting	*uwindaji*	oo·ween·*da*·jee
nuclear testing	*majaribio*	ma·ja·ree·*bee*·oh
	ya nyuklia	ya *nyook*·lee·a
ozone layer	*tabaka la hewa*	ta·*ba*·ka la *hay*·wa
	ya ozoni	ya oh·*zoh*·nee
pesticides	*viuavisumbufu*	vee·oo·a·vee·soom·*boo*·foo
petroleum	*utumiaji ovyo*	oo·too·mee·*a*·jee *oh*·vyoh
resource	*wa maliasili*	wa ma·lee·a·*see*·lee
exploitation	*ya mafuta*	ya ma·*foo*·ta
poaching	*uwindaji*	oo·ween·*da*·jee
	kinyume	kee·*nyoo*·may
	na sheria	na shay·*ree*·a
pollution	*uchafuzi*	oo·cha·*foo*·zee
recycling	*mradi wa*	m·*ra*·dee wa
programme	*urejelezaji*	oo·ray·jay·lay·*za*·jee
toxic waste	*taka za sumu*	*ta*·ka za *soo*·moo
water supply	*upatikanaji*	oo·pa·tee·ka·*na*·jee
	wa maji	wa *ma*·jee
Is it a	*... inahifadhiwa?*	ee·na·hee·fa·*dhee*·wa ...
protected ...?		
park	*Mbuga*	m·*boo*·ga
species	*Spishi*	*spee*·shee

where to go

kuenda wapi

What's there to do in the evenings?
Kuna nini kufanya   koo·na *nee*·nee koo·*fa*·nya
saa za jioni?   sa za jee·*oh*·nee

What's on …?	*Nini*	*nee*·nee
	inatokea …?	ee·na·toh·*kay*·a …
this weekend	*wikendi hii*	wee·*kayn*·dee hee
tonight	*usiku huu*	oo·*see*·koo hoo

I feel like going to a …	*Nataka kwenda kwenye …*	na·*ta*·ka *kwayn*·da *kway*·nyay …
bar	*baa*	ba
beer club	*kilabu*	kee·*la*·boo
café	*mgahawa*	m·ga·*ha*·wa
casino	*kasino*	ka·*see*·noh
coffee house	*mgahawa*	m·ga·*ha*·wa
dance and drumming performance	*ngoma*	n·*goh*·ma
concert	*kusikiliza*	koo·see·kee·*lee*·za
	muziki	moo·*zee*·kee
film	*filamu*	fee·*la*·moo
karaoke bar	*karaoke*	ka·ra·*oh*·kay
nightclub	*klabu ya usiku*	*kla*·boo ya oo·*see*·koo
party	*sherehe*	shay·*ray*·hay
pub	*baa*	ba
restaurant	*hoteli kula*	hoh·*tay*·lee koo·la

Are gay people bothered here?
Wasenge huteswa hapa?   wa·*sayn*·gay hoo·*tays*·wa *ha*·pa

Is there a local … guide?	Kuna mwongozo wa mji kuhusu …?	koo·na mwohn·goh·zoh wa m·jee koo·hoo·soo …
entertainment	burudani	boo·roo·da·nee
film	filamu	fee·la·moo
gay	wasenge	wa·sayn·gay
music	muziki	moo·zee·kee

Where can I find …?	… iko wapi?	… ee·koh wa·pee
clubs	Kilabu/Vilabu	kee·la·boo/vee·la·boo
gay venues	Mahali pa wasenge	ma·ha·lee pa wa·sayn·gay
places to eat	Hoteli kula	hoh·tay·lee koo·la
pubs	Baa	ba

For more on bars and drinks, see **eating out**, page 153.

invitations

mialiko

What are you doing …?	Unafanya nini …?	oo·na·fa·nya nee·nee …
this weekend	wikendi hii	wee·kayn·dee hee
tonight	usiku huu	oo·see·koo hoo

Would you like to go (for a) …?	Unataka kwenda (kwa) …?	oo·na·ta·ka kwayn·da (kwa) …
dancing	kucheza densi	koo·chay·za dayn·see
drink	kunywa vinywaji	koo·nywa vee·nywa·jee
meal	chakula	cha·koo·la
walk	kutembea	koo·taym·bay·a

My round.
Ofa yangu.   oh·fa yan·goo

Do you know a good restaurant?
Unajua hoteli nzuri kula?   oo·na·joo·a hoh·tay·lee n·zoo·ree koo·la

We're having a party.
Tutakuwa na sherehe. too·ta·*koo*·wa na shay·*ray*·hay·

You should come.
Uje. *oo*·jay

responding to invitations

Sure!
Sawa! *sa*·wa

Yes, I'd love to.
Sawa, nitafurahi. *sa*·wa nee·ta·foo·*ra*·hee

It's very kind of you to invite me.
Wewe ni mwema *way*·way nee *mway*·ma
kunialika. koo·nee·a·*lee*·ka

Where shall we go?
Twende wapi? *twayn*·day *wa*·pee

No, I'm afraid I can't.
Asante, lakini siwezi. a·*san*·tay la·*kee*·nee see·*way*·zee

What about tomorrow?
Kesho, je? *kay*·shoh jay

arranging to meet

What time will we meet?
Tukutane saa ngapi? too·koo·*ta*·nay sa n·*ga*·pee

Where will we meet?
Tukutane wapi? too·koo·*ta*·nay *wa*·pee

Let's meet at …	*Tukutane …*	too·koo·*ta*·nay …
(eight) o'clock	*saa (mbili)*	sa (m·*bee*·lee)
the entrance	*mlango wa*	m·*lan*·goh wa
	kuingia	koo·een·*gee*·a

I'll pick you up.
Nitakuja kukuchukua.   nee·ta·*koo*·ja koo·koo·choo·*koo*·a

Are you ready?
Tayari?   ta·*ya*·ree

I'm ready.
Mimi ni tayari.   *mee*·mee nee ta·*ya*·ree

I'll be coming later.
Nitakuja baadaye.   nee·ta·*koo*·ja ba·a·*da*·yay

See you later/tomorrow.
Tutaonana baadaye/   too·ta·oh·*na*·na ba·a·*da*·yay/
kesho.   *kay*·sho

I'm looking forward to it.
Natarejea sana.   na·ta·ray·*jay*·a *sa*·na

Sorry I'm late.
Samahani kwa   sa·ma·*ha*·ni kwa
kuchelewa.   koo·chay·*lay*·wa

Never mind.
Usijali.   oo·see·*ja*·lee

For the Swahili time system, go to **time & dates**, page 39.

drugs

I don't take drugs.
Situmii madawa   see·too·*mee* ma·*da*·wa
ya kulevya.   ya koo·*lay*·vya

I take (*miraa*) occasionally.
Natumia (miraa)   na·too·*mee*·a (mee·*ra*)
mara kwa mara.   *ma*·ra kwa *ma*·ra

Do you want to have a smoke?
Unataka kuvuta?   oo·na·*ta*·ka koo·*voo*·ta

Do you have a light?
Una kibiriti?   oo·na kee·bee·*ree*·tee

I'm high.
Nimelewa.   nee·may·*lay*·wa

asking someone out

Where would you like to go (tonight)?
Unataka kwenda　　　　oo·na·*ta*·ka *kwayn*·da
wapi (jioni hii)?　　　　wa·pee (jee·*oh*·nee hee)

Would you like to do something (tomorrow)?
Unataka kupanga　　　　oo·na·*ta*·ka koo·*pan*·ga
pamoja (kwa kesho)?　　pa·*moh*·ja (kwa *kay*·shoh)

Yes, I'd love to.
Asante, ndiyo.　　　　　a·*san*·tay n·*dee*·yoh

Sorry, I can't.
Asante, siwezi.　　　　　a·*san*·tay see·*way*·zee

local talk

He/She is a babe.
Huyu ni mrembo.　　　　hoo·yoo nee m·*raym*·boh

He/She is hot.
Huyu amependeza　　　　hoo·yoo a·may·payn·*day*·za
sana sana.　　　　　　　*sa*·na *sa*·na

He's a bastard.
Yeye ni mshenzi.　　　　*yay*·yay nee m·*shayn*·zee

She's a bitch.
Yeye ni jahili.　　　　　*yay*·yay nee ja·*hee*·lee

He/She gets around.
Yeye ni jamvi la　　　　*yay*·yay nee *jam*·vee la
wageni.　　　　　　　　wa·*gay*·nee

pick-up lines

Would you like a drink?
Unywe kinywaji? oony·way keeny·wa·jee

You look like someone I know.
Unafanana mtu oo·na·fa·na·na m·too
ninayejua. nee·na·yay·joo·a

You're a fantastic dancer.
Wewe ni mchezadensi way·way nee m·chay·za·dayn·se
mzuri sana. m·zoo·ree sa·na

Can I dance with you?
Tucheze densi? too·chay·zay dayn·see

Can I sit here?
Naomba nikae hapa? na·ohm·ba nee·ka·ay ha·pa

Can I accompany you to your home?
Nikusindikize kwako? nee·koo·seen·dee·kee·zay kwa·koh

Can I take you to my place?
Twende kwangu? twayn·day kwan·goo

rejections

No, thank you.
Hapana, asante. ha·pa·na a·san·tay

I'd rather not.
Nisingependa, asante. nee·seen·gay·payn·da a·san·tay

I'm here with my girlfriend/boyfriend.
Nipo na mpenzi wangu. nee·poh na m·payn·zee wan·goo

Excuse me, I have to go now.
Samahani, lazima sa·ma·ha·nee la·zee·ma
niondoke sasa. nee·ohn·doh·kay sa·sa

Leave me alone (now)!
Niache (sasa)! nee·a·chay (sa·sa)

Piss off!
Toka! toh·ka

getting closer

I like you very much.
Nakupenda sana. — na·koo·*payn*·da *sa*·na

You're great.
Wewe ni mzuri sana. — *way*·way nee m·*zoo*·ree *sa*·na

Can I kiss you?
Nikubusu? — nee·koo·*boo*·soo

Do you want to come inside for a while?
Unataka kuingia — oo·na·*ta*·ka koo·een·*gee*·a
ndani kidogo? — n·*da*·nee kee·*doh*·goh

Do you want a massage?
Unataka kuchuliwa? — oo·na·*ta*·ka koo·choo·*lee*·wa

Can I stay over?
Nikae usiku huu? — nee·*ka*·ay oo·*see*·koo hoo

sex

Kiss me.
Nibusu. — nee·*boo*·soo

I want you.
Nakutaka. — na·koo·*ta*·ka

Let's go to bed.
Twende kitandani. — *twayn*·day kee·tan·*dan*·ee

Touch me here.
Niguse hapa. — nee·*goo*·say *ha*·pa

Do you like this?
Unapenda hii? — oo·na·*payn*·da hee

I like that.
Napenda hiyo. — na·*payn*·da *hee*·yoh

I don't like that.
Sipendi hiyo. — see·*payn*·dee *hee*·yoh

I think we should stop now.
Tusimame sasa. — too·see·*ma*·may *sa*·sa

Do you have a condom?
Una kondom? — oo·na *kohn*·dom

I have a condom.
Nina kondom. — *nee*·na *kohn*·dom

Let's use a condom.
Tutumie kondom. — too·too·*mee*·ay *kohn*·dom

I won't do it without protection.
Sitafanya bila kinga. — see·ta·*fa*·nya *bee*·la *keen*·ga

It's my first time.
Ni mara yangu ya kwanza. — nee *ma*·ra *yan*·goo ya *kwan*·za

Don't worry, I'll do it myself.
Usiwe na wasiwasi, — oo·*see*·way na wa·see·*wa*·see
nitafanya mwenyewe. — nee·ta·*fa*·nya mway·*nyay*·way

It helps to have a sense of humour.
Husaidia kuweza — hoo·sa·ee·*dee*·a koo·*way*·za
kucheka. — koo·*chay*·ka

Oh my God!
Mwenyezi Mungu! — mway·*nyay*·zee *moon*·goo

That's great.
Safi sana. — *sa*·fee *sa*·na

Easy, lion!
Tulia, simba! — too·*lee*·a *seem*·ba

faster	*kwa mwendo*	kwa *mwayn*·doh
harder	*kwa nguvu*	kwa n·*goo*·voo
slower	*pole pole*	*poh*·lay *poh*·lay
softer	*punguza nguvu*	poon·*goo*·za n·*goo*·voo
That was …	*Ilikuwa …*	ee·lee·*koo*·wa …
amazing	*barabara*	ba·*ra*·ba·ra
animalistic	*kama wanyama*	*ka*·ma wa·*nya*·ma
like a dream	*kama ndoto*	*ka*·ma n·*doh*·toh

love

upenzi

Will you go out with me?
Utakuwa mpenzi wangu?   oo·ta·*koo*·wa m·*payn*·zee *wan*·goo

Will you meet my parents?
Utakutana na wazazi   oo·ta·koo·*ta*·na na wa·*za*·zee
wangu?   *wan*·goo

I think we're good together.
Nafikiri tunafaa   na·fee·*kee*·ree too·na·*fa*
pamoja.   pa·*moh*·ja

I love you.
Nakupenda.   na·koo·*payn*·da

Will you marry me? (man asking woman)
Niolewe.   nee·oh·*lay*·way

Will you marry me? (woman asking man)
Nioe.   nee·*oh*·ay

is it a he or a she?

Swahili doesn't distinguish between 'he' and 'she' – the language treats all people the same, regardless of gender. The only exceptions are verbs like 'to marry' (a woman is married, while a man marries), and certain sexual terms.

romance

problems

Are you seeing someone else?
Umekuwa unatembea oo·may·*koo*·wa oo·na·taym·*bay*·a
na mwengine? na mwayn·*gee*·nay

He/She is just a friend.
Yeye ni rafiki tu. *yay*·yay nee ra·*fee*·kee too

You're just using me for sex.
Unanitumia kwa oo·na·nee·too·*mee*·a kwa
mapenzi tu. ma·*payn*·zee too

I never want to see you again.
Sitaki kukuona see·*ta*·kee koo·koo·*oh*·na
tena daima. *tay*·na da·*ee*·ma

I don't think it's working out.
Sidhani inafaa. see·*dha*·nee ee·na·*fa*

We'll work it out.
Itafanikiwa. ee·ta·fa·nee·*kee*·wa

leaving

I have to leave (tomorrow).
Inabidi niondoke ee·na·*bee*·dee nee·ohn·*doh*·kay
(kesho). (*kay*·sho)

I'll keep in touch.
Nitakuwasiliana. nee·ta·koo·wa·see·lee·*a*·na

I'll miss you.
Nitakukosa. nee·ta·koo·*koh*·sa

I'll visit you.
Nitakutembelea. nee·ta·koo·taym·bay·*lay*·a

beliefs & cultural differences
imani na tofauti za utamaduni

religion

What's your religion?
Wewe ni dini gani? — way·way nee *dee*·nee *qa*·nee

I'm not religious.
Sina dini. — see·na *dee*·nee

I'm ...	*Mimi ni ...*	mee·mee nee ...
agnostic	*agnostiki*	ag·noh·*stee*·kee
Buddhist	*Mbudisti*	m·boo·*dee*·stee
Catholic	*Mkatoliki*	m·ka·toh·*lee*·kee
Christian	*Mkristo*	m·*kree*·stoh
Hindu	*Mhindu*	m·*heen*·doo
Jewish	*Myahudi*	m·ya·*hoo*·dee
Lutheran	*Mluteri*	m·loo·*tay*·ree
Muslim	*Mwislamu*	mwee·*sla*·moo
Protestant	*Mprotestanti*	m·proh·tay·*stan*·tee
Sikh	*Msiik*	m·*seek*

I believe/don't	*Naamini/*	na·a·*mee*·nee/
believe in ...	*Siamini*	see·a·*mee*·nee
	mambo ya ...	*mam*·boh ya ...
fate	*majaliwa*	ma·ja·*lee*·wa
God	*Mungu*	moon·goo

Where can I ...?	*Naweza ... wapi?*	na·*way*·za ... *wa*·pee
attend mass	*kuhudhuria*	koo·hoo·dhoo·*ree*·a
	misa	*mee*·sa
attend a	*kuhudhuria*	koo·hoo·dhoo·*ree*·a
service	*ibada*	ee·*ba*·da
pray	*kusali*	koo·*sa*·lee
worship	*kutoa huduma*	koo·*toh*·a hoo·*doo*·ma

Could I visit the mosque?
Naweza kutembelea   na·*way*·za koo·taym·bay·*lay*·a
msikiti?   m·see·*kee*·tee

Have you been on a Haj?
Umekwenda   oo·may·*kwayn*·da
kwenye Haji?   *kway*·nyay *ha*·jee

Are you planning to do a Haj?
Unategemea kwenda   oo·na·tay·gay·*may*·a *kwayn*·da
kwenye Haji?   *kway*·nyay *ha*·jee

cultural differences

tofauti za utamaduni

Is this a local or national custom?
Je, ni mila ya watu   jay nee *mee*·la ya *wa*·too
wa hapa, au ni mila   wa *ha*·pa *a*·oo nee *mee*·la
ya taifa nzima?   ya ta·*ee*·fa n·*zee*·ma

I don't want to offend you.
Sitaki kukusafihi.   see·*ta*·kee koo·koo·sa·*fee*·hee

I'm not used to this.
Sijazoea kufanya hivyo.   see·ja·zoh·*ay*·a koo·*fa*·nya *heev*·yoh

I'd rather not join in.
Napendelea   na·payn·day·*lay*·a
kutoshiriki.   koo·toh·shee·*ree*·kee

I'll try it.
Nitajaribu.   nee·ta·ja·*ree*·boo

This is different.
Ni tofauti.   nee toh·fa·*oo*·tee

This is interesting.
Ni ya kuvutia.   nee ya koo·voo·*tee*·a

It's against my beliefs.
Inavuka imani zangu.   ee·na·*voo*·ka ee·*ma*·nee *zan*·goo

I didn't mean to do/say anything wrong.
Sikukusudia kufanya/   see·koo·koo·soo·*dee*·a koo·*fa*·nya/
kusema vibaya.   koo·*say*·ma vee·*ba*·ya

When's the gallery/museum open?
Nyumba ya sanaa/
makumbusho
hufungua saa ngapi?
nyoom·ba ya sa·na/
ma·koom·boo·shoh
hoo·foon·goo·a sa n·ga·pee

What kind of art are you interested in?
Unapenda sanaa
ya aina gani?
oo·na·payn·da sa·na
ya a·ee·na ga·nee

What's in the collection?
Kuna sanaa gani hapa?
koo·na sa·na ga·nee ha·pa

What do you think of ...?
Unafikiriaje
kuhusu ...?
oo·na·fee·kee·ree·a·jay
koo·hoo·soo ...

It's an exhibition of ...
Ni onyesho la ...
nee oh·nyay·shoh la ...

I'm interested in ...
Napenda ...
na·payn·da ...

I like the works of ...
Napenda kazi ya ...
na·payn·da ka·zee ya ...

It reminds me of ...
Inanikumbusha
kuhusu ...
ee·na·nee·koom·boo·sha
koo·hoo·soo ...

... art	sanaa ya ...	sa·na ya ...
African	kiafrika	kee·a·free·ka
contemporary	kisasa	kee·sa·sa
figurative	tamathali	ta·ma·tha·lee
graphic	grafu	gra·foo
performance	uigizaju	oo·ee·gee·za·jee

art

139

architecture	ujenzi	oo·jayn·zee
artwork	usanii	oo·sa·nee
curator	afisa mkuu	a·fee·sa m·koo
	wa sanaa	wa sa·na
design	usanifu	oo·sa·nee·foo
drawing	mchoro	m·choh·roh
etching	uchoraji picha	oo·choh·ra·jee pee·cha
	kwa asidi	kwa a·see·dee
exhibit	onyesho	oh·nyay·shoh
exhibition hall	chumba cha	choom·ba cha
	maonyesho	ma·oh·nyay·shoh
installation	ufungaji	oo·foon·ga·jee
Makonde	uchongaji wa	oo·chohn·ga·jee wa
carvings	Makonde	ma·kohn·day
opening	ufunguzi	oo·foon·goo·zee
painter	msanii wa rangi	m·sa·nee wa ran·gee
painting	picha ya	pee·cha ya
(canvas)	uchoraji	oo·choh·ra·jee
painting	uchoraji	oo·choh·ra·jee
(the art)	kwa rangi	kwa ran·gee
period	kipindi	kee·peen·dee
permanent	makusanyo	ma·koo·sa·nyoh
collection	ya kudumu	ya koo·doo·moo
print	picha	pee·cha
sculptor	mchongaji	m·chohn·ga·jee
sculpture	uchongaji	oo·chohn·ga·jee
statue	sanamu	sa·na·moo
studio	chumba cha	choom·ba cha
	msanii	m·sa·nee
style	mtindo	m·teen·doh
technique	mbinu	m·bee·noo
Tingatinga	tingatinga	teen·ga·teen·ga
paintings		
wood carving	uchongaji	oo·chohn·ga·jee
	wa mbao	wa m·ba·oh

sporting interests

kupenda michezo

What sport do you …?	… mchezo gani?	… m·*chay*·zoh *ga*·nee
play	Unacheza	oo·na·*chay*·za
follow	Unafuata	oo·na·foo·*a*·ta
I play/do …	Nacheza …	na·*chay*·za …
I follow …	Nafuata …	na·foo·*a*·ta …
athletics	michezo ya riadha	mee·*chay*·zo ya ree·*a*·dha
basketball	mpira wa kikapu	m·*pee*·ra wa kee·*ka*·poo
boxing	ndondi	n·*dohn*·dee
football (soccer)	soka	*so*·ka
karate	kareti	ka·*ray*·tee
netball	netibali	nay·tee·*ba*·lee
running	kukimbia	koo·keem·*bee*·a
swimming	kuogelea	koo·oh·gay·*lay*·a
tennis	tenesi	tay·*nay*·see
volleyball	mpira wa wavu	m·*pee*·ra wa *wa*·voo

Do you like (cricket)?
Unapenda (kriketi)?   oo·na·*payn*·da (kree·*kay*·tee)

Yes, very much.
Ndiyo, sana.   n·*dee*·yoh *sa*·na

Not really.
Siyo sana.   *see*·yo *sa*·na

I like watching it.
Napenda kutazama.   na·*payn*·da koo·ta·*za*·ma

Who's your favourite ...?	*Unapendelea* *... gani?*	oo·na·payn·day·*lay*·a ... *ga*·nee
long-distance runner	*mkimbiaji*	m·keem·bee·*a*·jee
sportsperson	*mwanamichezo*	mwa·na·mee·*chay*·zoh
team	*timu*	*tee*·moo

For more sports, see the **dictionary**.

going to a game

Would you like to go to a game?
> *Unataka kwenda* *kwenye mchezo?*
> oo·na·*ta*·ka *kwayn*·da *kwa*·nyay m·*chay*·zoh

Who are you supporting?
> *Unapendelea nani?*
> oo·na·payn·day·*lay*·a *na*·nee

Who's playing/winning?
> *Nani wanacheza/* *wanashinda?*
> *na*·nee wa·na·*chay*·za/ wa·na·*sheen*·da

That was a bad/great game!
> *Mchezo ulikuwa* *mbaya/safi sana!*
> m·*chay*·zoh oo·lee·*koo*·wa m·*ba*·ya/*sa*·fee *sa*·na

scoring

What's the score?
> *Nini matokeo?*
> *nee*·nee ma·toh·*kay*·oh

It's (a) ...	*Ni* ...	nee ...
draw/even	*sare*	*sa*·ray
love (zero)	*bila*	*bee*·la
match point	*pointi* *ya mechi*	poh·*een*·tee ya *may*·chee
nil (zero)	*sifuri*	see·*foo*·ree

playing sport

Do you want to play?
Unataka kucheza?   oo·na·*ta*·ka koo·*chay*·za

Can I join in?
Naweza kucheza?   na·*way*·za koo·*chay*·za

That would be great.
Safi.   sa·fee

I can't.
Siwezi.   see·*way*·zee

I have an injury.
Nimejeruhiwa.   nee·may·jay·roo·*hee*·wa

Your/My point.
Pointi yako/yangu.   poh·*een*·tee ya·koh/*yan*·goo

Kick/Pass it to me!
Nitoe pasi!   nee·*toh*·ay pa·see

You're a good player.
Wewe ni mchezaji   *way*·way nee m·chay·*za*·jee
mzuri.   m·*zoo*·ree

Thanks for the game.
Asante kwa mchezo.   a·*san*·tay kwa m·*chay*·zoh

Where's a good place to …?	*Wapi ni pazuri …?*	*wa*·pee nee pa·*zoo*·ree …
fish	*kuvua samaki*	koo·*voo*·a sa·*ma*·kee
go horse riding	*kutembea kwa farasi*	koo·taym·*bay*·a kwa fa·*ra*·see
run	*kukimbia*	koo·keem·*bee*·a

Where's a …?	Kuna … wapi?	koo·na … wa·pee
golf course	uwanja wa gofu	oo·wan·ja wa goh·foo
gym	kilabu ya mazoezi	kee·la·boo ya ma·zoh·ay·zee
swimming pool	bwawa la kuogelea	bwa·wa la koo·oh·gay·lay·a
tennis court	kiwanja cha tenesi	kee·wan·ja cha tay·nay·see

What's the charge per …?	Ni bei gani kwa …?	nee bay ga·nee kwa …
day	siku	see·koo
game	mchezo	m·chay·zoh
hour	saa	sa
visit	kutembelea	koo·taym·bay·lay·a

Do I have to be a member to attend?

Ni lazima kuwa	nee la·zee·ma koo·wa
mwanachama	mwa·na·cha·ma
ili kuingia?	ee·lee koo·een·gee·a

Is there a women-only session?

Kuna kipindi kwa	koo·na kee·peen·dee kwa
wanawake tu?	wa·na·wa·kay too

Where are the changing rooms?

Chumba cha kubadilisha	choom·ba cha koo·ba·dee·lee·sha
nguo kiko wapi?	n·goo·oh kee·koh wa·pee

Can I hire a (court)?

Naweza kukodisha	na·way·za koo·koh·dee·sha
(kiwanja)?	kee·wan·ja

---

sports talk

What a …!	… gani!	… ga·nee
goal	goli	goh·lee
hit	ushindi	oo·sheen·dee
kick	teke	tay·kay
pass	pasi	pa·see
performance	onyesho	oh·nyay·shoh

SOCIAL

144

football/soccer

Who plays for (Yanga)?
Nani ni wachezaji — na·nee nee wa·chay·za·jee
wa (Yanga)? — wa (yan·ga)

He's a great (player).
Yeye ni (mchezaji) — yay·yay nee (m·chay·za·jee)
mzuri sana. — m·zoo·ree sa·na

Which team is at the top of the league?
Timu gani ni juu ya ligi? — tee·moo ga·nee nee joo ya lee·gee

What a great/terrible team!
Timu hiyo ni safi/ — tee·moo hee·yoh nee sa·fee/
mbaya sana! — m·ba·ya sa·na

ball	mpira	m·pee·ra
fan	mshabiki	m·sha·bee·kee
goal	mlango	m·lan·goh
player	mchezaji wa mpira	m·chay·za·jee wa m·pee·ra
red card	kadi nyekundu	ka·dee nyay·koon·doo
referee	rifa/refa	ree·fa/ray·fa

water sports

Where's a good diving site?
Wapi ni pazuri — wa·pee nee pa·zoo·ree
kuzamia? — koo·za·mee·a

Can I book a lesson?
Naweza kupanga — na·way·za koo·pan·ga
mafunzo? — ma·foon·zoh

Is the equipment regularly maintained?
Vifaa huthibitishwa — vee·fa hoo·thee·bee·tee·shwa
vizuri? — vee·zoo·ree

Can I hire (a) …?	Nataka kukodisha …	na·ta·ka koo·koh·dee·sha …
boat	boti	boh·tee
canoe	mtumbwi	m·toom·bwee
diving gear	vifaa vya kuzamia	vee·fa vya koo·za·mee·a
kayak	kayaki	ka·ya·kee
life jacket	jaketi la kuokolea	ja·kay·tee la ku·oh·koh·lay·a
water-skis	skii za maji	skee za ma·jee
wetsuit	vazi la kuzamia	va·zee la koo·za·mee·a

Are there any …?	Kuna …?	koo·na …
currents	mikondo	mee·kohn·doh
reefs	miamba	mee·am·ba
rips	mikondo	mee·kohn·doh
sharks	papa	pa·pa
water hazards	hatari katika maji	ha·ta·ree ka·tee·ka ma·jee
whales	nyangumi	nyan·goo·mee

cave	pango	pan·goh
coral formations	mwamba wa tumbawe	mwam·ba wa toom·ba·way
diving boat	boti ya safari za kuzamia	boh·tee ya sa·fa·ree za koo·za·mee·a
guide	kiongozi	kee·ohn·goh·zee
motorboat	motaboti	moh·ta·boh·tee
night dive	kuzamia wakati wa usiku	koo·za·mee·a wa·ka·tee wa oo·see·koo
sailing boat	chombo chenye tanga	chohm·boh chay·nyay tan·ga
surfboard	ubao wa kutelezea	oo·ba·oh wa koo·tay·lay·zay·a
wall dive	kuzamia kwenye ukuta	koo·za·mee·a kway·nyay oo·koo·ta
(wind)surfing	kuteleza (na tanga)	koo·tay·lay·za (na tan·ga)
wreck	msambaratiko	m·sam·ba·ra·tee·koh

hiking

kutembea porini

Where can I …?	Naweza … wapi?	na·way·za … wa·pee
buy supplies	kununua	koo·noo·noo·a
	mahitaji	ma·hee·ta·jee
find someone	kumkuta mtu	koom·koo·ta m·too
who knows	anayejua	a·na·yay·joo·a
this area	eneo hili	ay·nay·oh hee·lee
get a map	kununua	koo·noo·noo·a
	ramani	ra·ma·nee
hire hiking	kukodisha	koo·koh·dee·sha
gear	vifaa vya	vee·fa vya
	kutembea	koo·taym·bay·a
	porini	poh·ree·nee
Do we need	Inabidi	ee·na·bee·dee
to take …?	tuchukue …?	too·choo·koo·ay …
food	chakula	cha·koo·la
a sheet	shuka na	shoo·ka na
and cover	tandiko	tan·dee·koh
water	maji	ma·jee

We'd like to go wildlife spotting.

Tunataka kwenda too·na·ta·ka kwayn·da
kutafuta wanyama pori. koo·ta·foo·ta wa·nya·ma poh·ree

Can you recommend a trekking company?

Unaweza kupendekeza oo·na·way·za koo·payn·day·kay·za
kampuni ya safari kam·poo·nee ya sa·fa·ree
kwa miguu? kwa mee·goo

Do we need a guide?

Inabidi tuwe na ee·na·bee·dee too·way na
kiongozi? kee·ohn·goh·zee

Are there guided treks?
Kuna safari kwa miguu   koo·na sa·*fa*·ree kwa mee·*goo*
kwenye viongozi?   kway·nyay vee·ohn·*goh*·zee

Are park fees included?
Ada za hifadhi   *a*·da za hee·*fa*·dhee
zinazingatiwa?   zee·na·zeen·ga·*tee*·wa

Will we be staying in huts?
Tutakaa kibandani?   too·ta·*ka* kee·ban·*dan*·ee

Will we be camping?
Tutapiga hema?   too·ta·*pee*·ga *hay*·ma

I'd like to hire a porter.
Nataka kuajiri   na·*ta*·ka koo·a·*jee*·ree
mchukuzi.   m·choo·*koo*·zee

Can I see your permit?
Naomba kuona   na·*ohm*·ba koo·*ohn*·a
kibali chako.   kee·*ba*·lee *cha*·koh

Which route would you recommend?
Unapendekeza   oo·na·payn·day·*kay*·za
njia gani?   n·*jee*·a *ga*·nee

How high is the climb?
Ni mita ngapi juu?   nee *mee*·ta n·*ga*·pee joo

How long is the trail?
Njia ni urefu gani?   n·*jee*·a nee oo·*ray*·foo *ga*·nee

Is it safe?
Ni salama?   nee sa·*la*·ma

Which is the	*Njia gani*	n·*jee*·a *ga*·nee
… route?	*… zaidi?*	… za·*ee*·dee
easiest	*ni rahisi*	nee ra·*hee*·see
shortest	*ni fupi*	nee *foo*·pee

Is the track …?	*Njia …?*	n·*jee*·a …
icy	*yenye barafu*	*yay*·nyay ba·*ra*·foo
(well-)marked	*iliotiwa*	ee·lee·oh·*tee*·wa
	alama (nzuri)	a·*la*·ma (n·*zoo*·ree)
very steep	*huongezeka*	hoo·ohn·gay·*zay*·ka
	ghafla	*ga*·fla

Does this path go to …?
  Njia hii inaenda …? n·*jee*·a hee ee·na·*ayn*·da …

Is the water OK to drink?
  Maji yananywika? ma·*jee* ya·nany·*wee*·ka

I think I'm suffering from altitude sickness.
  Nadhani nimeugua na·*dha*·nee nee·may·oo·*goo*·a
  kwa sababu ya kimo. kwa sa·*ba*·boo ya *kee*·moh

I need to descend immediately.
  Ni lazima nee *la*·zee·ma
  nitelemke sasa hivi. nee·tay·*laym*·kay sa·sa *hee*·vee

Thanks for running a great trek.
  Asante kwa kuongoza a·*san*·tay kwa koo·ohn·*goh*·za
  safari nzuri sana. sa·*fa*·ree n·*zoo*·ree *sa*·na

Thanks for carrying our bags.
  Asante kwa kubeba a·*san*·tay kwa koo·*bay*·ba
  mizigo yetu. mee·*zee*·goh *yay*·too

Where can I find the …?	*… iko wapi?*	*… ee*·koh *wa*·pee
camping ground	*Uwanja wa kupiga kambi*	oo·*wan*·ja wa koo·*pee*·ga kam·bee
nearest village	*Kijiji jirani*	kee·*jee*·jee jee·*ra*·nee
showers	*Bafuni*	ba·*foo*·nee
toilet	*Choo*	cho

active volcano	*volkeno hai*	vol·*kay*·noh *ha*·ee
forest	*msitu*	m·*see*·too
glacier	*uwanja wa barafu*	oo·*wan*·ja wa ba·*ra*·foo
grassland	*ukanda wa mbuga*	oo·*kan*·da wa m·*boo*·ga
mountain peak	*kilele cha mlima*	kee·*lay*·lay cha m·*lee*·ma
national park	*hifadhi ya taifa*	hee·*fa*·dhee ya ta·*ee*·fa
summit	*kilele*	kee·*lay*·lay
wildlife reserve	*hifadhi ya wanyama*	hee·*fa*·dhee ya wa·*nya*·ma

outdoors

149

beach

Where's the ...	*Ufukwe ...*	oo·*fook*·way ...
beach?	*uko wapi?*	oo·koh wa·pee
nearest	*karibu zaidi*	ka·*ree*·boo za·*ee*·dee
nudist	*kwa watu uchi*	kwa *wa*·too oo·chee
public	*kwa hadhara*	kwa ha·dha·ra
How much	*Ni bei gani*	nee bay *ga*·nee
for a/an ...?	*kwa ...?*	kwa ...
chair	*kiti*	*kee*·tee
hut	*kibanda*	kee·*ban*·da
umbrella	*mwamvuli*	mwam·*voo*·lee
Where can	*... iko wapi?*	... ee·koh wa·pee
I find the ...?		
showers	*Bafuni*	ba·*foo*·nee
toilets	*Choo*	cho

Do we have to pay?
  Ni lazima kulipa?   nee *la*·zee·ma koo·*lee*·pa

Is it safe to dive/swim here?
  Ni salama kuzamia/   nee sa·*la*·ma koo·za·*mee*·a/
  kuogelea hapa?   koo·oh·gay·*lay*·a ha·pa

What time is high/low tide?
  Maji kujaa/kupwa   *ma*·jee koo·*ja*/*koop*·wa
  ni saa ngapi?   nee sa n·*ga*·pee

signs		
Usipige	oo·see·*pee*·gay	**No Diving**
Mbizi	m·*bee*·zee	
Usiogelee	oo·see·oh·gay·*lay*	**No Swimming**

weather

What's the weather like?
Hali ya hewa ikoje? · · · · · · · · · ha·lee ya *hay*·wa ee·*koh*·jay

It's ...

cold	*Ni baridi.*	nee ba·*ree*·dee
hot	*Ni joto.*	nee *joh*·toh
raining	*Inanyesha mvua.*	ee·na·*nyay*·sha m·*voo*·a
snowing	*Theluji*	thay·*loo*·jee
	inaanguka.	ee·na·an·*goo*·ka
sunny	*Kuna jua.*	koo·na *joo*·a
windy	*Kuna upepo.*	koo·na oo·*pay*·poh
... season	*kipindi cha ...*	kee·*peen*·dee cha ...
cold	*baridi*	ba·*ree*·dee
dry	*kiangazi*	kee·an·*ga*·zee
harvest	*kuvuna*	koo·*voo*·na
hot	*joto*	*joh*·toh
rainy	*mvua*	m·*voo*·a

Where can
I buy ...? *... wapi?* · · · · · · nee·noo·*noo*·ay
Ninunue ... *wa*·pee
| a rain jacket | *koti la mvua* | *koh*·tee la m·*voo*·a |
| an umbrella | *mwamvuli* | mwam·*voo*·lee |

flora & fauna

What ... is that?	*Ni ... gani?*	nee ... *ga*·nee
animal	*mnyama*	m·*nya*·ma
plant	*mmea*	m·*may*·a

Is it ...?	*Ni ...?*	nee ...
dangerous	*yenye hatari*	*yay*·nyay ha·*ta*·ree
endangered	*spishi zilizo*	*spee*·shee zee·*lee*·zoh
	hatarini	ha·ta·*ree*·nee
poisonous	*yenye sumu*	*yay*·nyay *soo*·moo
protected	*hifadhiwa*	hee·fa·*dhee*·wa

What's it used for?
Ina matumizi gani?   *ee*·na ma·too·*mee*·zee *ga*·nee

Can you eat the fruit?
Tunda linalika?   *toon*·da lee·na·*lee*·ka

We're very keen to see (elephants).
Tunataka sana   too·na·*ta*·ka *sa*·na
kuona (tembo).   koo·*oh*·na (*taym*·boh)

Yesterday we saw (impala).
Jana tuliona (swala).   *ja*·na too·lee·*oh*·na (*swa*·la)

local plants & animals

baobab	*mbuyu*	m·*boo*·yoo
coconut palm	*mnazi*	m·*na*·zee
mangrove	*mkoko*	m·*koh*·koh
miombo woodland	*msitu wa*	m·*see*·too wa
	miombo	mee·*ohm*·boh
rainforest	*msitu wa*	m·*see*·too wa
	mvua	m·*voo*·a
savanna	*mbuga*	m·*boo*·ga
buffalo	*mbogo*	m·*boh*·goh
camel	*ngamia*	nga·*mee*·a
crocodile	*mamba*	*mam*·ba
elephant	*ndovu/*	n·*doh*·voo/
	tembo	*taym*·boh
gazelle	*swala/swara*	*swa*·la/*swa*·ra
giraffe	*twiga*	*twee*·ga
hippopotamus	*kiboko*	kee·*boh*·koh
leopard	*chui*	*choo*·ee
lion	*simba*	*seem*·ba
monkey	*tumbili*	toom·*bee*·lee
python	*chatu*	*cha*·too
rhinoceros	*kifaru*	kee·*fa*·roo
sable antelope	*pala hala*	*pa*·la *ha*·la
spitting cobra	*swila*	*swee*·la
zebra	*punda*	*poon*·da
	milia	mee·*lee*·a

basics

misingi

breakfast	*chai ya asubuhi*	*cha*·ee ya a·soo·*boo*·hee
lunch	*chakula cha mchana*	cha·*koo*·la cha m·*cha*·na
dinner	*chakula cha jioni*	cha·*koo*·la cha jee·*oh*·nee
snack	*kumbwe*	*koom*·bway
eat v	*kula*	*koo*·la
drink v	*kunywa*	*koony*·wa

Is there food?
Kuna chakula? koo·na cha·*koo*·la

Can you cook for us?
Unaweza kutupikia chakula? oo·na·*way*·za koo·too·pee·*kee*·a cha·*koo*·la

I'd like …
Nataka … na·*ta*·ka …

I'm starving!
Nina njaa kali! *nee*·na n·*ja ka*·lee

finding a place to eat

kutafuta mahali kula

Can you recommend a …?	*Unaweza kupendekeza …?*	oo·na·*way*·za koo·payn·day·*kay*·za …
bar	*baa*	ba
café/coffee house	*mgahawa*	m·ga·*ha*·wa
restaurant	*hoteli kula*	hoh·*tay*·lee *koo*·la

Where would you go for ...?	Unapenda kwenda wapi kwa ...?	oo·na·payn·da kwayn·da wa·pee kwa ...
a celebration	sherehe	shay·ray·hay
a cheap meal	chakula rahisi	cha·koo·la ra·hee·see
Chinese food	chakula cha kichina	cha·koo·la cha kee·chee·na
European food	chakula cha kiulaya	cha·koo·la cha kee·oo·la·ya
Indian food	chakula cha kihindi	cha·koo·la cha kee·heen·dee
local specialities	chakula cha kienyeji	cha·koo·la cha kee·ay·nyay·jee

I'd like to reserve a table for ...	Nataka kuhifadhi meza kwa ...	na·ta·ka koo·hee·fa·dhee may·za kwa ...
(two) people	watu (wawili)	wa·too (wa·wee·lee)
(eight) o'clock	saa (mbili)	sa (m·bee·lee)

I'd like ..., please.	Naomba ...	na·ohm·ba ...
a children's menu	menyu kwa watoto	may·nyoo kwa wa·toh·toh
the drink list	orodha ya vinywaji	oh·roh·dha ya veeny·wa·jee
a half portion	nusu	noo·soo
a menu (in English)	menyu (kwa Kiingereza)	may·nyoo (kwa kee·een·gay·ray·za)
a table for (five)	meza kwa (watano)	may·za kwa (wa·ta·noh)
the nonsmoking section	eneo ambalo hakuna sigara	ay·nay·oh am·ba·loh ha·koo·na see·ga·ra
the smoking section	eneo kwa kuvuta sigara	ay·nay·oh kwa koo·voo·ta see·ga·ra

Are you still serving food?
Kuna chakula bado?   koo·na cha·*koo*·la *ba*·doh

How long is the wait?
Inabidi kusubiri   ee·na·*bee*·dee koo·soo·*hee*·ree
kwa muda gani?   kwa *moo*·da *ga*·nee

restaurant

hoteli

What would you recommend?
Chakula gani ni   cha·*koo*·la *ga*·nee nee
kizuri?   kee·*zoo*·ree

What's in that dish?
Chakula hicho   cha·*koo*·la *hee*·choh
kinapikwaje?   kee·na·peek·*wa*·jay

I'll have that.
Nataka hicho.   na·*ta*·ka *hee*·choh

eating out

155

Does it take long to prepare?

Inachukua muda	ee·na·choo·*koo*·a *moo*·da
mrefu kuandaa?	m·*ray*·foo koo·an·*da*

Are the meals freshly cooked?

Milo hupikwa sasa	*mee*·loh hoo·*peek*·wa *sa*·sa
hivi au zamani kidogo?	*hee*·vee *a*·oo za·*ma*·ni kee·*doh*·goh

Is it self-serve?

Ni lazima kujihuduma?	nee *la*·zee·ma koo·jee·hoo·*doo*·ma

Is there a cover charge?

Kuna bei ya kuingia?	*koo*·na bay ya koo·een·*gee*·a

Is service included in the bill?

Bili inazingatia	*bee*·lee ee·na·zeen·*ga*·tee·a
huduma?	hoo·*doo*·ma

Are these complimentary?

Hizi ni bure?	*hee*·zee nee *boo*·ray

---

look for ...

Kiamsha Hamu	kee·*am*·sha *ha*·moo	Appetisers
Supu	*soo*·poo	Soups
Chakula Kikuu	cha·*koo*·la kee·*koo*	Main Courses
Saladi	sa·*la*·dee	Salads
Vinginevyo	veen·gee·*nay*·vyo	Side Dishes
Kitindamlo	kee·teen·da·m·loh	Desserts
Vinywaji	veeny·*wa*·jee	Drinks
Soda	*soh*·da	Soft Drinks
Pombe Kali	*pohm*·bay *ka*·lee	Spirits
Bia	*bee*·a	Beers
Mvinyo	m·*vee*·nyoh	Sparkling Wines
Mwenye Povu	mway·nyay *poh*·voo	
Mvinyo	m·*vee*·nyoh	White Wines
Mweupe	mway·*oo*·pay	
Mvinyo	m·*vee*·nyoh	Red Wines
Mwekundu	mway·*koon*·doo	

For more words you might see on a menu, see the **culinary reader**, page 173.

I'd like ...	Nataka ...	na·ta·ka ...
a local	chakula maalum	cha-koo-la ma-loom
speciality	cha kienyeji	cha kee-ay-nyay-jee
a meal fit	chakula kama	cha-koo-la ka-ma
for a king	kingefaa kwa	keen-gay-fa kwa
	mfalme	m-fal-may
a sandwich	sandwichi	sand-wee-chee
that dish	chakula hicho	cha-koo-la hee-choh
the chicken	kuku	koo-koo

I'd like it with/	Nataka na/	na·ta·ka na/
without ...	bila ...	bee·la ...
cheese	chizi	chee·zee
chilli (sauce)	(mchuzi wa)	(m-choo-zee wa)
	pilipili	pee·lee-pee·lee
	hoho	hoh·hoh
garlic	kitunguu	kee-toon-goo
	saumu	sa-oo-moo
peanuts	karanga	ka-ran-ga
oil	mafuta	ma-foo-ta
pepper	pilipili	pee·lee-pee·lee
salad	saladi	sa-la-dee
salt	chumvi	choom-vee
vinegar	siki	see-kee
tomato sauce/	mchuzi wa	m-choo-zee wa
ketchup	nyanya	nya-nya

For additional items, see the **culinary reader**. For other specific meal requests, see **vegetarian & special meals**, page 171.

---

listen for ...

Unapenda...?	
oo·na·payn·da ...	Do you like ...?
Napendekeza ...	
na·payn·day·kay·za ...	I suggest the ...
Unapenda kipikwaje?	How would you like
oo·na·payn·da kee·peek·wa·jay	that cooked?

at the table

Please bring …	Lete …	lay·tay …
a cloth	kitambaa	kee·tam·ba
	kufunika meza	koo·foo·nee·ka may·za
a (wine-)	glasi	gla·see
glass	(ya mvinyo)	(ya m·vee·nyoh)
a serviette	kitambaa cha	kee·tam·ba cha
	mikono	mee·koh·noh
the bill	bili	bee·lee

I didn't order that.
Sikuagiza hicho.　　　see·koo·a·gee·za hee·choh

There's a mistake in the bill.
Kuna kosa kwenye bili.　　koo·na koh·sa kwayn·yay bee·lee

I'll pay!
Nitalipa!　　nee·ta·lee·pa

I invited you, you're my guest.
Nilikukaribisha,　　nee·lee·koo·ka·ree·bee·sha
wewe ni mgeni wangu.　　way·way nee m·gay·nee wan·goo

ashtray
chombo cha majivu
chohm·boh cha ma·jee·voo

spoon
kijiko
kee·jee·koh

fork
uma
oo·ma

plate
sahani
sa·ha·nee

knife
kisu
kee·soo

wineglass
glasi ya mvinyo
gla·see ya m·vee·nyoh

glass
glasi
gla·see

table
meza
may·za

talking food

I love this dish.
Napenda sana   na·*payn*·da *sa*·na
chakula hiki.   cha·*koo*·la *hee*·kee

I love the local cuisine.
Napenda sana   na·*payn*·da *sa*·na
chakula cha kienyeji.   cha·*koo*·la cha kee·ay·*nyay*·jee

That was delicious!
Chakula kitamu sana!   cha·*koo*·la kee·*ta*·moo *sa*·na

street food

chapati	cha·*pa*·tee	a round bread cooked like a pancake
chipsi	*chee*·psee	deep-fried potatoes
chipsi mayai	*chee*·psee ma·*ya*·ee	omelette made with chips
chungwa	*choon*·gwa	orange (usually eaten by squeezing the juice into your mouth)
kande	*kan*·day	a stew with beans & whole kernels of maize
mahindi	ma·*heen*·dee	grilled corn on the cob
mkate wa mayai	m·*ka*·tay wa ma·*ya*·ee	a mixture of eggs, ground meat, onion & spices, fried until brown
mishkaki	meesh·*ka*·kee	meat on a skewer, grilled until crisp
samosa/ sambusa	sa·*moh*·sa/ sam·*boo*·sa	a mixture of meat, onions, vegetables & spices fried in a triangular pastry
supu	*soo*·poo	soup with a piece of meat
wali maharagwe	*wa*·lee ma·ha·*ra*·gway	cooked rice & beans

My compliments to the chef.
Mwambie mpishi chakula ni kizuri.	mwam·*bee*·ay m·*pee*·shee cha·*koo*·la nee kee·*zoo*·ree

I'm full.
Nimeshiba.	nee·may·*shee*·ba

This isn't very good.
Chakula hiki si kizuri sana.	cha·*koo*·la *hee*·kee see kee·*zoo*·ree *sa*·na

This is too spicy.
Chakula hiki ni mno chenye viungo.	cha·*koo*·la *hee*·kee nee m·noh *chay*·nyay vee·*oon*·goh

methods of preparation

mibinu ya kuandaa

I'd like it …	*Nataka …*	na·*ta*·ka …
I don't want it …	*Sitaki …*	si·*ta*·kee …
boiled	*ya kuchemshwa*	ya koo·*chaym*·shwa
broiled	*ya kuchomwa*	ya koo·*chohm*·wa
fried	*ya kukaangwa*	ya koo·*kan*·gwa
grilled	*ya kuchomwa*	ya koo·*chohm*·wa
mashed	*ya kuponda*	ya koo·*pohn*·da
medium	*ya kuiva*	ya koo·*ee*·va
	wastani	*wa*·sta·nee
rare	*ya kuiva*	ya koo·*ee*·va
	kidogo	kee·*doh*·goh
reheated	*kiwekwe*	kee·*wayk*·way
	moto tena	*moh*·toh *tay*·na
steamed	*ya kupikwa*	ya koo·*pee*·kwa
	kwa mvuke	kwa m·*voo*·kay
well-done	*ya kuiva sana*	ya koo·*ee*·va *sa*·na
with the	*kwenye*	*kway*·nyay
dressing/sauce	*mchuzi*	m·*choo*·zee
on the side	*pembeni*	paym·*bay*·nee
without …	*bila …*	*bee*·la …

in the bar

Excuse me!
Samahani!
sa·ma·*ha*·nee

I'm next.
Zamu yangu ijayo.
za·moo yan·goo ee·*ja*·yoh

I'll have …
Nipe …
nee·pay …

Same again, please.
Hiki tena.
hee·kee *tay*·na

No ice, thanks.
Bila barafu, asante.
bee·la ba·*ra*·foo a·*san*·tay

I'll buy you a drink.
Nitakununulia kinywaji.
nee·ta·koo·noo·noo·*lee*·a keeny·*wa*·jee

What would you like?
Unataka nini?
oo·na·*ta*·ka *nee*·nee

I don't drink alcohol.
Sinywi pombe.
seeny·wee *pohm*·bay

It's my round.
Mzunguko wangu.
m·*zoon*·goo·koh *wan*·goo

How much is that?
Ni bei gani?
nee bay *ga*·nee

Do you serve meals here?
Kuna chakula hapa?
koo·na cha·*koo*·la *ha*·pa

listen for …

Unakunywa nini? oo·na·*koony*·wa *nee*·nee	**What are you having?**
Nafikiri umekunywa ya kutosha. na·fee·*kee*·ree oo·may·*koony*·wa ya koo·*toh*·sha	**I think you've had enough.**
Maagizo ya mwisho. ma·a·*gee*·zoh ya *mwee*·shoh	**Last orders.**

nonalcoholic drinks

All water sold in sealed bottles in East Africa is clean, but usually flat – the only water you'll find with bubbles is soda water. If you can't find water in a bottle, make sure any water you drink has been boiled.

Has this water been boiled?

| Maji haya | ma·jee ha·ya |
| yalichemshwa? | ya·lee·chaym·shwa |

... water	maji ...	ma·jee ...
boiled	yaliyochemshwa	ya·lee·yoh·chaym·shwa
bottled	kwenye chupa	kway·nyay choo·pa
cold	ya baridi	ya ba·ree·dee
hot	ya moto	ya moh·toh
mineral	ya madini	ya ma·dee·nee

orange juice	maji ya	ma·jee ya
	machungwa	ma·choon·gwa
soda water	klub soda	kloob soh·da
(cold) soft drink	soda (ya baridi)	soh·da (ya ba·ree·dee)

(cup of) ...	(kikombe cha) ...	(kee·kohm·bay cha) ...
ginger tea	chai ya	cha·ee ya
	tangawizi	tan·ga·wee·zee
spiced tea	chai masala	cha·ee ma·sa·la
tea	chai	cha·ee

(cup of)	(kikombe cha)	(kee·kohm·bay cha)
coffee ...	kahawa ...	ka·ha·wa ...
with milk	na maziwa	na ma·zee·wa
with lemon	na limau	na lee·ma·oo
with spices	na viungo	na vee·oon·goh
without (sugar)	bila (sukari)	bee·la (soo·ka·ree)

FOOD

162

East Africans drink tea and coffee at all hours, even on a hot afternoon. It's different in Central Africa, where cool drinks are the go on hot days. You might be offered a soda or a beer instead of a hot drink – but it's quite common that soft drinks or beer will be served at room temperature.

… coffee	kahawa …	ka·ha·wa …
black	ya rangi	ya ran·gee
decaffeinated	bila kafini	bee·la ka·fee·nee
iced	baridi yenye	ba·ree·dee yay·nyay
	barafu	ba·ra·foo
strong	yenye	yay·nyay
	nguvu	n·goo·voo
weak	isiye na	ee·see·yay na
	nguvu	n·goo·voo
white	ya maziwa	ya ma·zee·wa

alcoholic drinks

pombe

Most East Africans drink their beer warm. When you order, you should specify whether you want your beer *baridi* ba·ree·dee (cold) or *ya moto* ya moh·toh (warm).

a … of beer	… ya bia	… ya bee·a
glass	glasi	gla·see
half liter	nusu lita	noo·soo lee·ta
jug	lita	lee·ta
large bottle	chupa kubwa	choo·pa koob·wa
pint	painti	pa·een·tee
small bottle	chupa ndogo	choo·pa n·doh·goh

There are different types of home-made brews in East Africa, depending on the region, but the most common ones are made of maize, millet or banana. Local brews are usually drunk from a shared plastic pot called *lita lee*·ta, though you can agree to pour from the pot into glasses. When joining a group of people drinking *pombe pohm*·bay (alcoholic drink) the accepted practice is to promptly order another litre which then gets added to the pot. If you're tempted to partake in drinking local brews, be aware of the health risks that are often associated with the consumption of some of them.

Can I have a glass, please?
    Naomba bilauri.   na·*ohm*·ba bee·la·*oo*·ree

mbege	m·*bay*·gay	banana beer
pombe	*pohm*·bay	alcoholic beverage
pombe	*pohm*·bay	home-made brew
ya kienyeji	ya kee·ay·*nyay*·jee	
konyagi	koh·*nya*·gee	local distilled spirit

a bottle/glass	*chupa/glasi*	*choo*·pa/*gla*·see
of ... wine	*ya mvinyo ...*	ya m·*vee*·nyoh ...
dessert	*tamu*	*ta*·moo
red	*mwekundu*	mway·*koon*·doo
rosé	*pinki*	*peen*·kee
sparkling	*yenye*	*yay*·nyay
	mapovu	ma·*poh*·voo
white	*mweupe*	mway·*oo*·pay

a shot of ...	*toti ya ...*	*toh*·tee ya ...
gin	*gini*	*gee*·nee
rum	*rumi*	*roo*·mee
tequila	*tekila*	tay·*kee*·la
vodka	*vodka*	*vohd*·ka
whisky	*wiski*	*wee*·skee

drinking up

Cheers!
Heri!   hay·ree

This is hitting the spot.
Inatosheka.   ee·na·toh·*shay*·ka

I feel fantastic!
Nasikia nzuri sana!   na·see·*kee*·a n·*zoo*·ree *sa*·na

I think I've had one too many.
Nafikiri   na·fee·*kee*·ree
nimekunywa   nee·may·*koony*·wa
moja mno.   *moh*·ja m·noh

I'm feeling drunk.
Nimelewa.   nee·may·*lay*·wa

I feel ill.
    Nasikia mgonjwa.   na·see·*kee*·a m·*gohn*·jwa

Where's the toilet?
    Choo kiko wapi?   choh *kee*·koh *wa*·pee

I'm tired, I'd better go home.
    Nimechoka, nirudi   nee·may·*choh*·ka nee·*roo*·dee
    nyumbani.   nyoom·*ba*·nee

Can you call a taxi for me?
    Niitie teksi.   nee·ee·*tee*·ay *tayk*·see

I don't think you should drive.
    Sidhani ni salama kwa   see·*dha*·nee nee sa·*la*·ma kwa
    wewe kuendesha.   *way*·way koo·ayn·*day*·sha

dining East African style

Being invited to share a meal with East Africans at home is a treat not to be turned down, but be prepared for some customs that are different from what you might be used to.

Before eating, a bowl and a pitcher of water are often passed around for washing hands. The usual procedure is to hold your hands over the bowl while your host pours water over them. Sometimes soap is provided, as is a towel for drying off.

The centre of the meal itself is usually *ugali* oo·*ga*·lee (a staple made from maize or cassava flour) which is normally taken with the right hand from a communal pot, rolled into a small ball with the fingers, dipped into some sort of sauce and eaten. Food is never handled or eaten with the left hand.

At the end of the meal, try to avoid being the one who takes the last handful from the communal bowl, as this may leave your hosts worrying they haven't provided enough. After the meal, the water and wash basin are brought around again so that everyone can wash their hands.

Sharing a meal with others forms the basis for social life in East Africa, but don't be surprised if conversation stops while the food is being eaten.

buying food

kununua chakula

What's the local speciality?
Chakula cha kienyeji   cha·*koo*·la cha kee·ay·*nyay*·jee
gani ni maalum sana?   *ga*·nee nee ma·loom *sa*·na

What's that?
Hicho ni nini?   hee·choh nee *nee*·nee

Can I taste it?
Naomba nionje.   na·*ohm*·ba nee·*ohn*·jay

How much is a kilo of (mangoes)?
Kilo ya (maembe)   *kee*·loh ya (ma·*aym*·bay)
ni bei gani?   nee bay *ga*·nee

Can I have a bag, please?
Nipe mfuko.   *nee*·pay m·*foo*·koh

food stuff

cooked	*kupikwa*	koo·*pee*·kwa
cured	*kutiwa na chumvi*	koo·*tee*·wa na *choom*·vee
	na kukaushwa	na koo·ka·*oo*·shwa
dried	*kukaushwa*	koo·ka·*oo*·shwa
fresh	*mbichi*	m·*bee*·chee
frozen	*kugandishwa*	koo·gan·*dee*·shwa
	katika barafu	ka·*tee*·ka ba·*ra*·foo
smoked	*kukaushwa*	koo·ka·*oo*·shwa
	na moshi	na *moh*·shee
raw	*mbichi*	m·*bee*·chee

I'd like ...	Nataka ...	na·*ta*·ka ...
(200) grams	gramu	*gra*·moo
	(mia mbili)	(*mee*·a m·*bee*·lee)
a dozen	kumi na mbili	*koo*·mee na m·*bee*·lee
half a kilo	nusu kilo	*noo*·soo *kee*·loh
a kilo	kilo moja	*kee*·loh *moh*·ja
(two) kilos	kilo (mbili)	*kee*·loh (m·*bee*·lee)
a bottle	chupa	*choo*·pa
a jar	chupa ndogo	*choo*·pa n·*doh*·goh
a piece	kipande	kee·*pan*·day
(three) pieces	vipande	vee·*pan*·day
	(vitatu)	(vee·*ta*·too)
(six) slices	slaisi (sita)	sla·*ee*·see (*see*·ta)
(just) a little	kidogo (tu)	kee·*doh*·goh (too)
more	zaidi	za·*ee*·dee
some ...	kiasi ...	kee·*a*·see ...
this/that one	hiki/hicho	*hee*·kee/*hee*·choh

Less.	Punguza.	poon·*goo*·za
A bit more.	Ongeza kidogo.	ohn·*gay*·za kee·*doh*·goh
Enough.	Bas.	bas

Do you have ...?	Kuna ...?	*koo*·na...
anything	rahisi	ra·*hee*·see
cheaper	zaidi	za·*ee*·dee
other kinds	aina	a·*ee*·na
	nyingine	nyeen·*gee*·nay

Where's the ... section?	... iko wapi?	... *ee*·koh *wa*·pee
dairy	Ma ziwa	ma·*zee*·wa
fish	Samaki	sa·*ma*·kee
frozen goods	Vyakula vilivyo- gandishwa katika barafu	vya·*koo*·la vee·lee·vyo· gan·*dee*·shwa ka·*tee*·ka ba·*ra*·foo
fruit and vegetables	Matunda na mboga	ma·*toon*·da na m·*boh*·ga
meat	Nyama	*nya*·ma
poultry	Kuku	*koo*·koo

listen for ...

Nikusaidie? nee·koo·sa·ee·*de*·ay	Can I help you?
Unataka nini? oo·na·*ta*·ka *nee*·nee	What would you like?
Kiasi gani? kee·*a*·see *ga*·nee	How much? (quantity)
Kitu kingine? *kee*·too keen·*gee*·nay	Anything else?
Hamna/Hakuna. *ham*·na/ha·*koo*·na	There isn't any.

self-catering

cooking utensils

Could I please	*Naomba*	na·*ohm*·ba
borrow a ...?	*kuazima ...*	koo·a·*zee*·ma ...
I need a ...	*Nahitaji ...*	na·hee·*ta*·jee ...
chopping board	*bao la kukatia*	*ba*·oh la koo·ka·*tee*·a
frying pan	*kikaango*	kee·ka·*an*·goh
knife	*kisu*	*kee*·soo
meat cleaver	*kisu kikubwa*	*kee*·soo kee·*koob*·wa
	cha nyama	cha *nya*·ma
saucepan	*sufuria*	soo·foo·*ree*·a

For more cooking implements, see the **dictionary**.

vegetarian & special meals
kutokula nyama na milo maalum

ordering food

Is there a ...	Kuna hoteli	koo·na hoh·tay·lee
restaurant	ya chakula ...	ya cha·koo·la ...
near here?	hapa karibuni?	ha·pa ka·ree·boo·nee
Do you have	Mna chakula ...?	m·na cha·koo·la ...
... food?		
halal	halali	ha·la·lee
vegetarian	bila nyama	bee·la nya·ma

I don't eat ...	Sili ...	see·lee ...
butter	siagi	see·a·gee
eggs	mayai	ma·ya·ee
fish	samaki	sa·ma·kee
fish stock	supu ya	soo·poo ya
	samaki	sa·ma·kee
meat stock	supu ya nyama	soo·poo ya nya·ma
oil	mafuta	ma·foo·ta
pork	nyama	nya·ma
	nguruwe	n·goo·roo·way
poultry	kuku	koo·koo
red meat	nyama	nya·ma

Is this ...?	Hiki ...?	hee·kee ...
decaffeinated	ni bila kafini	nee bee·la ka·fee·nee
low-fat	ni chenye	nee chay·nyay
	mafuta	ma·foo·ta
	machache	ma·cha·chay
low in	ni chenye	nee chay·nyay
sugar	sukari	soo·ka·ree
	kidogo tu	kee·doh·goh too
salt-free	bila chumvi	bee·la choom·vee

Is it cooked in/with …?
Kinapikwa na …? kee·na·*pee*·kwa na …

Could you prepare a meal without …?
Unaweza kuandaa oo·na·*way*·za koo·an·*da*
mlo bila …? m·loh *bee*·la …

special diets & allergies

I'm on a special diet.
Nakula vyakula na·*koo*·la vya·*koo*·la
maalum tu. ma·loom too

I'm vegetarian.
Mimi ni mlaji wa *mee*·mee nee m·*la*·jee wa
mboga za majani tu. m·*boh*·ga za ma·*ja*·nee too

I'm vegan.
Mimi ni mtu asiyetumia *mee*·mee nee a·see·yay·too·*mee*·a
aina yoyote ya a·*ee*·na yoh·*yoh*·tay
mazao ya mnyama. ma·za·oh ya m·*nya*·ma

I'm (a) …	*Mimi ni …*	*mee*·mee nee …
Buddhist	*Mbudisti*	m·boo·*dee*·stee
Hindu	*Mhindu*	m·*heen*·doo
Jewish	*Myahudi*	m·ya·*hoo*·dee
Muslim	*Mwislamu*	mwee·*sla*·moo

I'm allergic to …	*Nina mzio wa …*	*nee*·na m·*zee*·oh wa …
dairy	*mazao ya*	ma·za·oh ya
produce	*maziwa*	ma·*zee*·wa
eggs	*mayai*	ma·*ya*·ee
gelatine	*jelatini*	jay·la·*tee*·nee
honey	*asali*	a·*sa*·lee
MSG	*msg*	aym·*ays*·gee
nuts	*kokwa*	*koh*·kwa
peanuts	*karanga*	ka·*ran*·ga
seafood	*vyakula kutoka*	vya·*koo*·la koo·*toh*·ka
	baharini	ba·ha·*ree*·nee
shellfish	*kombe*	*kohm*·bay

This miniguide to Swahili cuisine lists dishes and ingredients in Swahili alphabetical order. It's designed to help you get the most out of your gastronomic experience by providing you with food terms that you may see on the menu. For certain dishes we've marked the region or city where they're most popular.

A

achari a·cha·ree
  pickles • chutney • relish
aiskrimu a·ee·skree·moo *ice cream*
alizeti a·lee·zay·tee *sunflower seeds*
asali a·sa·lee *honey*

B

balungi ba·loon·gee *grapefruit*
bamia ba·mee·a *okra*
barafu ba·ra·foo *ice*
baridi ba·ree·dee *cold* ⓐ
bata ba·ta *duck*
  — mdogo m·doh·goh *duckling*
bekoni bay·koh·nee *bacon*
bia bee·a *beer*
  — baridi ba·ree·dee *cold*
  — ya moto ya moh·toh *warm*
biriani bee·ree·a·nee *Indian & Pakistani-inspired dish – a mixture of rice & spices, usually with meat or beans*
biringani bee·reen·ga·nee
  eggplant • aubergine
biskuti bees·koo·tee *biscuit • cookie*
blue bandi bloo ban·dee *margarine*
boha boh·ha *sugar cane* **pombe**
bokuboku boh·koo·boh·koo *festive dish with a pasty texture made from cooked ground wheat & meat cooked in spices, served over fried onion (Zanzibar)*
brokoli broh·koh·lee *broccoli*
buni boo·nee *coffee beans*
busi boo·see *barley* **pombe**

C

chai cha·ee *tea*
  — masala ma·sa·la *spiced sweet tea (often with cardamom)*
  — tangawizi tan·ga·wee·zee *tea flavoured with ginger*
  — ya asubuhi ya a·soo·boo·hee *breakfast*
chakula cha·koo·la *food*
  — cha jioni cha jee·oh·nee *dinner*
  — cha kichina cha kee·chee·na *Chinese food*
  — cha kihindi cha kee·heen·dee *Indian food*
  — kikuu kee·koo *main courses*
  — cha mchana cha m·cha·na *lunch*
  — kutoka bahari koo·toh·ka ba·ha·ree *seafood*
chang'aa chang·a *home-brewed firewater – not recommended for health reasons*
chapati cha·pa·tee *round bread cooked like a pancake – you tear off pieces to pick up other food*
chaza cha·za *oyster*
chenja chayn·ja *drink made by soaking uncooked rice in water with sugar*
chenye viungo chay·nyay vee·oon·goh *spicy*
chenza chayn·za *mandarin*
chewa chay·wa *rock cod*
chipsi chee·psee *deep-fried potatoes (chips or French fries) – commonly used to bulk up a meal*
  — mayai ma·ya·ee *greasy omelette made with chips – very popular fast food*

chizi chee·zee (cottage) cheese (also known as **jibini**)

chumvi choom·vee salt

chungwa choon·gwa orange

D

dafu da·foo coconut (green)

dagaa da·ga freshwater sardines fried & eaten whole

dalasini da·la·see·nee cinnamon

dengu dayn·goo lentils

E

embe aym·bay mango

— **mafuta** ma·foo·ta avocado

G

gini gee·nee gin

giligilani gee·lee·gee·la·nee coriander seeds

glukos gloo·kohs plain sweet biscuits

gogwe gohg·way tree tomato

gongo gohn·goh illegal distilled cashew nut drink

H

halua hal·oo·a Turkish delight

heringi hay·reen·gee herring

I

iliki ee·lee·kee cardamom

irio ee·ree·oh potato, cabbage & beans mashed together (also known as **kienyeji**)

J

jibini jee·bee·nee see **chizi**

jodari joh·da·ree tuna

jusi joo·see juice

— **ya makwaju** ya ma·kwa·joo tamarind juice

— **ya mananasi** ya ma·na·na·see pineapple juice

— **ya pasheni** ya pa·shay·nee passion fruit juice

K

kaa ka crab

kababu ka·ba·boo small kebabs – a popular snack food

kabichi ka·bee·chee cabbage

kahawa ka·ha·wa coffee

— **baridi yenye barafu** ba·ree·dee yay·nyay ba·ra·foo iced coffee

— **ya maziwa** ya ma·zee·wa white coffee

— **ya rangi** ya ran·gee black coffee

kamba kam·ba crayfish

kambakoche kam·ba·koh·chay rock lobster

kande kan·day stew made with beans & whole kernels of maize

kangara kan·ga·ra maize & honey **pombe**

kapile ka·pee·lay cooked food sold in the market

karafuu ka·ra·foo clove (the spice)

karanga ka·ran·ga peanut

karoti ka·roh·tee carrot

kasezi bong ka·say·zee bong undistilled Ugandan millet-based alcohol (not recommended for health reasons)

keki kay·kee cake

kiamsha hamu kee·am·sha ha·moo appetisers

kiazi (ulaya) kee·a·zee (oo·la·ya) (European) potato

— **kikuu** kee·koo yam potato

— **kitamu** kee·ta·moo sweet potato

kienyeji kee·ay·nyay·jee see **irio**

kima kee·ma mincemeat

kimbo keem·boh cooking fat (brand name)

kisibiti kee·see·bee·tee cumin

kisutuo kee·soo·too·oh food received as a thank you for helping someone

kitindamlo kee·teen·da·m·loh dessert

kitumbuo kee·toom·boo·oh deep-fried rice bread

kitunguu kee-toon-*goo* onion
— **saumu** sa-*oo*-moo garlic
klub soda kloob *soh*-da soda water
koko *koh*-koh cocoa
kokteli kohk-*tay*-lee cocktail
kokwa *koh*-kwa nut
komoni *koh*-moh-nee local millet beer
konyagi koh-*nya*-gee general name for
locally produced liquor • local gin-like
spirit
korosho koh-*roh*-shoh cashew nut – often
sold roasted as a street food
kuku *koo*-koo chicken
— **choma** *cho*-ma roast chicken
kunde *koon*-day cowpea (tropical pea)
kupikwa katika majani koo-*peek*-wa
ka-*tee*-ka ma-*ja*-nee baked in leaves
kwaju *kwa*-joo tamarind

L

lager *la*-gayr lager beer
limau lee-*ma*-oo lemon
lozi *loh*-zee almond

M

maandazi man-*da*-zee semisweet
deep-fried doughnut-like pastry, often
containing coconut milk & sometimes
spiced – popular snack food
mabuyu ma-*boo*-yoo
sweet & sour baobab seeds
madafu ma-*da*-foo
fresh juice of a green coconut
mafuta ma-*foo*-ta oil
maharagwe ma-ha-*rag*-way red kidney
beans (often cooked with coconut)
mahindi ma-*heen*-dee
corn • maize • roast corn cobs
maji *ma*-jee water
— **ya dafu** ya *da*-foo coconut milk
— **ya madini** ya ma-*dee*-nee mineral
water
— **ya machungwa** ya ma-*choon*-gwa
orange juice
— **ya ndimu** ya n-*dee*-moo lime juice
makaroni ma-ka-*roh*-nee see **spageti**

manjano man-*ja*-noh turmeric
mastafeli ma-sta-*fay*-lee soursop
matapa ma-*ta*-pa cassava leaves cooked
in peanut sauce often served with
prawns (Mozambique)
matoke ma-*toh*-kay green bananas or
plantains boiled, steamed or mashed &
eaten as a staple
mayai ma-*ya*-ee eggs (also called **yai**)
— **yaliyochemshwa**
ya-lee-yoh-*chem*-shwa hard-boiled eggs
— **yaliyokaangwa**
ya-lee-yo-ka-*ang*-wa fried eggs
— **yaliyovurugwa**
ya-lee-yo-voo-*roog*-wa scrambled eggs
maziwa ma-*zee*-wa milk
— **ganda** *gan*-da yoghurt
— **ya unga** ya *oon*-ga powdered milk
maziwalala ma-zee-wa-*la*-la 'sleeping
milk' – yoghurt-like fermented milk
mbege m-*bay*-gay banana beer
mbichi m-*bee*-chee raw
mbivu m-*bee*-voo ripe
mboga m-*boh*-ga vegetable • vegetables
or relish served as a side dish with ugali
mchaichai m-cha-*ee*-cha-ee lemongrass
mchele m-*chay*-lay uncooked white rice
mchicha m-*chee*-cha spinach – sometimes
cooked with onion & tomato
mchuzi m-*choo*-zee sauce (often spicy)
eaten with **ugali**, containing either fish,
meat, beans or spinach • any sauce •
curry
— **wa nyama** wa *nya*-ma beef stew –
in Zanzibar, can be a curry with lemon
juice & spices including turmeric
— **wa nyanya** wa *nya*-nya
tomato sauce
— **wa pilipili hoho**
wa pee-lee-*pee*-lee *hoh*-hoh chilli sauce
mgiligilani m-gee-lee-gee-*la*-nee
fresh coriander leaves
miche ya mianzi mee-chay ya mee-*an*-zee
bamboo shoots
mishikaki mee-shee-*ka*-kee meat on
a skewer grilled until crisp – popular
roadside snack served with salt &
possibly chilli

mkate m·*ka*·tay *bread*
— **mayai** ma·*ya*·ee
'egg bread' – dough wrapped around minced meat & fried egg
— **wa mayai** wa ma·*ya*·ee *mixture of eggs, ground meat, onion & spices fried until brown and eaten hot (popular on the East African Coast)*
— **wa ngano asilia** wa n·*ga*·noh a·*see*·*lee*·a *wholemeal bread*
mkizi m·*kee*·zee *grey mullet*
mlenda m·*layn*·da *green sticky vegetable similar to okra*
mnofu m·*noh*·foo *beefsteak (also known as **steki**)*
mpishi m·*pee*·shee *flavoured cooking fat (brand name) • cook (chef)*
mtama m·*ta*·ma *sorghum • millet (often cooked into a gruel as a breakfast food)*
mtande m·*tan*·day *food hung to dry*
mtindi m·*teen*·dee *cultured milk product similar to yoghurt • cream (usually skim from boiled milk)*
mtori m·*toh*·ree *banana soup*
muhogo moo·*hoh*·goh *cassava • grilled cassava topped with chilli sauce (a roadside snack)*
muwa moo·wa *sugar cane*
mvinyo m·*vee*·nyoh *wine*
— **mwekundu** mway·*koon*·doo *red wine*
— **mwenye povu** mway·nyay *poh*·voo *sparkling wine*
— **mweupe** mway·oo·pay *white wine*

N

nanasi na·*na*·see *pineapple*
nazi *na*·zee *coconut (ripe)*
ndimu n·*dee*·moo *lime*
ndizi n·*dee*·zee *banana*
— **ko kastad** koh *ka*·stad *custard made from sliced bananas & chopped peanuts, spiced with cloves, cinnamon & nutmeg (Zanzibar)*
— **ya kupika** ya koo·*pee*·ka *plantain*
nduwalo n·doo·*wa*·loh *sailfish*
ngisi n·*gee*·see *squid*
njegere n·jay·*gay*·ray *pigeon pea*

nusu noo·soo *half portion*
nyama *nya*·ma *meat*
— **choma** *choh*·ma *grilled meat – often goat meat – cooked over a charcoal pit & sold in bite-sized pieces*
— **mamba** *mam*·ba *crocodile meat*
— **mbuni** m·*boo*·nee *ostrich meat*
— **mbuzi** m·*boo*·zee
goat meat • mutton
— **ng'ombe** ng·*ohm*·bay *beef*
— **nguruwe** n·goo·*roo*·way *pork – not widely available as many of the Swahili-speaking areas are Muslim*
— **punda milia** *poon*·da mee·*lee*·a *zebra meat*
— **swala** *swa*·la *impala meat*
— **twiga** *twee*·ga *giraffe meat*
— **ya mkebe** ya m·*kay*·bay *tinned meat*
— **ya kopo** ya *koh*·poh *tinned meat*
— **ya wanyama pori** ya wa·*nya*·ma *poh*·ree *game meat – may be legally farmed or illegally poached*
nyanya *nya*·nya *tomato*
— **ya mkebe** ya m·*kay*·bay *tomato paste*

O

oluwombo o·loo·*wohm*·boh *dish made from meat or even peanuts mixed with mushrooms (Uganda)*
omlet ohm·*layt* *omelette*

P

papa *pa*·pa *shark*
papai pa·*pa*·ee *papaya • pawpaw*
parachichi pa·ra·*chee*·chee *avocado*
pasheni pa·*shay*·nee *passion fruit*
pera *pay*·ra *guava*
peremende pay·ray·*mayn*·day *sweet* ⓝ
pilau pee·*la*·oo *rice, vegetables & meat cooked in a seasoned broth*
pilipili pee·lee·*pee*·lee *pepper*
— **hoho** *hoh*·hoh
hot pepper • chilli • chilli sauce
— **manga** *man*·ga
black pepper • black peppercorn
— **mbichi** m·*bee*·chee *green pepper*

pipi *pee-pee* candy
piripiri *pee-ree-pee-ree* very hot sauce made from chilli pepper & lemon juice, eaten with meat, fish & shellfish
pojo *poh-joh* mung beans
pombe *pohm-bay* popular home-made beer-like brew made from maize, millet, banana, or other local produce
 — **kali** *ka-lee* spirits
popkon *pohp-kohn* popcorn
posho *poh-shoh* see **ugali**
pweza *pway-za* octopus

R

rasiberi *ra-see-bay-ree* raspberry
rojorojo *roh-joh-roh-joh* viscous food (especially sauce)
rubisi *roo-bee-see* banana wine
rumi *roo-mee* rum

S

saladi *sa-la-dee* lettuce • salad
samaki *sa-ma-kee* fish
 — **ya kupaka** *ya koo-pa-ka* fish cooked in a spicy coconut sauce
 — **ya kuwonga** *ya koo-wohn-ga* fish croquettes (Zanzibar)
 — **ya mkebe/kopo** *ya m-kay-bay/koh-poh* tinned sardines
sambusa *sam-boo-sa* mixture of meat, onion, vegetables & spices fried in a triangular-shaped pastry & eaten as a snack (also known as **samosa**)
samosa *sa-moh-sa* see **sambusa**
sandwichi *sand-wee-chee* sandwich
shampeni *sham-pay-nee* champagne
shayiri *sha-yee-ree* barley • oats
siagi *see-a-gee* butter
siki *see-kee* vinegar
simsim *seem-seem* sesame seeds • sesame candy (Zanzibar)
slaisi *sla-ee-see* slice (see also **tosti**)
soda *soh-da* soft drink
sorpotel *sohr-poh-tayl* stew of beef & pork flavoured with a rich spice mix (Zanzibar)
soseji ya nyama nguruwe *soh-say-jee ya nya-ma n-goo-roo-way* pork sausage

spageti *spa-gay-tee* spaghetti (see also **makaroni**)
stauti *sta-oo-tee* stout beer
steki *stay-kee* see **mnofu**
stroberi *stroh-bay-ree* strawberry
sukari *soo-ka-ree* sugar
sukuma wiki *soo-koo-ma wee-kee* mixture of basic greens (eg spinach) often served with meat dishes
supu *soo-poo* soup • broth (sometimes spicy) made from pieces of chicken, meat or fish
 — **ya kuku** *ya koo-koo* chicken soup with onion, cabbage, tomato & celery

T

tangawizi *tan-ga-wee-zee* ginger
tembo *taym-boh* palm wine
tende *tayn-day* date
tikiti (maji) *tee-kee-tee (ma-jee)* melon • watermelon
tilapia *tee-la-pee-a* tilapia (Nile perch)
tofaa *toh-fa* apple
topetope *toh-pay-toh-pay* cherimoya • custard apple
tosti *toh-stee* slice of bread (often toasted), also known as **slaisi**
tunda *toon-da* fruit

U

ubwabwa *oo-bwa-bwa* rice cooked with coconut
ugali *oo-ga-lee* traditional dish made by mixing maize and/or cassava flour in hot water until it becomes like a stiff porridge & eaten in the hand to form a small ball which is then dipped in sauce before eating (also known as **posho** in Uganda)
uji *oo-jee* thin sweet porridge
ulanzi *oo-lan-zee* bamboo juice **pombe**
umanga *oo-man-ga* plain food (without relish)
unga wa kahawa wa moja kwa moja *oon-ga wa ka-ha-wa wa moh-ja kwa moh-ja* instant coffee

unga wa mahindi *oon*-ga wa
ma-*heen*-dee *maize/corn meal*
unga wa pilipili hoho *oon*-ga wa
pee-lee-*pee*-lee *hoh*-hoh *chilli powder*
unga wa viazi vikuu *oon*-ga wa vee-*a*-zee
vee-ku-*u* *yam flour*
uraka oo-*ra*-ka *brewed cashew nut drink*
utumbo wa nyama oo-*toom*-boh wa
nya-ma *offal • intestines*

V

vinginevyo veen-gee-*nay*-vyo *side dishes*
vinywaji veeny-*wa*-jee *drinks*
vitambua vee-tam-*boo*-a
small cakes made with rice flour

W

wanzuki wan-*zoo*-kee *honey beer*
wali *wa*-lee *cooked rice (available with a
variety of meats or sauces)*
— **maharagwe** ma-ha-*ra*-gway
cooked rice and beans
waragi wa-*ra*-gee
millet-based alcohol (Uganda)

Y

yai *see* mayai
ya kuchemshwa ya koo-*chaym*-shwa
boiled
ya kuchomwa ya koo-*choh*-mwa
broiled • grilled
ya kuiva kidogo
ya koo-*ee*-va kee-*doh*-goh *rare (meat)*
ya kuiva kubisa/sana ya koo-*ee*-va
koo-*bee*-sa/*sa*-na *well-done*
ya kuiva wastani ya koo-*ee*-va wa-*sta*-nee
medium (meat)
ya kukaanga ya koo-ka-*a*-nga *fried*
ya kuoka ya koo-*oh*-ka *roasted*
ya kuokwa ya koo-*ok*-wa *baked*
ya kupikwa ya koo-*peek*-wa
cooked • heated

Z

zabibu za-*bee*-boo *grapes*
— **nyeupe zilizokaushwa** nyay-oo-*pay*
zee-lee-zoh-ka-oo-shwa *sultanas*
zabibubata za-bee-boo-*ba*-ta
cape gooseberries (Kenya)

emergencies

dharura

Careful!	*Angalia!*	an·ga·*lee*·a
Help!	*Saidia!*	sa·ee·*dee*·a
Stop!	*Simama!*	see·*ma*·ma
Go away!	*Toka!*	*toh*·ka
Thief!	*Mwizi!*	*mwee*·zee
Fire!	*Moto!*	*moh*·toh
Watch out!	*Angalia!*	an·ga·*lee*·a

Leave me alone!
  Niache! nee·*a*·chay

I won't give you any money!
  Sitakupa hela! see·ta·*koo*·pa *hay*·la

It's an emergency.
  Ni dharura. nee dha·*roo*·a

There's been an accident.
  Ajali imetokea. a·*ja*·lee ee·may·toh·*kay*·a

Call the police.
  Waite polisi. wa·*ee*·tay poh·*lee*·see

Call a doctor.
  Mwite daktari. m·*wee*·tay dak·*ta*·ree

Call an ambulance.
  Ita gari la hospitali. ee·ta *ga*·ree la ho·spee·*ta*·lee

signs

Dharura	dha·*roo*·ra	**Emergency Department**
Hospitali	hoh·spee·*ta*·lee	**Hospital**
Polisi	poh·*lee*·see	**Police**

Could you please help?
Saidia, tafadhali.   sa·ee·*dee*·a ta·fa·*dha*·lee

Can I use your phone?
Naomba kutumia   na·*ohm*·ba koo·too·*mee*·a
simu yako.   *see*·moo ya·koh

I'm lost.
Nimejipotea.   nee·may·jee·poh·*tay*·a

Where are the toilets?
Vyoo viko wapi?   vyoh *vee*·ko wa·pee

Is it safe ...?	Ni salama ...?	nee sa·*la*·ma ...
at night	usikuni	oo·see·*koo*·nee
for gay people	kwa wasenge	kwa wa·*sayn*·gay
for travellers	kwa watalii	kwa wa·ta·*lee*
for women	kwa wanawake	kwa wa·na·*wa*·kay
on your own	kuwa pekee	koo·wa pay·*kay*

police

polisi

Where's the police station?
Kituo cha polisi   kee·*too*·oh cha poh·*lee*·see
kiko wapi?   *kee*·koh wa·pee

I want to report an offence.
Nataka kutoa   na·*ta*·ka koo·*toh*·a
taarifa ya jinai.   ta·*ree*·fa ya jee·*na*·ee

Can I see your police identification card?
Nionyeshe kadi   nee·oh·*nyay*·shay *ka*·dee
ya kitambulisho   ya kee·tam·boo·*lee*·shoh
ya polisi.   ya poh·*lee*·see

It was him/her.
Alikuwa yeye.   a·lee·*koo*·wa *yay*·yay

I have insurance.
Nina bima.   *nee*·na *bee*·ma

My (backpack) was stolen.
(Shanta) iliibwa.   (*shan*·ta) ee·lee·*ee*·bwa

I've been ...

assaulted	*Nilishambuliwa.*	nee·lee·sham·boo·*lee*·wa
mugged	*Nilivamiwa.*	nee·lee·va·*mee*·wa
raped	*Nilibakwa.*	nee·lee·*ba*·kwa
robbed	*Niliibiwa.*	nee·lee·ee·*bee*·wa

He/She tried to ... me. — *Alijaribu ...* — a·lee·ja·*ree*·boo ...

assault	*kunishambulia*	koo·nee·sham·boo·*lee*·a
rape	*kunibaka*	koo·nee·*ba*·ka
rob	*kuniibia*	koo·nee·ee·*bee*·a
trick	*kunidanganya*	koo·nee·dan·*ga*·nya

I've lost my ... — *Nilipoteza ...* — nee·lee·poh·*tay*·za ...

bags	*mizigo yangu*	mee·*zee*·goh *yan*·goo
car	*gari langu*	*ga*·ree *lan*·goo
credit card	*kadi ya benki*	*ka*·dee ya *bayn*·kee
money	*pesa yangu*	*pay*·sa *yan*·goo
passport	*pasipoti yangu*	pa·see·*poh*·tee *yan*·goo

What am I accused of?
Nashtakiwa na nini? — na·shta·*kee*·wa na *nee*·nee

I'm sorry.
Nasikia majuto. — na·see·*kee*·a ma·*joo*·toh

I didn't realise I was doing anything wrong.
Nilikuwa sielewi — nee·lee·*koo*·wa see·ay·*lay*·wee
kwamba nilifanya — *kwam*·ba nee·lee·*fa*·nya
kosa lolote. — *koh*·sa loh·*loh*·tay

I didn't do it.
Sikuifanya. — see·koo·ee·*fa*·nya

Can I pay an on-the-spot fine?
Naweza kulipa faini — na·*way*·za koo·*lee*·pa fa·*ee*·nee
hapa hapa? — *ha*·pa *ha*·pa

Can I make a phone call?
Naweza kutumia simu? — na·*way*·za koo·too·*mee*·a *see*·moo

I want to contact my embassy/consulate.
Nataka kuwasiliana — na·*ta*·ka koo·wa·see·lee·*a*·na
na ubalozi wangu. — na oo·ba·*loh*·zee *wan*·goo

Can I have a lawyer (who speaks English)?

Naomba mwanasheria	na·*ohm*·ba mwa·na·*shay*·*ree*·a
(anayesema Kiingereza).	(a·na·yay·*say*·ma kee·een·gay·*ray*·za)

This drug is for personal use.

Dawa hili ni kwa	*da*·wa *hee*·lee nee kwa
matumizi yangu	ma·too·*mee*·zee *yan*·goo
mwenyewe.	mway·*nyay*·way

I have a prescription for this drug.

Nina agizo la daktari	*nee*·na a·*gee*·zoh la dak·*ta*·ree
kwa dawa hili.	kwa *da*·wa *hee*·lee

---

the police may say …

Unashitakiwa	oo·na·shee·ta·*kee*·wa	**You're charged**
na …	na …	**with …**
Anashitakiwa	a·na·shee·ta·*kee*·wa	**He/She is**
na …	na …	**charged with …**
kubaki	koo·*ba*·kee	**overstaying**
baada ya	ba·*a*·da ya	**your visa**
visa kuisha	*vee*·sa koo·*ee*·sha	
kuiba dukani	koo·*ee*·ba doo·*ka*·nee	**shoplifting**
kutokuwa	koo·toh·*koo*·wa	**not having**
na visa	na *vee*·sa	**a visa**
kuvuruka	koo·voo·*roo*·ka	**disturbing**
amani	a·*ma*·nee	**the peace**
kuwa na (kitu	*koo*·wa na (*kee*·too	**possession**
kinyume	kee·*nyoo*·may	**(of illegal**
cha sheria)	cha shay·*ree*·ya)	**substances)**
shambulio	sham·boo·*lee*·oh	**assault**

Ni faini ya kuegesha gari.
nee fa·*ee*·nee ya   **It's a parking fine.**
koo·ay·*gay*·sha *ga*·ree

Ni faini ya kwenda mwendo kubwa mno.
nee fa·*ee*·nee ya *kwayn*·da   **It's a speeding fine.**
mwayn·do *koob*·wa *m*·noh

doctor

daktari

Where's the nearest …?	… hapo karibuni iko wapi?	… ha·poh ka·ree·boo·nee ee·koh wa·pee
dentist	Daktari wa meno	dak·ta·ree wa may·noh
doctor	Daktari	dak·ta·ree
emergency department	Wadi ya dharura	wa·dee ya dha·roo·ra
hospital	Hospitali	hoh·spee·ta·lee
medical centre	Kituo cha afya	kee·too·oh cha af·ya
(night) pharmacist	Duka la madawa (la saa za manane)	doo·ka la ma·da·wa (la sa za ma·na·nay)
optometrist	Daktari wa macho	dak·ta·ree wa ma·choh
rural clinic	Kliniki	klee·nee·kee

I need a doctor (who speaks English).
Nahitaji daktari   na·hee·ta·jee dak·ta·ree
(anayesema   (a·na·yay·say·ma
Kiingereza).   kee·een·gay·ray·za)

Could I see a female doctor?
Inawezekana nione   ee·na·way·zay·ka·na nee·oh·nay
daktari mwanamke?   dak·ta·ree mwa·nam·kay

Could the doctor come here?
Daktari anaweza   dak·ta·ree a·na·way·za
kuja hapa?   koo·ja ha·pa

Is there an after-hours emergency number?
Kuna simu ya dharura   koo·na see·moo ya dha·roo·ra
kupiga baada ya   koo·pee·ga ba·a·da ya
saa za kazi?   sa za ka·zee

I've run out of my medication.
Dawa langu limekwisha.   da·wa lan·goo lee·may·kwee·sha

This is my usual medicine.

Hili ni dawa langu   *hee*·lee nee *da*·wa lan·goo
la kawaida.   la ka·wa·*ee*·da

My child weighs (20 kilos).

Mtoto wangu ana uzito   m·*toh*·toh *wan*·goo *a*·na oo·*zee*·toh
wa (kilo ishirini).   wa (*kee*·loh ee·shee·*ree*·nee)

What's the correct dosage?

Niambie kipimo halisi?   nee·am·*bee*·ay kee·*pee*·moh ha·*lee*·see

I don't want a blood transfusion.

Sitaki damu kutoka   see·*ta*·kee *da*·moo koo·*toh*·ka
mtu mwengine.   m·too mwayn·*gee*·nay

Please use a new syringe.

Tumia sindano mpya.   too·*mee*·a seen·*da*·noh m·pya

I have my own syringe.

Nina sindano yangu.   *nee*·na seen·*da*·noh *yan*·goo

---

the doctor may say ...

Kuna shida gani?
koo·na *shee*·da *ga*·nee   **What's the problem?**

Una maumivu wapi?
oo·na ma·oo·*mee*·voo *wa*·pee   **Where does it hurt?**

Una homa?
oo·na *hoh*·ma   **Do you have a temperature?**

Umekuwa hivyo kwa muda gani?
oo·may·*koo*·wa *heev*·yoh
kwa *moo*·da *ga*·nee   **How long have you been like this?**

Imetokea kabla?
ee·may·toh·*kay*·a *ka*·bla   **Have you had this before?**

Umekunywa maji yasiyo salama?
oo·may·*koony*·wa *ma*·jee
ya·*see*·yoh sa·*la*·ma   **Have you drunk any unsafe water?**

Umekula chakula kisicho salama?
oo·may·*koo*·la cha·*koo*·la
kee·*see*·choh sa·*la*·ma   **Have you eaten any unsafe food?**

the doctor may say ...

Wewe hufanya mapenzi?
  way·way hoo·*fa*·nya
  ma·*payn*·zee
Are you sexually active?

Umewahi kufanya mapenzi bila kinga?
  oo·may·*wa*·hee koo·*fa*·nya
  ma·*payn*·zee *bee*·la *keen*·ga
Have you had unprotected sex?

Unakunywa?
  oo·na·*koony*·wa
Do you drink?

Unavuta sigara?
  oo·na·*voo*·ta see·*ga*·ra
Do you smoke?

Unatumia madawa ya kulevya?
  oo·na·too·*mee*·a ma·*da*·wa
  ya koo·*lay*·vya
Do you take drugs?

Una mzio wa kitu chochote?
  oo·na m·*zee*·oh wa *kee*·too
  choh·*choh*·tay
Are you allergic to anything?

Unatumia dawa lolote?
  oo·na·too·*mee*·a *da*·wa
  loh·*loh*·tay
Are you on medication?

Unasafiri kwa muda gani?
  oo·na·sa·*fee*·ree kwa
  moo·da *ga*·nee
How long are you travelling for?

Inabidi ulazwe hospitalini.
  ee·na·*bee*·dee oo·*laz*·way
  hoh·spee·ta·*lee*·nee
You need to be admitted to hospital.

Inatakiwa daktari akuangalie ukifika nyumbani.
  ee·na·ta·*kee*·wa dak·*ta*·ree
  a·koo·an·ga·*lee*·ay oo·kee·*fee*·ka
  nyoom·*ba*·nee
You should have it checked when you go home.

Afadhali urudi kwenu kwa matibabu.
  a·fa·*dha*·lee oo·*roo*·dee
  kway·noo kwa ma·tee·*ba*·boo
You should return home for treatment.

Wewe huwaza magonjwa yasiyoonekana.
  way·way hoo·*wa*·za ma·*gohn*·jwa
  ya·see·yoh·oh·nay·*ka*·na
You're a hypochondriac.

I'm vaccinated against …	Nimechanjwa kwa …	nee·may·chan·jwa kwa …
hepatitis A/B/C	uvimbe wa ini A/B/C	oo·veem·bay wa ee·nee a/bay/say
meningitis	homa ya uti wa mgongo	hoh·ma ya oo·tee wa m·gohn·goh
rabies	kichaa cha mbwa	kee·cha cha m·bwa
tetanus	pepopunda	pay·poh·poon·da
typhoid	homa ya matumbo	hoh·ma ya ma·toom·boh
yellow fever	homa ya manjano	hoh·ma ya man·ja·noh

I need new …	Nahitaji … mpya.	na·hee·ta·jee … m·pya
contact lenses	lenzi mboni	layn·zee m·boh·nee
glasses	miwani	mee·wa·nee

My prescription is …
Agizo la daktari ni …   a·gee·zoh la dak·ta·ree nee …

Can I have a receipt for my insurance?
Niandikie risiti kwa   nee·an·dee·kee·ay ree·see·tee kwa
kampuni yangu ya bima.   kam·poo·nee yan·goo ya bee·ma

symptoms & conditions

dalili na uhali

I'm sick.
Mimi ni mgonjwa.   mee·mee nee m·gohn·jwa

My friend is (very) sick.
Rafiki yangu ni   ra·fee·kee yan·goo nee
mgonjwa (sana).   m·gohn·jwa (sa·na)

My child is (very) sick.
Mwanangu ni   mwa·nan·goo nee
mgonjwa (sana).   m·gohn·jwa (sa·na)

He/She is having a/an …

allergic reaction	Ana matatizo ya mzio.	a·na ma·ta·tee·zoh ya m·zee·oh
asthma attack	Anashambuliwa na pumu.	a·na·sham·boo·lee·wa na poo·moo
baby	Anajifungua.	a·na·jee·foon·goo·a
epileptic fit	Anashambuliwa na kifafa.	a·na·sham·boo·lee·wa na kee·fa·fa
heart attack	Ameshambuliwa na maradhi ya moyo.	a·may·sham·boo·lee·wa na ma·ra·dhee ya moh·yoh

I've been …

injured	Nimejeruhiwa.	nee·may·jay·roo·hee·wa
vomiting	Nimekuwa natapika.	nee·may·koo·wa na·ta·pee·ka

I feel … · *Nasikia …* · na·see·kee·a …

anxious	wasiwasi	wa·see·wa·see
better	afadhali	a·fa·dha·lee
depressed	huzuni	hoo·zoo·nee
dizzy	kizunguzungu	kee·zoon·goo·zoon·goo
hot and cold	joto na baridi	joh·toh na ba·ree·dee
nauseous	kichefuchefu	kee·chay·foo·chay·foo
shivery	mitetemeko	mee·tay·tay·may·koh
strange	siyo kawaida	see·yoh ka·wa·ee·da
weak	hafifu	ha·fee·foo
worse	mbaya zaidi	m·ba·ya za·ee·dee

It hurts here.
Inauma hapa. — ee·na·oo·ma ha·pa

I'm dehydrated.
Nimekausha maji. — nee·may·ka·oo·sha ma·jee

I can't sleep.
Siwezi kulala. — see·way·zee koo·la·la

I think it's the medication I'm on.
Nadhani ni dawa ninalomeza. — na·dha·nee nee da·wa nee·na·loh·may·za

I'm on medication for …
Ninameza dawa kwa … nee·na·*may*·za *da*·wa kwa …
He/She is on medication for …
Anameza dawa kwa … a·na·*may*·za *da*·wa kwa …
I have (a/an) …
Nina … nee·na …
He/She has (a/an) …
Ana … a·na …

AIDS	*ukimwi*	oo·*keem*·wee
amoebic	*ugonjwa*	oo·*gohn*·jwa
dysentery	*wa amoeba*	wa a·moh·*ay*·ba
asthma	*pumu*	*poo*·moo
bedbugs	*kunguni*	koon·*goo*·nee
bilharzia	*kichocho*	kee·*choh*·choh
cholera	*kipindupindu*	kee·peen·doo·*peen*·doo
cold n	*mafua*	ma·*foo*·a
constipation	*hali ya*	*ha*·lee ya
	kufunga choo	koo·*foon*·ga cho
cough	*kikohozi*	kee·koh·*hoh*·zee
diabetes	*kisukari*	kee·soo·*ka*·ree
diarrhoea	*kuhara*	koo·*ha*·ra
fever	*homa*	*hoh*·ma
headache	*maumivu ya*	ma·oo·*mee*·voo ya
	kichwa	*kee*·chwa
HIV	*VVU*	vee·vee·*yoo*
malaria	*malaria*	ma·*la*·ree·a
meningitis	*homa ya uti*	*hoh*·ma ya oo·tee
	wa mgongo	wa m·*gohn*·goh
nausea	*kichefuchefu*	kee·chay·foo·*chay*·foo
pain	*maumivu*	ma·oo·*mee*·voo
runny nose	*pua yenye*	*poo*·a yay·nyay
	makamasi	ma·ka·*ma*·see
sore throat	*koo lenye*	koh *lay*·nyay
	maumivu	ma·oo·*mee*·voo
intestinal worms	*minyoo*	mee·*nyoh*
typhoid	*homa ya*	*hoh*·ma ya
	matumbo	ma·*toom*·boh

women's health

(I think) I'm pregnant.
(Nafikiri) mimi ni (na·fee·*kee*·ree) *mee*·mee nee
mja mzito. *m*·ja m·*zee*·toh

I'm on the pill.
Natumia vidonge vya na·too·*mee*·a vee·*dohn*·gay vya
uzazi wa mpango. oo·*za*·zee wa m·*pan*·goh

I haven't had my period for (six) weeks.
Sijaingia mwezini see·ja·een·*gee*·a mway·*zee*·nee
kwa wiki (sita). kwa *wee*·kee (*see*·ta)

I've noticed a lump here.
Nimegundua nee·may·goon·*doo*·a
uvimbe hapa. oo·*veem*·bee *ha*·pa

Do you have something for (period pain)?
Una dawa kwa oo·na *da*·wa kwa
(maumivu ya (ma·oo·*mee*·voo ya
mwezini)? mway·*zee*·nee)

the doctor may say ...

Ulipopata hedhi ilikuwa lini?
oo·lee·poh·*pa*·ta *hay*·dhee **When did you last**
ee·lee·*koo*·wa *lee*·nee **have your period?**

Umepata hedhi?
oo·may·*pa*·ta *hay*·dhee **Are you menstruating?**

Unatumia uzazi wa mpango?
oo·na·too·*mee*·a oo·*za*·zee **Are you using**
wa m·*pan*·goh **contraception?**

Wewe ni mja mzito?
way·way nee *m*·ja m·*zee*·toh **Are you pregnant?**

Wewe ni mja mzito.
way·way nee *m*·ja m·*zee*·toh **You're pregnant.**

I have a ...	Nina ...	nee·na ...
urinary tract infection	ambukizo la mfumo wa mkojo	am·boo·kee·zoh la m·foo·moh wa m·koh·joh
yeast infection	ambukizo la hamira	am·boo·kee·zoh la ha·mee·ra
I need ...	Nahitaji ...	na·hee·ta·jee ...
a pregnancy test	kupima kama mimi ni mja mzito	koo·pee·ma ka·ma mee·mee nee m·ja m·zee·toh
contraception	uzuiaji mimba	oo·zoo·ee·a·jee meem·ba
the morning-after pill	kidonge cha kuzuia mimba kumeza baada ya mahusiano	kee·dohn·gay cha koo·zoo·ee·a meem·ba koo·may·za ba·a·da ya ma·hoo·see·a·noh

allergies

mzio

I'm allergic to ...	Nina mzio wa ...	nee·na m·zee·oh wa ...
He/She is allergic to ...	Ana mzio wa ...	a·na m·zee·oh wa ...
antibiotics	viuavija-sumu	vee·oo·a·vee·ja·soo·moo
anti-inflammatories	madawa ya kupunguza uvimbe	ma·da·wa ya koo·poon·goo·za oo·veem·bee
aspirin	aspirini	as·pee·ree·nee
bees	nyuki	nyoo·kee
penicillin	penisilini	pay·nee·see·lee·nee
pollen	chavua	cha·voo·a
sulphur-based drugs	madawa yenye sulfa ndani	ma·da·wa yay·nyay sool·fa n·da·nee

I have a skin allergy.
Nina mzio wa ngozi.   nee·na m·zee·oh wa n·goh·zee

inhaler	*kivutia pumzi*	kee-voo-*tee*-a *poom*-zee
injection	*sindano*	seen-*da*-noh
antimalarials	*madawa kuzuia*	ma-*da*-wa koo-zoo-*ee*-a
	malaria	ma-*la*-ree-a

For food-related allergies, see **vegetarian & special meals**, page 172.

alternative treatments

matibabu mengine

I don't use (Western medicine).
Situmii (uganga   see-too-*mee* (oo-*gan*-ga
wa Ulaya).   wa oo-*la*-ya)

Can I see someone who practices acupuncture?
Naomba kuona   na-*ohm*-ba koo-*oh*-na
mtaalamu wa tiba ya   m-ta-*la*-moo wa *tee*-ba ya
kuchoma sindano.   koo-*choh*-ma seen-*da*-noh

Can I see someone who practices naturopathy?
Naomba kuona   na-*ohm*-ba koo-*oh*-na
mtaalamu wa   m-ta-*la*-moo wa
matibabu asilia.   ma-tee-*ba*-boo a-see-*lee*-a

better safe than sorry

Here are a few terms you might need to know while you're in East Africa, just to be on the safe side:

(DEET) insect repellent
dawa la kufukuza   *da*-wa la koo-foo-*koo*-za
wadudu (aina ya dit)   wa-*doo*-doo (a-*ee*-na ya deet)
(permethrin) insect repellent
dawa la kufukuza   *da*-wa la koo-foo-*koo*-za
wadudu (aina ya   wa-*doo*-doo (a-*ee*-na ya
permethrin)   payr-*may*-threen)
water purification tablets
vidonge vya   vee-*dohn*-gay vya
kusafisha maji   koo-sa-*fee*-sha *ma*-jee

parts of the body

My ... hurts.
... *yangu inauma.* ... *yan*·goo ee·na·*oo*·ma

I can't move my ...
Siwezi kuhamisha see·*way*·zee koo·ha·*mee*·sha
... *yangu.* ... *yan*·goo

I have a cramp in my ...
Nina mkakamao *nee*·na m·ka·ka·*ma*·oh
kwenye ... yangu. *kway*·nyay ... *yan*·goo

My ... is swollen.
... *yangu imevimba.* ... *yan*·goo ee·may·*veem*·ba

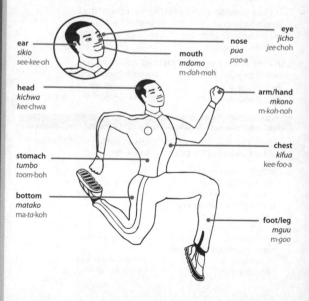

ear
sikio
see·*kee*·oh

nose
pua
poo·a

mouth
mdomo
m·*doh*·moh

eye
jicho
jee·choh

head
kichwa
kee·chwa

arm/hand
mkono
m·*koh*·noh

stomach
tumbo
toom·boh

chest
kifua
kee·*foo*·a

bottom
matako
ma·*ta*·koh

foot/leg
mguu
m·*goo*

pharmacist

I need something for (a headache).
*Nahitaji dawa kwa
(maumivu ya kichwa).*
na·hee·*ta*·jee *da*·wa kwa
(ma·oo·*mee*·voo ya *kee*·chwa)

Do I need a prescription for …?
*Inabidi niwe na
agizo la daktari kwa …?*
ee·na·*bee*·dee *nee*·way na
a·*gee*·zoh la dak·*ta*·ree kwa …

I have a prescription.
Nina agizo la daktari.
nee·na a·*gee*·zoh la dak·*ta*·ree

How many times a day?
Mara ngapi kwa siku?
ma·ra n·*ga*·pee kwa *see*·koo

Will it make me drowsy?
Itanisinzisha?
ee·ta·nee·seen·*zee*·sha

antiseptic n	*dawa ya*	*da*·wa ya
	kusafisha jeraha	koo·sa·*fee*·sha jay·*ra*·ha
condoms	*kondom*	*kohn*·dohm
contraceptives	*kingamimba*	keen·ga·*meem*·ba
iodine	*iodini*	ee·oh·*dee*·nee
painkillers	*viondoa*	vee·ohn·*doh*·a
	maumivu	ma·oo·*mee*·voo
rehydration	*dawa ya*	*da*·wa ya
salts	*kuongeza*	koo·ohn·*gay*·za
	maji mwilini	*ma*·jee mwee·*lee*·nee

the pharmacist may say …

Mara mbili kwa siku (pamoja na chakula).
ma·ra m·*bee*·lee
kwa *see*·koo (pa·*moh*·ja na
cha·*koo*·la)
Twice a day (with food).

Umewahi kumeza hili?
oo·may·*wa*·hee
koo·*may*·za *hee*·lee
Have you taken this before?

Ni lazima umalize kosi.
nee *la*·zee·ma
oo·ma·*lee*·zay *koh*·see
You must complete
the course.

dentist

I have a ...	Nina ...	nee·na ...
broken	jino	jee·noh
tooth	lililovunjika	lee·lee·loh·voon·jee·ka
cavity	kutokoka	koo·toh·koh·ka
	kwa jino	kwa jee·noh
toothache	maumivu	ma·oo·mee·voo
	ya jino	ya jee·noh

I need (a/an) ...	Nahitaji ...	na·hee·ta·jee ...
anaesthetic	ganzi	gan·zee
filling	kijazio	kee·ja·zee·oh

I've lost a filling.
Nimepoteza kijazio.   nee·may·poh·tay·za kee·ja·zee·oh

My gums hurt.
Ufizi unaniumiza.   oo·fee·zee oo·na·nee·oo·mee·za

I don't want it extracted.
Sitaki ung'oaji.   see·ta·kee oong·oh·a·jee

the dentist may say ...

Fumbua sana. foom·boo·a sa·na	Open wide.
Haitauma hata kidogo. ha·ee·ta·oo·ma ha·ta kee·doh·goh	This won't hurt a bit.
Tafuna na kamata. ta·foo·na na ka·ma·ta	Bite down on this.
Usihame. oo·see·ha·may	Don't move.
Sukutua! soo·koo·too·a	Rinse!
Rejea, sijamaliza. ray·jay·a see·ja·ma·lee·za	Come back, I haven't finished.

Verbs are shown in the dictionary in their root forms, with a hyphen in front. To express a series of functions in a sentence, the verb can have several prefixes, infixes and suffixes. Some adjectives will also have a hyphen in front as they take different prefixes depending on certain characteristics of the thing being described. For more details on verbs and adjectives, see the **phrasebuilder**. You'll also find words marked as adjective ⓐ, noun ⓝ, verb ⓥ, singular sg or plural pl where necessary. A Swahili dictionary is also available online at www.yale.edu/swahili.

A

aboard *chomboni* chohm·*boh*·nee
abortion *kutoa mimba*
    koo·*toh*·a *meem*·ba
about *kuhusu* koo·*hoo*·soo
above *juu ya* joo ya
abroad *nchi za nje* n·chee za n·jay
accident *ajali* a·*ja*·lee
accommodation *malazi* ma·*la*·zee
account (bank) *akaunti* a·ka·*oon*·tee
across *ng'ambo* ng·*am*·boh
activist *mhamisishaji*
    m·ha·mee·see·*sha*·jee
actor *mwigizaji* mwee·gee·*za*·jee
acupuncture
    tibu yu kuchòma na sindano
    tee·*ba* ya koo·*choh*·ma na seen·*da*·noh
adaptor *adapta* a·*dap*·ta
address *anwani* an·*wa*·nee
administration *usimamizi*
    oo·see·ma·*mee*·zee
admission (price) *bei ya kuingia*
    bay ya koo·een·*gee*·a
admit *·laza* ·*la*·za
adult ⓝ *mtu mzima* m·too m·*zee*·ma
advertisement *tangazo* tan·*ga*·zoh
advice *ushauri* oo·sha·oo·ree
aeroplane *ndege* n·*day*·gay
Africa *Afrika* a·*free*·ka
after *baada ya* ba·*a*·da ya
afternoon *mchana* m·*cha*·na
aftershave *losheni baada ya kunyoa*
    ndevu loh·*shay*·nee ba·*a*·da ya
    koo·*nyoh*·a n·*day*·voo
again *tena* *tay*·na
age *umri* oom·ree

agree *·kubali* ·koo·*ba*·lee
agriculture *kilimo* kee·*lee*·moh
ahead *mbele* m·*bay*·lay
AIDS *ukimwi* oo·*keem*·wee
air (outside) *hewa* *hay*·wa
air (in a tyre) *upepo* oo·*pay* poh
air-conditioned *kwenye a/c*
    kway·nyay ay·*see*
air conditioning *a/c* ay·*see*
airline *kampuni ya ndege*
    kam·*poo*·nee ya n·*day*·gay
airmail *barua kwa ndege*
    ba·roo·a kwa n·*day*·gay
airplane *ndege* n·*day*·gay
airport *uwanja wa ndege*
    oo·*wan*·ja wa n·*day*·gay
airport tax *kodi ya uwanja wa ndege*
    koh·dee ya oo·*wan*·ja wa n·*day*·gay
aisle (on plane) *njia* n·*jee*·a
alarm clock *saa yenye kengele*
    sa *yay*·nyay kayn·*gay*·lay
alcohol *kilevi* kee·*lay*·vee
alcoholic drink *pombe* pohm·bay
all *zote* zoh·tay
allergy *mzio* m·*zee*·oh
almond *lozi* loh·zee
almost *karibu na* ka·ree·boo na
alone *pekee* pay·*kay*
already *tayari* ta·ya·ree
also *pia* pee·a
altar *madhahabu* ma·dha·*ha*·boo
altitude *kimo* kee·moh
always *daima* da·ee·ma
ambassador *balozi* ba·*loh*·zee
ambulance *gari la hospitali*
    ga·ree la hoh·spee·*ta*·lee
America *Marekani* ma·ray·*ka*·nee

American football *futbol ya kimarekani*
foot·bohl ya kee·ma·ray·ka·nee
anaemia *upungufu wa damu*
oo·poon·goo·foo wa da·moo
anarchist *mshabiki wa utawala huria*
m·sha·bee·kee wa oo·ta·wa·la hoo·ree·a
ancient *ya kale ya ka·lay*
and *na na*
angry *mwenye hasira*
mway·nyay ha·see·ra
animal *mnyama* m·nya·ma
ankle *kiwiko cha mguu*
kee·wee·koh cha m·goo
another *nyingine* nyeen·gee·nay
answer *jibu* jee·boo
ant *sungusungu* soon·goo·soon·goo
antelope *palahala* pa·la·ha·la
antibiotic *kiuavijasumu*
kee·oo·a·vee·ja·soo·moo
antinuclear *dhidi ya nyuklia*
dhee·dee ya nyoo·klee·a
antique ⓝ *ya zamani ya za·ma·nee*
antiseptic ⓝ *dawa ya kusafisha jeraha*
da·wa ya koo·sa·fee·sha jay·ra·ha
any *yoyote* yoh·yoh·tay
apartment *fleti* flay·tee
appendix (body) *kibole* kee·boh·lay
apple *tofaa* to·fa
appointment *miadi* mee·a·dee
April *mwezi wa nne* mway·zee wa n·nay
archaeological *ya elimu kale*
ya ay·lee·moo ka·lay
architect *msanifu wa majengo*
m·sa·nee·foo wa ma·jayn·goh
architecture *ujenzi* oo·jayn·zee
argue *-bisha* ·bee·sha
arm *mkono* m·koh·noh
aromatherapy *tiba ya harufu*
tee·ba ya ha·roo·foo
arrest *-kamata* ·ka·ma·ta
arrivals *wanaofika* wa·na·oh·fee·ka
arrive *-fika* ·fee·ka
art *sanaa* sa·na
art gallery *nyumba ya sanaa*
nyoom·ba ya sa·na
artist *msanii* m·sa·nee
ashtray *chombo cha majivu*
chohm·boh cha ma·jee·voo
Asia *Asia* a·see·a
ask (a question) *-uliza* ·oo·lee·za
ask (for something) *-omba* ·ohm·ba
aspirin *aspirini* a·spee·ree·nee
asthma *pumu* poo·moo

at *kwenye* kway·nyay
athletics *michezo ya riadha*
mee·chay·zoh ya ree·a·dha
atmosphere *hewa* hay·wa
aubergine *biringani* bee·reen·ga·nee
August *mwezi wa nane*
mway·zee wa na·nay
aunt *shangazi* shan·ga·zee
Australia *Australia* a·oo·stra·lee·a
automated teller machine (ATM)
mashine ya kutolea pesa
ma·shee·nay ya koo·toh·lay·a pay·sa
autumn *kipindi cha baridi kidogo*
kee·peen·dee cha ba·ree·dee
kee·doh·goh
avenue *barabara* ba·ra·ba·ra
avocado *embe mafuta* aym·bay ma·foo·ta
awful *mbaya sana* m·ba·ya sa·na

B

B&W (film) *nyeusi na nyeupe*
nyay·oo·see na nyay·oo·pay
baboon *nyani* nya·nee
baby *mtoto mchanga*
m·toh·toh m·chan·ga
baby food *chakula cha mtoto mchanga*
cha·koo·la cha m·toh·toh m·chan·ga
baby powder *pauda kwa mtoto*
pa·oo·da kwa m·toh·toh
babysitter *yaya* ya·ya
back (body) *mgongo* m·gohn·goh
back (position) *nyuma* nyoo·ma
backpack *shanta* shan·ta
bacon *bekoni* bay·koh·nee
bad *mbaya* m·ba·ya
bag *mfuko* m·foo·koh
baggage *mizigo* mee·zee·goh
baggage allowance *uzito usiolipiwa*
oo·zee·toh oo·see·oh·lee·pee·wa
baggage claim *sehemu ya
kuchukulia mizigo* say·hay·moo ya
koo·choo·koo·lee·a mee·zee·goh
bakery *duka la mkate* doo·ka la m·ka·tay
balance (account) *urari* oo·ra·ree
balcony *ubaraza* oo·ba·ra·za
ball *mpira* m·pee·ra
ballet *ngoma ya kuigiza hadithi*
n·goh·ma ya koo·ee·gee·za ha·dee·thee
banana *ndizi* n·dee·zee
band (music) *kikundi* kee·koon·dee
bandage *plasta* pla·sta

Band-Aid *elasto* ay-*la*-stoh
bank *benki* bayn-kee
bank account *akaunti ya benki*
a-ka-*oon*-tee ya bayn-kee
banknote *noti* noh-tee
baptism *ubatizo* oo-ba-*tee*-zoh
bar *baa* ba
bar work *kazi kwenye baa*
ka-zee kway-nyay ba
barber *kinyozi* kee-*nyoh*-zee
basket *kikapu* kee-*ka*-poo
basketball *mpira wa kikapu*
m-*pee*-ra wa kee-*ka*-poo
bath *bafu* ba-*foo*
bathing suit *nguo za kuogelea*
n-*goo*-oh za koo-oh-gay-*lay*-a
bathroom (for bathing) *bafuni*
ba-*foo*-nee
bathroom (toilet) *choo* choh
battery *betri* bay-tree
be -*wa* -wa
beach *ufukwe* oo-*fook*-way
beach volleyball *mpira wa wavu ufukoni*
m-*pee*-ra wa wa-voo oo-foo-*koh*-nee
beans *maharagwe* ma-ha-*rag*-way
beansprouts *miche ya maharagwe*
mee-chay ya ma-ha-*rag*-way
beautiful *ya kupendeza*
ya koo-*payn*-day-za
beauty salon *saloni* sa-*loh*-nee
because *kwa sababu* kwa sa-*ba*-boo
bed *kitanda* kee-*tan*-da
bed linen *shuka* shoo-ka
bedding *shuka na tandiko*
shoo-ka na tan-*dee*-koh
bedroom *chumba cha kulala*
choom-ba cha koo-*la*-la
bee *nyuki* nyoo-kee
beef *nyama ng'ombe* nya-ma ng-*ohm*-bay
beer *bia* bee-a
beetroot *kiazisukari* kee-a-zee-soo-*ka*-ree
before *kabla* ka-bla
beggar *mwombaji* mwohm-*ba*-jee
behind *nyuma* nyoo-ma
Belgium *Ubelgiji* oo-bayl-*gee*-jee
below *chini* chee-nee
beside *jirani* jee-*ra*-nee
best *nzuri kabisa* n-zoo-ree ka-*bee*-sa
bet *dau* da-oo
better *afadhali* a-fa-*dha*-lee
between *katikati* ka-tee-*ka*-tee
Bible *Biblia* beeb-*lee*-a
bicycle *baisikeli* ba-ee-see-*kay*-lee

big *kubwa* koob-wa
bigger *kubwa zaidi* koob-wa za-ee-dee
biggest *kubwa kabisa* koob-wa ka-*bee*-sa
bike *baisikeli* ba-ee-see-*kay*-lee
bike chain *mnyororo wa baisikeli*
m-nyoh-*roh*-roh wa ba-ee-see-*kay*-lee
bike lock *kufuli ya baisikeli*
koo-*foo*-lee ya ba-ee-see-*kay*-lee
bike path *njia ya baisikeli*
n-*jee*-a ya ba-ee-see-*kay*-lee
bike shop *duka la baisikeli*
doo-ka la ba-ee-see-*kay*-lee
bill (restaurant etc) *bili* bee-lee
binoculars *darubini* da-roo-*bee*-nee
bird *ndege* n-*day*-gay
birth certificate *cheti cha kuzaliwa*
chay-tee cha koo-za-*lee*-wa
birthday *sikukuu ya kuzaliwa*
see-koo-koo ya koo-za-*lee*-wa
biscuit *biskuti* bee-*skoo*-tee
bite (dog, insect etc) ⓝ *uma* oo-ma
bitter *chungu* choon-goo
black *nyeusi* nyay-oo-see
bladder *kibofu* kee-*boh*-foo
blanket *blanketi* blan-*kay*-tee
blind *kipofu* kee-*poh*-foo
blister *lengelenge* layn-gay-*layn*-gay
blockage *kizuizi* kee-zoo-ee-zee
blood *damu* da-moo
blood group *aina ya damu*
a-ee-na ya da-moo
blood pressure *shinikizo la damu*
shee-nee-*kee*-zoh la da-moo
blood test *kipimo cha damu*
kee-*pee*-moh cha da-moo
blue *buluu* boo-loo
board (a plane etc) -*panda* -*pan*-da
boarding house *nyumba ya wageni*
nyoom-ba ya wa-*gay*-nee
boarding pass *pasi ya kupanda ndege*
pa-see ya koo-*pan*-da n-*day*-gay
boat *boti* boh-tee
body *mwili* mwee-lee
boiled *ya kuchemshwa*
ya koo-*chaym*-shwa
bone *mfupa* m-*foo*-pa
book ⓝ *kitabu* kee-*ta*-boo
book ⓥ -*fanya buking* -*fa*-nya boo-keeng
booked out *hakuna nafasi*
ha-*koo*-na na-*fa*-see
bookshop *duka la vitabu*
doo-ka la vee-*ta*-boo
boots (footwear) *mabuti* ma-*boo*-tee

border *mpaka* m·pa·ka
bored *-choshwa* ·choh·shwa
boring *ya kuchosha* ya koo·choh·sha
borrow *-kopa* ·koh·pa
botanic garden *bustani ya kibotania* boo·sta·nee ya kee·boh·ta·*nee*·a
both *mbili* m·*bee*·lee
bottle *chupa* choo·pa
bottle opener *kifungua chupa* kee·foon·goo·a choo·pa
bottle shop *duka la pombe kali* doo·ka la pohm·bay ka·lee
bottom (body) *matako* ma·ta·koh
bottom (position) *chini* chee·nee
bowl *bakuli* ba·koo·lee
box *sanduku* san·doo·koo
boxer shorts *chupi* choo·pee
boxing *ndondi* n·dohn·dee
boy *mvulana* m·voo·la·na
boyfriend *mpenzi* m·payn·zee
bra *sidiria* see·dee·ree·a
brakes *breki* bray·kee
brandy *brandi* bran·dee
brave *shupavu* shoo·pa·voo
bread *mkate* m·ka·tay
bread rolls *skonzi* skohn·zee
break *-vunja* ·voon·ja
break down *-vunjika* ·voon·jee·ka
breakfast *chai ya asubuhi* cha·ee ya a·soo·boo·hee
breast (body) *titi* tee·tee
breast-feed *-nyonyesha* ·nyoh·nyay·sha
breathe *-pumua* ·poo·moo·a
bribe *-toa rushwa* ·toh·a roosh·wa
bridge *daraja* da·ra·ja
briefcase *mkoba* m·koh·ba
bring *-leta* ·lay·ta
brochure *kijitabu* kee·jee·ta·boo
broken *ya kuvunjika* ya koo·voon·jee·ka
broken down *ya kuharibika* ya koo·ha·ree·bee·ka
bronchitis *mkamba* m·kam·ba
brother *kaka* ka·ka
brown *kahawia* ka·ha·wee·a
bruise *jeraha* jay·ra·ha
brush *burashi* boo·ra·shee
bucket *ndoo* n·doh
Buddhist *Mbudisti* m·boo·dee·stee
budget *bajeti* ba·jay·tee
buffalo *nyati* nya·tee
buffet *meza kujihudumia* may·za koo·jee·hoo·doo·mee·a
bug *mdudu* m·doo·doo

build *-jenga* ·jayn·ga
builder *mjenzi* m·jayn·zee
building *jengo* jayn·goh
burn ⑪ *jeraha la moto* jay·ra·ha la moh·toh
burnt *ya kuchomwa* ya koo·chohm·wa
Burundi *Burundi* boo·roon·dee
bus (city) *daladala/matatu* Tan/Ken da·la·da·la/ma·ta·too
bus (intercity) *basi* ba·see
bus station *stendi ya basi* stayn·dee ya ba·see
bus stop *kituo cha basi* kee·too·oh cha ba·see
business *biashara* bee·a·sha·ra
business class *daraja la wafanyabiashara* da·ra·ja la wa·fa·nya·bee·a·sha·ra
business person *mfanyabiashara* m·fa·nya·bee·a·sha·ra
business trip *safari kwa biashara* sa·fa·ree kwa bee·a·sha·ra
busker *mwimbaji barabarani* mweem·ba·jee ba·ra·ba·ra·nee
busy (person) *mwenye shughuli nyingi* mway·nyay shoo·goo·lee nyeen·gee
but *lakini* la·kee·nee
butcher *bucha* boo·cha
butcher's shop *bucha* boo·cha
butter *siagi* see·a·gee
butterfly *kipepeo* kee·pay·pay·oh
button *kifungo* kee·foon·goh
buy *-nunua* ·noo·noo·a

C

cabbage *kabichi* ka·bee·chee
café *mgahawa* m·ga·ha·wa
cake *keki* kay·kee
cake shop *duka la keki* doo·ka la kay·kee
calculator *kikokotoo* kee·koh·koh·toh·oh
calendar *kalenda* ka·layn·da
call *-ita* ·ee·ta
camel *ngamia* n·ga·mee·a
camera *kemra* kaym·ra
camera shop *duka la kemra* doo·ka la kaym·ra
camp *-piga kambi* ·pee·ga kam·bee
camp site *kiwanja cha kupigia kambi* kee·wan·ja cha kuu·pee·gee·a kam·bee
camping ground *uwanja wa kupigia kambi* oo·wan·ja cha kuu·pee·gee·a kam·bee

camping store *duka la vifaa vya kambi*
doo-ka la vee-*fa* vya kam-bee
can (be able) *-weza* -*way*-za
can (have permission) *-ruhusiwa*
-roo-hoo-*see*-wa
can (tin) *mkebe/kopo* m-*kay*-bay/*koh*-poh
can opener *opena ya kopo*
oh-*pay*-na ya *koh*-poh
Canada *Kanada* ka-na-da
cancel *-futa* -*foo*-ta
cancer *kansa* kan-sa
candle *mshumaa* m-shoo-*ma*
candy *pipi* pee-pee
cantaloupe *tikiti maji ndogo la rangi*
ya machungwa tee-*kee*-tee ma-jee
n-*doh*-goh la ran-gee ya ma-*choon*-gwa
capsicum *pilipili hoho*
pee-lee-*pee*-lee hoh-hoh
car *gari* ga-ree
car hire *kukodi gari* koo-*koh*-dee ga-ree
car owner's title *haki ya kisheria ya*
mmiliki wa gari ha-kee ya kee-shay-*ree*-a
ya m-mee-lee-kee wa ga-ree
car park *sehemu ya kuegesha magari*
say-*hay*-moo ya koo-ay-gay-*shay*-a
ma-ga-ree
car registration *usajili wa gari*
oo-sa-jee-lee wa ga-ree
caravan *lori la wasafiri*
loh-ree la wa-sa-*fee*-ree
cardiac arrest *kusimama kwa mapigo ya*
moyo koo-see-*ma*-ma kwa ma-*pee*-goh
ya moh-yoh
cards (playing) *karata* ka-*ra*-ta
care (for someone) *-tunza* -*toon*-za
carpenter *seremala* say-ray-*ma*-la
carrot *karoti* ka-*roh*-tee
carry *-beba* -*bay*-ba
carton *katoni* ka-*toh*-nee
cash ⓝ *fedha* fay-dha
cash register *rejista* ray-*gee*-sta
cash (a cheque) *-lipwa fedha kwa kutoa*
hundi -*leep*-wa fay-dha kwa koo-*toh*-a
hoon-dee
cashew *korosho* koh-*roh*-shoh
cashier *keshia* kay-*shee*-a
casino *kasino* ka-*see*-noh
cassette *kanda* kan-da
castle *husuni* hoo-soo-nee
casual work *kibarua* kee-ba-roo-a
cat *paka* pa-ka
cathedral *kanisa kuu* ka-nee-sa koo
Catholic (denomination)
Romani roh-*ma*-nee

Catholic (person) *Mkatoliki*
m-ka-toh-*lee*-kee
cauliflower *koliflawa* koh-lee-*fla*-wa
cave *pango* pan-goh
CD *CD* see-*dee*
CD-ROM *cd-rom* see-dee-*rohm*
celebration *sherehe* shay-*ray*-hay
cell phone *simu ya mkononi*
see-moo ya m-koh-*noh*-nee
cemetery *makaburini* ma-ka-boo-*ree*-nee
cent *senti* sayn-tee
centimetre *sentimita* sayn-tee-*mee*-ta
Central Africa *Afrika ya Kati*
a-*free*-ka ya ka-tee
centre *katikati* ka-tee-ka-tee
ceramics *ufinyanzi* oo-fee-*nyan*-zee
cereal *nafaka* na-fa-ka
certificate *cheti* chay-tee
chain *mnyororo* m-nyoh-*roh*-roh
chair *kiti* kee-tee
championships *mashindano ya ubingwa*
ma-sheen-*da*-noh ya oo-*been*-gwa
chance *nafasi* na-*fa*-see
change (coins) *sarafu* sa-*ra*-foo
change (money) *-badilisha hela*
-ba-dee-*lee*-sha hay-la
changing room (in shop) *chumba*
cha kubadilisha nguo choom-ba cha
koo-ba-dee-*lee*-sha n-*goo*-oh
charming *mwenye haiba*
mway-nyay ha-*ee*-ba
cheap *rahisi* ra-*hee*-see
cheat ⓝ *mdanganyi* m-dan-*ga*-nyee
check (banking) *hundi* hoon-dee
check (bill) *bili* bee-lee
check *-kagua* -ka-*goo*-a
check-in (desk) *mapokezi*
ma-poh-*kay*-zee
checkpoint *kituo cha ukaguzi*
kee-*too*-oh cha oo-ka-*goo*-zee
cheese *jibini* jee-bee-nee
cheetah *duma* doo-ma
chef *mpishi* m-*pee*-shee
chemist (pharmacy)
duka la dawa doo-ka la *da*-wa
chemist (person) *mfamasia* m-fa-ma-*see*-a
cheque (banking) *hundi* hoon-dee
cheque (bill) *bili* bee-lee
cherry *cheri* chay-ree
chess *sataranji* sa-ta-ran-jee
chessboard *ubao wa sataranji*
oo-*ba*-oh wa sa-ta-*ran*-jee
chest (body) *kufua* koo-*foo*-a

chewing gum *mpira* m-*pee*-ra
chicken *kuku* koo-koo
chicken pox *tetekuwanga*
tay-tay-koo-*wan*-ga
child *mtoto* m-*toh*-toh
child seat *kiti cha mtoto*
kee-tee cha m-*toh*-toh
childminding *ulezi wa mtoto*
oo-*lay*-zee wa m-*toh*-toh
children *watoto* wa-*toh*-toh
chilli *pilipili hoho* pee-lee-*pee*-lee hoh-hoh
chilli sauce *mchuzi wa pilipili hoho*
m-*choo*-zee wa pee-lee-*pee*-lee hoh-hoh
China *China* chee-na
chiropractor *tabibu wa maungo*
ta-*bee*-boo wa ma-*oon*-goh
choose *-chagua* -cha-*goo*-a
chopping board *bao la kukatia*
ba-oh la koo-ka-*tee*-a
Christian *Mkristo* m-*kree*-stoh
Christian name *jina la kwanza*
jee-na la *kwan*-za
Christmas *Krismasi* krees-*ma*-see
church *kanisa* ka-*nee*-sa
cigar *biri* bee-ree
cigarette *sigara* see-*ga*-ra
cigarette lighter *kiwashio* kee-wa-*shee*-oh
cinema *sinema* see-*nay*-ma
circus *sarakasi* sa-ra-*ka*-see
citizenship *uraia* oo-ra-ee-a
city *mji* m-jee
city centre *katikati ya mji*
ka-tee-*ka*-tee ya m-jee
civil rights *haki za binadamu*
ha-kee za been-a-*da*-moo
class (category) *tabaka* ta-*ba*-ka
class system *mfumo wa matabaka*
m-*foo*-moh wa ma-ta-*ba*-ka
classical *ya jadi* ya *ja*-dee
clay *udongo* oo-*dohn*-goh
clean ⓐ *safi* sa-fee
clean *-safisha* -sa-*fee*-sha
cleaning *usafi* oo-sa-fee
client *mteja* m-*tay*-ja
cliff *mwamba* mwam-ba
climb *-panda* -*pan*-da
cloakroom *chumba cha makoti*
choom-ba cha ma-*koh*-tee
clock *saa* sa
close *-funga* -*foon*-ga
closed *ya kufungwa* ya koo-*foon*-gwa
clothesline *kamba ya kukausha nguo*
kam-ba ya koo-ka-oo-sha n-*goo*-oh

clothing *nguo* n-*goo*-oh
clothing store *duka la nguo*
doo-ka la n-*goo*-oh
cloud *wingu* ween-goo
cloudy *kuna mawingu*
koo-na ma-*ween*-goo
clutch (car) *klachi* *kla*-chee
coach (bus) *basi* *ba*-see
coast *pwani* pwa-nee
coat *koti* koh-tee
cobra *koboko* koh-*boh*-koh
cocaine *kokeini* koh-kay-ee-nee
cockroach *mende* mayn-day
cocoa *kakao* ka-ka-oh
coconut *nazi* na-zee
coffee *kahawa* ka-*ha*-wa
coins *sarafu* sa-*ra*-foo
cold ⓐ *baridi* ba-ree-dee
cold (illness) *ugonjwa* oo-*gon*-jwa
colleague *mwenzi wangu*
mwayn-zee wan-goo
collect call *gharama kwa mpigiwa simu*
gha-*ra*-ma kwa m-pee-*gee*-wa see-moo
college *chuo* choo-oh
colour *rangi* ran-gee
comb *chanuo* cha-*noo*-oh
come *-ja* -ja
comedy *ya kuchekesha* ya koo-chay-*kay*-sha
comfortable *ya starehe* ya sta-*ray*-hay
commission *kamisheni* ka-mee-*shay*-nee
communications (profession)
mawasiliano ma-wa-see-lee-*a*-noh
communion *komunyo* koh-*moo*-nyoh
(The) Comoros Islands *Visiwa vya Komoros*
vee-*see*-wa vya koh-*moh*-rohs
companion *mwenzi* mwayn-zee
company *kampuni* kam-poo-nee
compass *dira* dee-ra
complaint *lalamiko* la-la-mee-koh
complimentary (free) *bure* boo-ray
computer *kompyuta* kohm-*pyoo*-ta
computer game
mchezo kwenye kompyuta
m-*chay*-zoh *kway*-nyay kom-*pyoo*-ta
concert *onyesho la muziki*
oh-*nyay*-shoh la moo-zee-kee
concussion *mshtuko wa ubongo*
m-*shtoo*-koh wa oo-*bohn*-goh
conditioner (hair)
dawa la kuboresha nywele
da-wa la koo-boh-*ray*-sha nyway-lay
condom *kondom* kohn-dohm
conference (big) *mikutano*
mee-koo-*ta*-noh

conference (small) *mkutano*
m·koo·*ta*·noh
confession *ungamo* oon·ga·moh
confirm (a booking) -*hakikisha*
·ha·kee·*kee*·sha
congratulations *hongera* hohn·*gay*·ra
conjunctivitis *uvimbe wa mboni*
oo·*veem*·bay wa m·*boh*·nee
connection *kiungo* kee·oon·goh
conservative *muhafidhina*
moo·ha·fee·*dhee*·na
constipation *uyabisi wa tumbo*
oo·ya·*bee*·see wa *toom*·boh
consulate *ubalozi mdogo*
oo·ba·*loh*·zee m·*doh*·goh
contact lenses *lenzi mboni*
layn·zee m·*boh*·nee
contact lenses solution
myeyuko wa lenzi mboni
m·*yay*·*yoo*·koh wa *layn*·zee m·*boh*·nee
contraceptives *kingamimba*
keen·ga·*meem*·ba
contract *mkataba* m·ka·*ta*·ba
convenience store
duka la bidhaa mbalimbali
doo·ka la bee·*dha* m·ba·lee·m·*ba*·lee
convent *jumuiya ya masista*
joo·moo·*ee*·ya ya ma·*see*·sta
cook ⓝ *mpishi* m·*pee*·shee
cook ⓥ -*pika* ·*pee*·ka
cookie *biskuti* bee·*skoo*·tee
cooling *kupika koo·pee·ka*
cool (temperature) *ya baridi*
ya ba·*ree*·dee
copper *shaba* *sha*·ba
corkscrew *kizibuo* kee·zee·boo·oh
corn *mahindi* ma·*heen*·dee
corner *kona* *koh*·na
corrupt *ya kula rushwa* ya koo·la *roosh*·wa
cost *gharama* ga·*ra*·ma
cotton *pamba* *pam*·ba
cotton balls *mafusha ya pamba* pl
ma·*foo*·sha ya *pam*·ba
cotton buds *vijiti vya pamba safi* pl
vee·*jee*·tee vya *pam*·ba sa·fee
cough *kikohozi* kee·koh·*hoh*·zee
cough medicine *dawa la kukohoa*
da·wa la koo·koh·*hoh*·a
count -*hesabu* ·*hay*·sa·boo
counter (at bar) *kaunta* ka·oon·ta
country *nchi* n·chee
countryside *nyika* *nyee*·ka
coupon *kuponi* koo·*pohn*·ee

courgette *mumunye ya kula*
moo·*moo*·nyay ya koo·la
court (legal) *mahakama* ma·ha·*ka*·ma
court (tennis) *kiwanja* kee·*wan*·ja
cover charge *bei ya kuingia*
bay ya koo·een·*gee*·a
cow *ng'ombe* ng·*ohm*·bay
cracker (biscuit) *mkate mkavu*
m·*ka*·tay m·ka·voo
crafts *vitu vya sanaa* vee·too vya sa·*na*
crash *mgongano* m·gohn·*ga*·noh
crazy *mwenye kichaa* mway·nyay kee·*cha*
cream *mtindi* m·*teen*·dee
credit *mkopo* m·*koh*·poh
credit card *kadi ya benki*
ka·dee ya *bayn*·kee
crocodile *mamba* *mam*·ba
crop *zao* za·oh
cross (religious) *msalaba* m·sa·*la*·ba
crowded *ya kujazana* ya koo·ja·*za*·na
cucumber *tango* tan·goh
cup *kikombe* kee·*kohm*·bay
cupboard *kabati* ka·ba·tee
currency exchange *kubadilisha hela*
koo·ba·dee·*lee*·sha *hay*·la
current (electricity) *mkondo* m·*kohn*·doh
curry *bizari* bee·za·ree
custom (tradition) *mila* *mee*·la
customs *forodha* foh·*roh*·dha
cut -*kata* ·*ka*·ta
cutlery *vitu vya* ▪▪▪
CV *maelezo binafsi ya ujuzi*
ma·ay·*lay*·zoh bee·*naf*·see ya oo·*joo*·zee
cycle -*panda baisikeli*
·*pan*·da ba·ee·*see*·*kay*·lee
cycling *kupanda baisikeli*
koo·*pan*·da ba·ee·see·*kay*·lee
cyclist *mpanda baisikeli*
m·*pan*·da ba·ee·see·*kay*·lee
cystitis *kuvimba kibofu*
koo·*veem*·ba kee·*boh*·foo

D

dad *baba* ba·ba
daily *kila siku* kee·la *see*·koo
dance -*cheza densi* ·*chay*·za *dayn*·see
dancing *densi* dayn·see
dangerous *hatari* ha·*ta*·ree
dark (at night) *giza* *gee*·za
dark (of colour) *nyeusi* nyay·*oo*·see
date (appointment) *miadi* mee·*a*·dee

date (fruit) *tende* tayn·day
date (day) *tarehe* ta·ray·hay
date (a person) *-wa marafiki*
·wa ma·ra·fee·kee
date of birth *tarehe ya kuzaliwa*
ta·ray·hay ya koo·za·lee·wa
daughter *binti* been·tee
dawn *kucha* koo·cha
day *siku* see·koo
(the) day after tomorrow *kesho kutwa*
kay·shoh koot·wa
(the) day before yesterday *juzi* joo·zee
dead *amekufa* a·may·koo·fa
deaf *ziwi* zee·wee
December *mwezi wa kumi na mbili*
mway·zee wa koo·mee na m·bee·lee
decide *-amua* a·moo·a
deep *-refu* ·ray·foo
deforestation *kuharibu misitu*
koo·ha·ree·boo mee·see·too
degrees (temperature) *nyuzi* nyoo·zee
delay *ucheleweshaji*
oo·chay·lay·way·sha·jee
deliver *-fikisha* ·fee·kee·sha
democracy *demokrasia*
day·moh·kra·see·a
demonstration (protest) *maandamano*
ma·an·da·ma·noh
Denmark *Denmarki* dayn·mar·kee
dental floss *uzi wa meno*
oo·zee wa may·noh
dentist *daktari wa meno*
dak·ta·ree wa may·noh
deodorant *diodorani* dee·oh·doh·ra·nee
depart *-ondoka* ·ohn·doh·ka
department store *duka lenye vitu vingi*
doo·ka lay·nyay vee·too veen·gee
departure *kuondoka* koo·ohn·doh·ka
departure gate *mlango wa kuondoka*
m·lan·goh wa koo·ohn·doh·ka
deposit (bank) *amana* a·ma·na
desert *jangwa* jan·gwa
design *rasimu* ra·see·moo
dessert *kitindamlo* kee·teen·da·m·loh
destination *kifiko* kee·fee·koh
details *vipengele* vee·payn·gay·lay
diabetes *kisukari* kee·soo·ka·ree
dial tone *mlio wa simu*
m·lee·oh wa see·moo
diaper *nepi* nay·pee
diaphragm (contraceptive) *kiwambo
cha kizuia mimba* kee·wam·boh cha
kee·zoo·ee·a meem·ba

diarrhoea *kuhara* koo·ha·ra
diary *kitabu cha kumbukumbu*
kee·ta·boo cha koom·boo·koom·boo
dice *dadu* da·doo
dictionary *kamusi* ka·moo·see
die *-fa* ·fa
diet ⓝ *mlo* m·loh
different *tofauti* to·fa·oo·tee
difficult *vigumu* vee·goo·moo
digital *dijiti* dee·jee·tee
dining car *bogi la kulia chakula*
boh·gee la koo·lee·a cha·koo·la
dinner *chakula cha jioni*
cha·koo·la cha jee·oh·nee
direct *moja kwa moja* moh·ja kwa moh·ja
direct dial *kupiga simu moja kwa moja*
koo·pee·ga see·moo moh·ja kwa moh·ja
direction *uelekeo* oo·ay·lay·kay·oh
director *mkurugenzi* m·koo·roo·gayn·zee
dirty *chafu* cha·foo
disabled *wasiojiweza*
wa·see·oh·jee·way·za
disco *disko* dees·koh
discount *punguzo* poon·goo·zoh
discrimination *ubaguzi* oo·ba·goo·zee
disease *maradhi* ma·ra·dhee
dish *chakula* cha·koo·la
disk *diski* dee·skee
disk (floppy) *disketi* dees·kay·tee
diving *kuzamia* koo·za·mee·a
diving equipment *vifaa vya kuzamia*
vee·fa vya koo·za·mee·a
divorced *kutalikiwa* koo·ta·lee·kee·wa
dizziness *kizunguzungu*
kee·zoon·goo·zoon·goo
do *-fanya* ·fa·nya
doctor *daktari* dak·ta·ree
documentary (film) *filamu ya hali halisi*
fee·la·moo ya ha·lee ha·lee·see
dog *mbwa* m·bwa
dole *posho* poh·shoh
doll *mwanasesere* mwa·na·say·say·ray
dollar *dola* doh·la
door *mlango* m·lan·goh
dope (drugs) *madawa ya kulevya*
ma·da·wa ya koo·lay·vya
double *mbilimbili* m·bee·lee·m·bee·lee
double bed *kitanda cha watu wawili*
kee·tan·da cha wa·too wa·wee·lee
double room *chumba cha watu wawili*
choom·ba cha wa·too wa·wee·lee
down *chini* chee·nee
downhill *kwa kuteremka*
kwa koo·tay·raym·ka

dozen kumi na mbili
   koo·mee na m·bee·lee
drama hadithi kama riwaya
   ha·dee·thee ka·ma ree·wa·ya
dream ndoto n·doh·toh
dress vazi va·zee
dried ya kukaushwa ya koo·ka·oosh·wa
dried fruit matunda yaliyokaushwa
   ma·toon·da ya·lee·yoh·ka·oosh·wa
drink ⓝ kinywaji kee·nywa·jee
drink -nywa ·nywa
drink (alcoholic) ⓝ pombe pohm·bay
drive -endesha ·ayn·day·sha
drivers license leseni ya kuendesha gari
   lay·say·nee ya koo·ayn·day·sha ga·ree
drug dawa da·wa
drug addiction utegemezi wa madawa
   ya kulevya oo·tay·gay·may·zee wa
   ma·da·wa ya koo·lay·vya
drug dealer mwuzaji wa madawa ya
   kulevya mwoo·za·jee wa ma·da·wa ya
   koo·lay·vya
drug trafficking
   kuuza madawa ya kulevya
   koo·oo·za ma·da·wa ya koo·lay·vya
drug user mtumiaji wa madawa ya
   kulevya m·too·mee·a·jee wa ma·da·wa
   ya koo·lay·vya
(illegal) drugs madawa (ya kulevya)
   ma·da·wa (ya koo·lay·vya)
drum ngoma n·goh·ma
(be) drunk -lewa ·lay·wa
dry -kausha ·ka·oo·sha
dry ⓐ kavu ka·voo
duck bata ba·ta
dummy (pacifier) nyonyo bandia
   nyoh·nyoh ban·dee·a
DVD dvd dee·vee·dee

E

each kila kee·la
ear sikio see·kee·oh
early mapema ma·pay·ma
earn -pata ·pa·ta
earplugs vizibo vya masikio
   vee·zee·boh vya ma·see·kee·oh
earrings herini hay·ree·nee
Earth Dunia doo·nee·a
earthquake tetemeko la ardhi
   tay·tay·may·koh la ar·dhee
east mashariki ma·sha·ree·kee

East Africa Afrika ya Mashariki
   a·free·ka ya ma·sha·ree·kee
Easter Pasaka pa·sa·ka
easy rahisi ra·hee·see
eat -la ·la
economy class daraja la tatu
   da·ra·ja la ta·too
ecstasy (drug) ekstasi ayk·sta·see
eczema ukurutu oo·koo·roo·too
education elimu ay·lee·moo
egg yai ya·ee
eggplant biringani bee·reen·ga·nee
election uchaguzi oo·cha·goo·zee
electrical store duka la bidhaa za umeme
   doo·ka la bee·dha za oo·may·may
electricity umeme oo·may·may
elephant ndovu/tembo
   n·doh·voo/taym·boh
elevator lifti leef·tee
email barua pepe ba·roo·a pay·pay
embarrassment aibu a·ee·boo
embassy ubalozi oo·ba·loh·zee
emergency dharura dha·roo·ra
emotional mwenye hisia
   mway·nyay hee·see·a
employee mfanyakazi m·fa·nya·ka·zee
employer mwajiri mwa·jee·ree
empty tupu too·poo
end mwisho mwee·shoh
endangered species spishi zilizo hatarini
   spee·shee zee·lee·zoh ha·ta·ree·nee
(I'm) engaged nimechumbiwa
   nee·may·choom·bee·wa
engagement (to be married)
   uchumba oo·choom·ba
engine injini een·jee·nee
engineer mhandisi m·han·dee·see
engineering uhandisi oo·han·dee·see
England Uingereza oo·een·gay·ray·za
English (language) Kiingereza
   kee·een·gay·ray·za
enjoy oneself -furahia ·foo·ra·hee·a
enough ya kutosha ya koo·toh·sha
enter -ingia ·een·gee·a
entertainment guide
   mwongozo wa burudani
   mwohn·goh·zoh wa boo·roo·da·nee
entry (access) mwingilio mween·gee·lee·oh
envelope bahasha ba·ha·sha
environment mazingira ma·zeen·gee·ra
epilepsy kifafa kee·fa·fa
equal opportunity fursa sawa foor·sa sa·wa
equality usawa oo·sa·wa

equipment *vifaa* vee·*fa*
escalator *eskaleta* ays·ka·*lay*·ta
estate agency *wakala wa shamba* wa·*ka*·la wa *sham*·ba
Ethiopia *Uhabeshi* oo·ha·*bay*·shee
euro *euro* ay·oo·roh
Europe *Ulaya* oo·*la*·ya
euthanasia *eutanasia* ay·oo·ta·*na*·see·a
evening *jioni* jee·oh·*nee*
every *kila* kee·la
everyone *wote* woh·*tay*
everything *kila kitu* kee·la kee·too
exactly *kamili* ka·*mee*·lee
example *mfano* m·*fa*·noh
excellent *barabara* ba·*ra*·ba·ra
excess baggage *mizigo ziada* mee·zee·goh zee·*a*·da
exchange *-badilisha* ·ba·dee·*lee*·sha
exchange rate *kiwango cha kubadilishia fedha* kee·*wan*·goh cha koo·ba·dee·*lee*·shee·a fay·dha
excluded *ya kuachwa* ya koo·*ach*·wa
exhaust (car) *mchemuo* m·*chay*·moo·oh
exhibition *maonyesho* ma·oh·*nyay*·shoh
exit *kutoka* koo·*toh*·ka
expensive *ghali* ga·lee
experience *uzoefu* oo·zoh·*ay*·foo
exploitation *utumiaji* oo·too·mee·*a*·jee
express ⓐ *ekspres* ayk·*sprays*
express mail *barua ya haraka* ba·*roo*·a ya ha·*ra*·ka
extension (visa) *uongezaji wa visa* oo·ohn·*gay*·za·jee wa *vee*·sa
eye *jicho* jee·*choh*
eye drops *matone ya macho* ma·*toh*·nay ya *ma*·choh
eyes *macho* ma·*choh*

fabric *kitambaa* kee·*tam*·ba
face (body) *uso* oo·*soh*
face cloth *kitambaa cha mkono* kee·*tam*·ba cha m·*koh*·noh
factory *kiwanda* kee·*wan*·da
factory worker *mfanyakazi wa kiwandani* m·fa·nya·*ka*·zee wa kee·wan·*da*·nee
fall (autumn) *kipindi cha baridi kidogo* kee·*peen*·dee cha ba·*ree*·dee kee·*doh*·goh
fall (down) *-anguka* ·*an*·goo·ka
family *familia* fa·mee·*lee*·a

family name *jina la familia* *jee*·na la fa·mee·*lee*·a
famous *maarufu* ma·a·*roo*·foo
fan (machine) *feni* fay·nee
fan (sport, etc) *mshabiki* m·sha·*bee*·kee
fanbelt *mkanda wa feni* m·*kan*·da wa *fay*·nee
far *mbali* m·*ba*·lee
farm *shamba* *sham*·ba
farmer *mkulima* m·koo·*lee*·ma
fare *nauli* na·oo·lee
fashion *mtindo* m·*teen*·doh
fast *ya kasi* ya ka·*see*
fat ⓐ *nene* nay·nay
father *baba* ba·ba
father-in-law *babamkwe* ba·ba·m·*kway*
faucet *bomba* bohm·ba
(someone's) fault *kosa* koh·sa
faulty *yenye kosa* *yay*·nyay koh·sa
fax machine *faksi* fak·see
February *mwezi wa pili* *mway*·zee wa *pee*·lee
feed *-lisha* ·lee·sha
feel (touch) *-hisi* ·hee·see
feeling (physical) *hisia* hee·*see*·a
feelings *hisia* hee·*see*·a
female *ya kike ya kee·kay*
fence *wigo* wee·goh
ferry *kivuko* kee·*voo*·koh
festival *tamasha* ta·*ma*·sha
fever *homa* hoh·ma
few *chache* cha·chay
fiancé *mchumba* m·*choom*·ba
fiancée *mchumba* m·*choom*·ba
fiction *uzushi* oo·*zoo*·shee
fig *tini* tee·nee
fight *pigano* pee·*ga*·noh
fill *-jaza* ·ja·za
fillet *sarara* sa·*ra*·ra
film (cinema) *filamu* fee·*la*·moo
film (for camera) *mkanda wa picha* m·*kan*·da wa *pee*·cha
film speed *mwendo wa mkanda* *mwayn*·doh wa m·*kan*·da
filtered *ya chujwa* ya *chooj*·wa
find *-gundua* ·goon·doo·a
fine ⓝ *faini* fa·*ee*·nee
fine ⓐ *nzuri* n·*zoo*·ree
finger *kidole* kee·*doh*·lay
finish ⓝ *mwisho* mwee·*shoh*
finish *-maliza* ·ma·lee·za
Finland *Ufini* oo·*fee*·nee
fire *moto* moh·toh

firewood *kuni* koo·nee
first *ya kwanza* ya kwan·za
first class *daraja la kwanza*
  da·ra·ja la kwan·za
first-aid kit *kisanduku cha huduma*
  ya kwanza kee·san·doo·koo cha
  hoo·doo·ma ya kwan·za
first name *jina la kwanza*
  jee·na la kwan·za
fish *samaki* sa·ma·kee
fishing *uvuvi* oo·voo·vee
fish shop *duka la samaki*
  doo·ka la sa·ma·kee
flag *bendera* bayn·day·ra
flamingo *heroe* hay·roh·ay
flashlight (torch) *tochi* toh·chee
flat ⓝ *fleti* flay·tee
flat ⓐ *tambalale* tam·ba·la·lay
flea *kiroboto* kee·roh·boh·toh
fleamarket *mnada* m·na·da
flight (of a bird) *mruko* m·roo·koh
flight (plane) *ndege* n·day·gey
flood *mafuriko* ma·foo·ree·koh
floor *sakafu* sa·ka·foo
floor (storey) *ghorofa* go·ro·fa
florist *duka la maua* doo·ka la ma·oo·a
flour *unga* oon·ga
flower *ua* oo·a
flu *fluu* floo
fly *-ruka* ·roo·ka
fog *ukungu* oo·koon·goo
follow *fuata* foo·a·ta
food *chakula* cha·koo·la
food supplies *akiba za chakula*
  a·kee·ba ya za·koo·la
food vendor *mwuzaji wa chakula*
  mwoo·za·jee wa cha·koo·la
foot *mguu* m·goo
football (soccer) *soka* soh·ka
footpath *njia ya miguu*
  n·jee·a ya mee·goo
foreign *ya kigeni* ya kee·gay·nee
forest *msitu* m·see·too
forever *milele* mee·lay·lay
forget *-sahau* ·sa·ha·oo
forgive *-samehe* ·sa·may·hay
fork *uma* oo·ma
fortnight *wiki mbili* wee·kee m·bee·lee
fortune teller *mtabiri* m·ta·bee·ree
foul (sport) *faulo* fa·oo·loh
foyer *sebule* say·boo·lay
fragile *ya kuvunjika kirahisi*
  ya koo·voon·jee·ka kee·ra·hee·see

France *Ufaransa* oo·fa·ran·sa
free (available) *kupatikana*
  koo·pa·tee·ka·na
free (gratis) *bure* boo·ray
free (not bound) *huru* hoo·roo
freeze *-ganda* ·gan·da
fresh *bichi* bee·chee
Friday *Ijumaa* ee·joo·ma
fridge *friji* free·jee
fried *ya kukaangwa* ya koo·ka·an·gwa
friend *rafiki* ra·fee·kee
from *kutoka* koo·toh·ka
frost *sakitu* sa·kee·too
frozen *ya kugandwa* ya koo·gan·dwa
fruit *tunda* toon·da
fry *-kaanga* ·ka·an·ga
frying pan *kikaango* kee·ka·an·goh
full *ya kujaa* ya koo·ja
full-time *ya muda kamili*
  ya moo·da ka·mee·lee
fun *burudani* boo·roo·da·nee
funeral *kilio* kee·lee·oh
funny *ya kuchekesha* ya koo·chay·kay·sha
furniture *fenicha* fay·nee·cha
future ⓝ *mbeleni* m·bay·lay·nee

G

game (sport) *mchezo* m·chay·zoh
game park *hifadhi ya wanyama*
  hee·*fa*·dhee ya wa·*nya*·ma
garage *gereji* gay·ray·jee
garbage *takataka* ta·ka·ta·ka
garbage can *pipa la taka* pee·pee la ta·ka
garden *bustani* boo·sta·nee
gardener *mtunza bustani*
  m·toon·za boo·sta·nee
gardening *kilimo cha bustani*
  kee·lee·moh cha boo·sta·nee
garlic *kitunguu saumu*
  kee·toon·goo sa·oo·moo
gas (for cooking) *mafuta ya taa*
  ma·foo·ta ya ta
gas (petrol) *mafuta* ma·foo·ta
gas cartridge *mtungi wa gesi*
  m·toon·gee wa gay·see
gate (airport, etc) *mlango* m·lan·goh
gauze *shashi* sha·shee
gay *msenge* m·sayn·gay
gazelle *swala* swa·la
Germany *Ujerumani* oo·jay·roo·ma·nee
get *-pata* ·pa·ta

get off (a train, etc) -shuka ·shoo·ka
gift zawadi za·wa·dee
gig (musical) onyesho oh·nyay·shoh
giraffe twiga twee·ga
girl msichana m·see·cha·na
girlfriend mpenzi m·payn·zee
give -pa ·pa
given name jina la kwanza
   jee·na la kwan·za
glandular fever homa ya matezi
   hoh·ma ya ma·tay·zee
glass (drinking) glesi glay·see
glasses (spectacles) miwani mee·wa·nee
gloves maglavu ma·gla·voo
glue gundi goon·dee
go -enda ·ayn·da
go out -enda nje ·ayn·da n·jay
go out with -rafikiana ·ra·fee·kee·a·na
go shopping -enda dukani
   ·ayn·da doo·ka·nee
goal goli goh·lee
goalkeeper kipa kee·pa
goat mbuzi m·boo·zee
God Mungu moon·goo
goggles (swimming) miwani ya kuogelea
   mee·wa·nee ya koo·oh·gay·lay·a
gold dhahabu dha·ha·boo
golf ball mpira wa gofu
   m·pee·ra wa goh·foo
golf course uwanja wa gofu
   oo·wan·ja wa goh·foo
good nzuri n·zoo·ree
government serikali say·ree·ka·lee
gram gramu gra·moo
grandchild mjukuu m·joo·koo
grandfather babu ba·boo
grandmother bibi bee·bee
grapefruit balungi ba·loon·gee
grapes zabibu za·bee·boo
grass nyasi nya·see
grateful mwenye shukrani
   mway·nyay shook·ra·nee
grave kaburi ka·boo·ree
gray kijivu kee·jee·voo
great (fantastic) nzuri sana
   n·zoo·ree sa·na
green kijani kee·ja·nee
greengrocer duka la mboga
   doo·ka la m·boh·ga
grey kijivu kee·jee·voo
groceries vyakula vya·koo·la
groundnut karanga ka·ran·ga
grow -mea ·may·a

guarantee dhamana dha·ma·na
guess -buni ·boo·nee
guesthouse gesti gay·stee
guide (audio) mwongozo wa sauti
   mwohn·goh·zoh (wa sa·oo·tee)
guide (person) kiongozi kee·ohn·goh·zee
guide dog mbwa wa kuongoza
   m·bwa wa koo·ohn·goh·za
guidebook kitabu cha mwongozo
   kee·ta·boo cha mwohn·goh·zoh
guided tour safari yenye kiongozi
   sa·fa·ree yay·nyay kee·ohn·goh·zee
guilty mwenye hatia mway·nyay ha·tee·a
guitar zeze zay·zay
gum mpira m·pee·ra
gun bunduki boon·doo·kee
gym (fitness room) ukumbi oo·koom·bee
gymnastics sarakasi sa·ra·ka·see
gynaecologist daktari wa akina mama
   dak·ta·ree wa a·kee·na ma·ma

H

hair nywele nyway·lay
hairbrush burashi ya nywele
   boo·ra·shee ya nyway·lay
haircut kukata nywele
   koo·ka·ta nyway·lay
hairdresser msusi m·soo·see
halal halali ha·la·lee
half nusu noo·soo
hallucination wazimu wa·zee·moo
ham nyama nguruwe
   nya·ma n·goo·roo·way
hammer nyundo nyoon·doh
hammock machela ma·chay·la
hand mkono m·koh·noh
handbag mkoba m·koh·ba
handball mpira wa mikono
   m·pee·ra wa mee·koh·noh
handicrafts kazi ya mikono
   ka·zee ya mee·koh·noh
handkerchief kitambaa cha mkono
   kee·tam·ba cha m·koh·noh
handlebars usukani pl oo·soo·ka·nee
handmade kutengenezwa kwa mkono
   koo·tun·gay·nayz·wa kwa m·koh·noh
handsome mrembo m·raym·boh
happy mwenye furaha
   mway·nyay foo·ra·ha
harassment usumbufu oo·soom·boo·foo
harbour bandari ban·da·ree

hard (not soft) *ngumu* n·goo·moo
hard-boiled egg *yai lililochemshwa*
ya·ee lee·lee·loh·chaym·shwa
hardware store *duka la vifaa vya ujenzi*
doo·ka la vee·fa·a vya oo·jayn·zee
hash *bangi* ban·gee
hat *kofia* koh·fee·a
have *-wa na* ·wa na
have a cold *-wa mgonjwa*
·wa m·gohn·jwa
have fun *-furahia* ·foo·ra·hee·a
hawker *mchuuzi* m·choo·oo·zee
hay fever *homa ya mzio*
hoh·ma ya m·zee·oh
he *yeye* yay·yay
head *kichwa* keech·wa
headache *maumivu ya kichwa*
ma·oo·mee·voo ya keech·wa
headlights *taa za mbele* ta za m·bay·lay
health *afya* af·ya
hear *-sikia* ·see·kee·a
hearing aid *chombo cha kusaidia kusikia*
chohm·boh cha koo·sa·ee·dee·a
koo·see·kee·a
heart *moyo* moh·yoh
heart attack *kushambuliwa na maradhi*
ya moyo koo·sham·boo·lee·wa na
ma·ra·dhee ya moh·yoh
heart condition *ugonjwa wa moyo*
oo·gohn·jwa wa moh·yoh
heat *joto* joh·toh
heated *yu moto ya moh·toh*
heater *kipasha moto* kee·pa·sha moh·toh
heating *joto* joh·toh
heavy *nzito* n·zee·toh
helmet *helmeti* hayl·may·tee
help ⓝ *msaada* m·sa·a·da
help *-saidia* ·sa·ee·dee·a
hepatitis *uvimbi wa ini*
oo·veem·bee wa ee·nee
her (ownership) *yake* ya·kay
herbs *mboga za majani*
m·boh·ga za ma·ja·nee
herbalist *mganga wa madawa ya
kienyeji* m·gan·ga wa ma·da·wa ya
kee·ay·nyay·jee
here *hapa* ha·pa
heroin *heroini* hay·roh·ee·nee
high *juu* joo
high school *shule ya msingi*
shoo·lay ya m·seen·gee
highchair *kiti juu cha mtoto*
kee·tee joh cha m·toh·toh

highway *barabara* ba·ra·ba·ra
hike *-tembea porini*
·taym·bay·a poh·ree·nee
hiking *kutembea porini*
koo·taym·bay·a poh·ree·nee
hiking boots *mabuti ya kutembea
porini* ma·boo·tee ya koo·taym·bay·a
poh·ree·nee
hiking route *njia ya kutembea porini*
n·jee·a ya koo·taym·bay·a poh·ree·nee
hill *mlima* m·lee·ma
Hindu *Mhindu* m·heen·doo
hippopotamus *kiboko* kee·boh·koh
hire *-kodi* ·koh·dee
his *yake* ya·kay
historical *ya kihistoria*
ya kee·hee·stoh·ree·a
history *historia* hee·stoh·ree·a
hitchhike *-omba lifti* ·ohm·ba leef·tee
HIV *VVU* vee·vee·yoo
holiday *sikukuu* see·koo·koo
holidays *likizo* lee·kee·zoh
home *nyumbani* nyoom·ba·nee
home brew *pombe ya kienyeji*
pohm·bay ya kee·ay·nyay·jee
homeless *bila nyumba* bee·la nyoom·ba
homemaker *mke anayekaa nyumbani*
m·kay a·na·yay·ka nyoom·ba·nee
homosexual *msenge* m·sayn·gay
honey *asali* a·sa·lee
honeymoon *fungate* foon·ga·tay
hoodlum *mhuni* m·hoo·nee
horn *honi* hoh·nee
horoscope *falaki* fa·la·kee
horse *farasi* fa·ra·see
horse riding *kupanda farasi*
koo·pan·da fa·ra·see
hospital *hospitali* hoh·spee·ta·lee
hospitality *ukarimu* oo·ka·ree·moo
hot *joto* joh·toh
hot water *maji ya moto*
ma·jee ya moh·toh
hotel *gesti* gay·stee
hour *saa* sa
house *nyumba* nyoom·ba
housework *kazi ya nyumbani*
ka·zee ya nyum·ba·nee
how *namna* nam·na
how much *kiasi gani* kee·a·see ga·nee
hug *-kumbatia* ·koom·ba·tee·a
huge *kubwa sana* koob·wa sa·na
human resources *uwezo wa watu*
oo·way·zoh wa wa·too

human rights *haki za binadamu* ha·kee za bee·na·da·moo
humanities *sayansi za jamii* sa·yan·see za ja·mee
hundred *mia* mee·a
hunger *njaa* n·ja
hunting *uwindaji* oo·ween·da·jee
hurt *-uma* ·oo·ma
husband *mume* moo·may
hyena *fisi* fee·see

I

I *mimi* mee·mee
ice *barafu* ba·ra·foo
ice axe *kishota cha kukatia barafu* kee·sho·ta cha koo·ka·tee·a ba·ra·foo
ice cream *aiskrimu* a·ee·skree·moo
ice hockey *hoki ya barafuni* hoh·kee ya ba·ra·foo·nee
identification card (ID) *kitambulisho* kee·tam·boo·lee·shoh
idiot *mjinga* m·jeen·ga
if *kama* ka·ma
ill *mgonjwa* m·gohn·jwa
immigration *uhamiaji* oo·ha·mee·a·jee
impala *swalapala* swa·la·pa·la
important *muhimu* moo·hee·moo
impossible *haiwezekani* ha·ee·way·zay·ka·nee
in *katika* ka·tee·ka
in a hurry *kwa haraka* kwa ha·ra·ka
in front of *mbele ya* m·bay·lay ya
included *ndani yake* n·da·nee ya·kay
income tax *kodi ya mapato* koh·dee ya ma·pa·toh
India *Uhindi* oo·heen·dee
Indian Ocean *Bahari Hindi* ba·ha·ree heen·dee
indicator *kionyeshi* kee·oh·nyay·shee
indigestion *kuvimbiwa* koo·veem·bee·wa
indoor *ndani* n·da·nee
industry *kiwanda* kee·wan·da
infection *ambukizo* am·boo·kee·zoh
inflammation *uvimbe* oo·veem·bay
influenza *fluu* floo
information *taarifa* ta·a·ree·fa
ingredient *kiambato* kee·am·ba·toh
inject *-choma sindano* ·choh·ma seen·da·noh
injection *dawa la sindano* da·wa la seen·da·noh
injury *jeraha* jay·ra·ha
inner tube *tyubu* tyoo·boo

innocent *asiye na hatia* a·see·yay na ha·tee·a
inside *ndani* n·da·nee
instructor *mwalimu* mwa·lee·moo
insurance *bima* bee·ma
interesting *ya kuvutia* ya koo·voo·tee·a
intermission *mapumziko* ma·poom·zee·koh
international *ya kimataifa* ya kee·ma·ta·ee·fa
Internet *mtandao wa kompyuta* m·tan·da·oh wa kohm·pyoo·ta
Internet café *intanet kafe* een·ta·nayt ka·fay
interpreter *mkalimani* m·ka·lee·ma·nee
interview *mahojiano* ma·hoh·jee·a·noh
invite *-karibisha* ·ka·ree·bee·sha
Ireland *Irelandi* ee·ray·layn·dee
iron (for clothes) *pasi* pa·see
island *kisiwa* kee·see·wa
Israel *Israeli* ees·ra·ay·lee
it *hii* hee
IT *teknolojia ya maarifa* tayk·noh·loh·jee·a ya ma·a·ree·fa
Italy *Italia* ee·ta·lee·a
itch *mwasho* mwa·shoh
itemised *kuandikwa kitu kimoja kimoja* koo·an·deek·wa kee·too kee·moh·ja kee·moh·jah
itinerary *ratiba ya safari* ra·tee·ba ya sa·fa·ree
IUD *kitanzi cha kuzuia kuzaa* kee·tan·zee cha koo·zoo·ee·a koo·za

J

jacket *jaketi* ja·kay·tee
jail *gereza* gay·ray·za
jam *jamu* ja·moo
January *mwezi wa kwanza* mway·zee wa kwan·za
Japan *Japani* ja·pa·nee
jar *chupa* choo·pa
jaw *taya* ta·ya
jealous *mwenye wivu* mway·nyay wee·voo
jeans *jinzi* jeen·zee
jeep *jipi* jee·pee
jet lag *kizunguzungu cha saa kutokana na kusafiri kwa ndege* kee·zoon·goo·zoon·goo cha sa koo·toh·ka·na na koo·sa·fee·ree kwa n·day·gay

jewellery *vipuli* vee·*poo*·lee
jewellery store *duka la vipuli* *doo*·ka la vee·*poo*·lee
Jewish *Myahudi* m·ya·*hoo*·dee
job *kazi* ka·zee
jogging *kukimbia taratibu* koo·keem·*bee*·a ta·ra·*tee*·boo
joke *soga* soh·ga
journalist *mwandishi wa habari* mwan·*dee*·shee wa ha·*ba*·ree
journey *safari* sa·fa·ree
judge *hakimu* ha·kee·moo
juice *jusi* joo·see
July *mwezi wa saba* mway·zee wa sa·ba
jump -*ruka* *roo*·ka
jumper (sweater) *sweta* sway·ta
jumper leads *kebo za kuwashia* kay·boh za koo·wa·shee·a
June *mwezi wa sita* mway·zee wa see·ta

K

Kenya *Kenya* kayn·ya
ketchup *mchuzi wa nyanya* m·choo·zee wa nya·nya
key *ufunguo* oo·foon·goo·oh
keyboard *kichapishi* kee·cha·pee·shee
kick -*piga teke* ·pee·ga tay·kay
kidney *figo* fee·goh
kilogram *kilo* kee·loh
kilometre *kilomita* kee·loh·*mee*·ta
kind (nice) *mkarimu* m·ka·*ree*·moo
kindergarten *chekechea* chay·kay·*chay*·a
king *mfalme* m·fal·may
kiosk *kioski* kee·oh·skee
kiss ⓝ *busu* boo·soo
kiss -*busu* ·boo·soo
kitchen *jiko* jee·koh
knee *goti* goh·tee
knife *kisu* kee·soo
know -*jua* ·joo·a
kosher *halali* ha·*la*·lee

L

labourer *mfanyakazi* m·fa·nya·ka·zee
laces *kamba za viatu* kam·ba za vee·a·too
lake *ziwa* zee·wa
lamb *mwanakondoo* mwa·na·kohn·doh
land *ardhi* ar·dhee
landlady/landlord *mwenye nyumba* mway·nyay nyoom·ba

language *lugha* loo·gha
laptop *kompyuta ya kubeba* kohm·pyoo·ta ya koo·bay·ba
large *kubwa* koob·wa
last (previous) *ya kabla* ya kab·la
last (final) *ya mwisho* ya mwee·shoh
last week *wiki iliyopita* wee·kee ee·lee·yoh·pee·ta
late *ya kuchelewa* ya koo·chay·lay·wa
later *baadaye* ba·a·da·yay
laugh -*cheka* ·chay·ka
launderette *dobi* doh·bee
laundry (clothes) *nguo kufua* n·goo·oh koo·foo·a
laundry (place) *udobi* oo·doh·bee
laundry (room) *chumba cha dobi* choom·ba cha doh·bee
law *sheria* shay·ree·a
lawyer *mwanasheria* mwa·na·shay·ree·a
laxative *dawa la kuendesha* da·wa la koo·ayn·day·sha
lazy *mvivu* m·vee·voo
leader *kiongozi* kee·ohn·goh·zee
leaf *jani* ja·nee
learn -*jifunza* ·jee·foon·za
leather *ngozi* n·goh·zee
lecturer *mhadhiri* m·ha·dhee·ree
ledge *mwamba* mwam·ba
left (direction) *kushoto* koo·shoh·toh
left luggage *mizigo iliyowekwa* mee·zee·goh ee·lee·yoh·wayk·wa
left-luggage office *chumba cha kuwekea mizigo* choom·ba cha koo·way·kay·a mee·zee·goh
left-wing *mrengo wa kushoto* m·rayn·goh wa koo·shoh·toh
leg *mguu* m·goo
legal *halali* ha·*la*·lee
legislation *sheria* shay·ree·a
legume *kundekunde* koon·day·koon·day
lemon *limau* lee·ma·oo
lemonade *maji ya limau* ma·jee ya lee·ma·oo
leopard *chui* choo·ee
lens (eye) *mboni* m·boh·nee
lentil *dengu* dayn·goo
lesbian *msagaji* m·sa·ga·jee
less *chache* cha·chay
letter (mail) *barua* ba·roo·a
lettuce *saladi* sa·la·dee
liar *mwongo* mwohn·goh
library *maktaba* mak·ta·ba
lice *chawa* cha·wa

license *laiseni* la·ee·say·nee
licence plate number *namba ya gari*
nam·ba ya *ga*·ree
lie (not stand) *-lala* ·*la*·la
life *maisha* ma·ee·sha
life jacket *jaketi la kuokolea*
ja·*kay*·tee la koo·oh·koh·*lay*·a
lift (elevator) *lifti* leef·tee
light (brightness) *mwanga* mwan·ga
light (lamp) *taa* ta
light (colour) *nyeupe* nyay·oo·pay
light (not heavy) *nyepesi* nyay·*pay*·see
light bulb *balbu ya taa* bal·boo ya ta
light meter *kipima mwanga*
kee·*pee*·ma mwan·ga
lighter (match) *kibiriti* kee·bee·*ree*·tee
lighter (cigarette) *kiwashio*
kee·wa·*shee*·oh
like *-penda* ·*payn*·da
lime (fruit) *ndimu* n·dee·moo
linen (material) *kitani* kee·ta·nee
linen (sheets etc) *mashuka* ma·shoo·ka
lion *simba* seem·ba
lip balm *dawa la midomo*
da·wa la mee·*doh*·moh
lips *midomo* mee·*doh*·moh
lipstick *rangi ya mdomo*
ran·gee ya m·doh·moh
liquor store *duka la pombe*
doo·ka la pohm·bay
listen *-sikiliza* ·see·kee·*lee*·za
little (not much) *chache* cha·chay
little (small) *-dogo* ·*doh*·goh
live (somewhere) *-ishi* ·ee·shee
liver *ini* ee·nee
lizard *mjusi* m·joo·see
local ⓐ *ya kienyeji* ya kee·ayn·*nyay*·jee
lock ⓝ *kufuli* koo·*foo*·lee
lock *-funga kwa ufunguo*
·*foon*·ga kwa oo·foon·goo·oh
locked *ya kufungwa* ya koo·*foon*·gwa
lollies *pipi* pee·pee
long *ndefu* n·*day*·foo
look *-angalia* ·an·ga·*lee*·a
look after *-tunza* ·toon·za
look for *-tafuta* ·ta·foo·ta
lookout *lindo* leen·doh
loose *kejekeje* kay·jay·*kay*·jay
loose change *pesa kichele*
pay·sa kee·*chay*·lay
lose *-potea* ·po·*tay*·a
lost *ya kupotezwa* ya koo·poh·*tayz*·wa

lost property office
chumba cha mali ya kuokota
choom·ba cha ma·lee ya koo·oh·koh·ta
(a) lot *nyingi* nyeen·gee
loud *kwa sauti* kwa sa·oo·tee
love ⓝ *upendo* oo·payn·doh
love ⓥ *-penda* ·payn·da
lover *mpenzi* m·*payn*·zee
low *chini* chee·nee
lubricant *kilainishio*
kee·la·ee·nee·shee·oh
luck *bahati* ba·*ha*·tee
lucky *mwenye bahati*
mway·nyay ba·*ha*·tee
luggage *mizigo* mee·zee·goh
luggage locker *sanduku la*
kuhifadhia mizigo san·doo·koo la
koo·hee·fa·dhee·a mee·zee·goh
luggage tag *tiketi ya mzigo*
tee·*kay*·tee ya m·zee·goh
lump *uvimbe* oo·*veem*·bay
lunch *chakula cha mchana*
cha·koo·la cha m·cha·na
lung *pafu* pa·foo
luxury *anasa* a·na·sa

M

machine *mashine* ma·*shee*·nay
Madagascar *Madagascar* ma·da·*ga*·skar
magazine *gazeti* ga·*zay*·tee
mail (letters) *barua* ba·*roo*·a
mail (postal system) *posta* poh·sta
mailbox *sanduku la posta*
san·doo·koo la poh·sta
main *-kuu* ·koo
main road *barabara kuu* ba·ra·*ba*·ra koo
make *-tengeneza* ·tayn·gay·*nay*·za
make-up *kipodozi* kee·poh·*doh*·zee
malaria *malaria* ma·*la*·ree·a
Malawi *Malawi* ma·*la*·wee
man *mwanamume* mwa·na·*moo*·may
manager (restaurant, hotel) *meneja*
may·*nay*·ja
manager (sales, sports) *mkurugenzi*
m·koo·roo·*gayn*·zee
mandarin *chenza* chayn·za
mango *embe* aym·bay
manual worker *mfanyakazi wa kutumia*
mikono m·fa·nya·*ka*·zee wa
koo·too·*mee*·a mee·*koh*·noh
many *nyingi* nyeen·gee

map *ramani* ra·ma·nee
March *mwezi wa tatu*
  mway·zee wa ta·too
margarine *blue bandi* bloo·ban·dee
marijuana *bangi* ban·gee
marital status *hadhi ya kindoa*
  ha·dhee ya kee·n·doh·a
market *soko* soh·koh
marmalade *jamu ya machungwa*
  ja·moo ya ma·choon·gwa
marriage *ndoa* n·doh·a
(I'm) married (man) *nimeoa*
  nee·may·oh·a
(I'm) married (woman) *nimeolewa*
  nee·may·oh·lay·wa
marry (man) *-oa* ·oh·a
marry (woman) *-olewa* ·oh·lay·wa
martial arts *mieleka* mee·ay·lay·ka
mass (Catholic) *misa* mee·sa
massage *kuchuliwa* koo·choo·lee·wa
masseur/masseuse *mchuaji* m·choo·a·jee
mat *mkeka* m·kay·ka
match (sports) *mechi* may·chee
matches (for lighting) *vibiriti*
  vee·bee·ree·tee
mattress *godolo* goh·doh·loh
May *mwezi wa tano* mway·zee wa ta·noh
maybe *labda* lab·da
mayonnaise *mayonezi* ma·yoh·nay·zee
mayor *mwenyekiti* mway·nyay·kee·tee
me *mimi* mee·mee
meal *mlo* m·loh
measles *surua* soo·roo·a
meat *nyama* nya·ma
mechanic *fundi* foon·dee
media *vyombo vya habari*
  vyohm·boh vya ha·ba·ree
medicine (study, profession) *udaktari*
  oo·dak·ta·ree
medicine (medication) *dawa* da·wa
meditation *kutaamali* koo·ta·a·ma·lee
meet *-kuta* ·koo·ta
melon *tikiti maji* tee·kee·tee ma·jee
member *mwanachama* mwa·na·cha·ma
menstruation *hedhi* hay·dhee
menu *menyu* may·nyoo
message *ujumbe* oo·joom·bay
metal ⓝ *metali* may·ta·lee
metre *mita* mee·ta
microwave (oven) *joko la mikrowevu*
  joh·koh la mee·kroh·way·voo
midday (noon) *saa sita mchana*
  sa see·ta m·cha·na

midnight *saa sita usiku*
  sa see·ta oo·see·koo
migraine *kipandauso* kee·pan·da·oo·soh
military ⓝ *jeshi* jay·shee
military service *kutumikia jeshi*
  koo·too·mee·kee·a jay·shee
milk *maziwa* ma·zee·wa
millimetre *milimita* mee·lee·mee·ta
million *milioni* mee·lee·oh·nee
mince *nyama ya kusaga*
  nya·ma ya koo·sa·ga
mineral water *maji ya madini*
  ma·jee ya ma·dee·nee
minute *dakika* da·kee·ka
mirror *kioo* kee·oh
miscarriage *kuharibu mimba*
  koo·ha·ree·boo meem·ba
Miss *Bibi* bee·bee
miss (feel absence of) *-kosa* ·koh·sa
mistake *kosa* koh·sa
mix *-changanyika* ·chan·ga·nyee·ka
mobile phone *simu ya mkononi*
  see·moo ya m·koh·noh·nee
modem *modemu* moh·day·moo
modern *ya kisasa* ya kee·sa·sa
moisturiser *krimu ya kulainisha ngozi*
  kree·moo ya koo·la·ee·nee·sha n·goh·zee
monastery *nyumba ya utawa wa*
  wanaume nyoom·ba ya oo·ta·wa wa
  wa·na·oo·may
Monday *Jumatatu* Joo·ma·ta·too
money *pesa* pay·sa
monk *mtawa* m·ta·wa
monkey *tumbili* toom·bee·lee
month *mwezi* mway·zee
monument *mnara* m·na·ra
moon *mwezi* mway·zee
more *zaidi* za·ee·dee
morning *asubuhi* a·soo·boo·hee
morning sickness *kichefuchefu cha*
  asubuhi kee·chay·foo·chay·foo cha
  a·soo·boo·hee
mosque *msikiti* m·see·kee·tee
mosquito *mbu* m·boo
mosquito net *chandarua* chan·da·roo·a
motel *gesti* gay·stee
mother *mama* ma·ma
mother-in-law *mamamkwe*
  ma·ma·m·kway
motorbike *pikipiki* pee·kee·pee·kee
motorboat *motaboti* moh·ta·boh·tee
motorcycle *pikipiki* pee·kee·pee·kee
motorway *barabara* ba·ra·ba·ra

mountain *mlima* m·*lee*·ma
mountain bike *baisikeli kwenye gia* ba·ee·see·*kay*·lee kway·nyay *gee*·a
mountain path *njia ya kupanda mlimani* n·*jee*·a ya koo·*pan*·da m·lee·*ma*·nee
mountain range *safu ya milima* sa·foo ya mee·*lee*·ma
mountaineering *kupanda milima* koo·*pan*·da mee·*lee*·ma
mouse *panya* pa·nya
mouth *mdomo* m·*doh*·moh
movie *filamu* fee·*la*·moo
Mozambique *Msumbiji* m·soom·*bee*·jee
Mr *Bwana* bwa·na
Mrs *Bi* bee
Ms (Miss) *Bibi* bee·bee
mud *matope* ma·*toh*·pay
mum *mama* ma·ma
mumps *machumbwichumbwi* ma·choom·bwee·*choom*·bwee
murder ⓝ *mauaji* ma·oo·*a*·jee
murder ⓥ *-ua* ·oo·a
muscle *musuli* moo·soo·lee
museum *makumbusho* ma·koom·boo·shoh
mushroom *uyoga* oo·*yoh*·ga
music *muziki* moo·*zee*·kee
music shop *duka la muziki* doo·ka la moo·*zee*·kee
musician *mwanamuziki* mwa·na·moo·*zee*·kee
Muslim *Mwislamu* mwee·*sla*·moo
mussel *kome* koh·*may*
mustard *mastadi* ma·*sta*·dee
mute *bubu* boo·boo
my *yangu* yan·goo

N

nail clippers *mkasi wa kucha* m·*ka*·see wa koo·cha
name *jina* jee·na
napkin *kitambaa cha mkono* kee·tam·*ba* cha m·*koh*·noh
nappy *nepi* nay·pee
nappy rash *upele wa nepi* oo·*pay*·lay wa nay·pee
national park *hifadhi ya wanyama* hee·*fa*·dhee ya wa·nya·ma
nationality *raia* ra·*ee*·a
nature *hali asili* ha·le a·*see*·lee
naturopathy *matibabu asilia* ma·tee·*ba*·boo a·see·*lee*·a

nausea *kichefuchefu* kee·chay·foo·*chay*·foo
near *karibu* ka·*ree*·boo
nearby *hapo karibuni* ha·poh ka·ree·*boo*·nee
nearest *karibu zaidi* ka·*ree*·boo za·ee·dee
necessary *lazima* la·*zee*·ma
necklace *mkufu* m·*koo*·foo
need *-hitaji* ·hee·ta·jee
needle (sewing) *sindano (ya kushonea)* seen·*da*·noh (ya koo·shoh·*nay*·a)
needle (syringe) *sindano (ya dawa)* seen·*da*·noh (ya *da*·wa)
negative ⓐ *ya kukana* ya koo·*ka*·na
neither *wala* wa·la
net *neti* nay·tee
Netherlands *Uholanzi* oo·hoh·*lan*·zee
never *kamwe* kam·way
new *mpya* m·pya
New Year's Day *Siku ya Mwaka Mpya* see·koo ya mwa·ka m·pya
New Year's Eve *Mkesha wa Mwaka Mpya* m·*kay*·sha wa mwa·ka m·pya
New Zealand *New Zealandi* noo zee·*lan*·dee
news *habari* ha·*ba*·ree
newsstand *duka la magazeti* doo·ka la ma·ga·*zay*·tee
newsagency *shirika la habari* shee·*ree*·ka la ha·*ba*·ree
newspaper *gazeti* ga·*zay*·tee
newspaper vendor *mwuzaji wa magazeti* mwoo·za·jee wa ma·ga·*zay*·tee
next *ijayo* ee·*ja*·yoh
next (month) *(mwezi) ujao* (mway·zee) oo·*ja*·oh
next to *kando ya* kan·doh ya
nice *mwema* mway·ma
nickname *jina la utani* jee·na la oo·*ta*·nee
night *usiku* oo·*see*·koo
night out *usiku nje* oo·*see*·koo n·jay
nightclub *klabu ya usiku* kla·boo ya oo·*see*·koo
no *hapana* ha·*pa*·na
no vacancy *hakuna nafasi* ha·koo·na na·*fa*·see
noisy *yenye kelele* yay·nyay kay·*lay*·lay
none *hakuna* ha·*koo*·na
nonsmoking *hakuna sigara* ha·koo·na see·*ga*·ra
noodles *tambi* tam·bee
noon *saa sita mchana* sa·*ee*·ta m·*cha*·na
north *kaskazini* kas·ka·*zee*·nee
North Africa *Afrika ya Kaskazini* a·*free*·ka ya ka·ska·*zee*·nee

Norway Norwei nohr-way-ee
nose pua poo-a
not hapana ha-pa-na
not yet bado ba-doh
notebook daftari daf-ta-ree
nothing hakuna kitu ha-koo-na kee-too
November mwezi wa kumi na moja
mway-zee wa koo-mee na moh-ja
now sasa sa-sa
nuclear energy nishati ya nyuklia
nee-sha-tee ya nyook-lee-a
nuclear testing majaribio ya nyuklia
ma-ja-ree-bee-oh ya nyook-lee-a
nuclear waste takataka za nyuklia
ta-ka-ta-ka za nyook-lee-a
number namba nam-ba
numberplate kipande cha namba ya gari
kee-pan-day cha nam-ba ya ga-ree
nun sista see-sta
nurse mwuguzi mwoo-goo-zee
nut kokwa kohk-wa

O

ocean bahari ba-ha-ree
October mwezi wa kumi
mway-zee wa koo-mee
off (spoiled) mbaya m-ba-ya
office ofisi oh-fee-see
office worker mfanyakazi ofisini
m-fa-nya-ka-zee n fee see nee
often mara nyingi ma-ra nyeen-gee
oil mufuta ma-foo-ta
old (a) ya zamani ya za-ma-nee
old person (n) mzee m-zay
olive zaituni za-ee-too-nee
olive oil mafuta ya zaituni
ma-foo-ta ya za-ee-too-nee
Olympic Games Michezo ya Olimpiki
mee-chay-zoh ya oh-leem-pee-kee
omelette omlet ohm-layt
on juu ya joo ya
on time kuwahi koo-wa-hee
once mara moja ma-ra moh-ja
one moja moh-ja
one-way ticket tiketi ya kwenda tu
tee-kay-tee ya kwayn-da too
onion kitungu kee-toon-goo
only tu too
open (v) -fungua -foon-goo-a
open (a) wazi wa-zee
opening hours masaa ya kufunguliwa
ma-sa ya koo-foon-goo-lee-wa

opera opera oh-pay-ra
opera house jumba la opera
joom-ba la oh-pay-ra
operation (medical) operesheni
oh-pay-ray-shay-nee
operator opareta oh-pa-ray-ta
opinion maoni ma-oh-nee
opposite kinyume kee-nyoo-may
optometrist daktari wa macho
dak-ta-ree wa ma-choh
or au a-oo
orange (fruit) chungwa choon-gwa
orange (colour) rangi ya machungwa
ran-gee ya ma-choon-gwa
orange juice maji ya machungwa
ma-jee ya ma-choon-gwa
orchestra okestra oh-kay-stra
order (n) agizo a-gee-zoh
order (v) -agiza -a-gee-za
ordinary kawaida ka-wa-ee-da
orgasm mshushio m-shoo-shee-oh
original ya awali ya a-wa-lee
oryx choroa choh-roh-a
ostrich mbuni m-boo-nee
other nyingine nyeen-gee-nay
our yetu yay-too
out of order imevunjika
ee-may-voon-jee-ka
outside nje n-jay
ovarian cyst uvimbe wa ovari
oo-veem-bay wa oh-va-ree
ovary ovari oh-va-ree
oven joko joh-koh
overcoat kabuti ka-boo-tee
overdose dozi kubwa mno ya dawa
doh-zee koob-wa m-noh ya da-wa
overnight kwa usiku mmoja
kwa oo-see-koo m-moh-ja
overseas nchi za nje n-chee za n-jay
owe -wa na deni -wa na day-nee
owner mwenye mway-nyay
oxygen oksijeni ohk-see-jay-nee
oyster chaza cha-za
ozone layer tabaka la hewa ya ozoni
ta-ba-ka la hay-wa ya oh-zoh-nee

P

pacemaker kirekebisho moyo
kee-ray-kay-bee-shoh moh-yoh
pacifier (dummy) nyonyo bandia
nyoh-nyoh ban-dee-a
package furushi foo-roo-shee

packet (general) *pakiti* pa·*kee*·tee
padlock *kufuli* koo·*foo*·lee
page *ukurasa* oo·koo·*ra*·sa
pain *maumivu* ma·oo·*mee*·voo
painful *ya kuumiza* ya koo·oo·*mee*·za
painkiller *kiondoa maumivu*
  kee·ohn·*doh*·a ma·oo·*mee*·voo
painter *msanii wa rangi*
  m·sa·*nee* wa *ran*·gee
painting (a work) *picha* *pee*·cha
painting (the art)
  sanaa ya uchoraji wa rangi
  sa·*na* ya oo·choh·*ra*·jee wa *ran*·gee
pair (couple) *wawili wawili*
  wa·*wee*·lee wa·*wee*·lee
palace *jumba* *joom*·ba
pan *kikaango* kee·*ka*·an·goh
pants (trousers) *suruali* soo·roo·*a*·lee
panty liners *kibandiko cha chupi* pl
  kee·ban·*dee*·koh cha *choo*·pee
paper *karatasi* ka·ra·*ta*·see
paperwork *kazi ya ukarani*
  ka·zee ya oo·ka·*ra*·nee
paraplegic *kilema* kee·*lay*·ma
parcel *kifurushi* kee·foo·*roo*·shee
parents *wazazi* wa·*za*·zee
park ⓝ *hifadhi* hee·*fa*·dhee
park (a car) *-egesha* ·ay·*gay*·sha
parliament *bunge* *boon*·gay
part (component) *sehemu* say·*hay*·moo
part-time *kibarua* kee·ba·*roo*·a
party (night out) *sherehe* shay·*ray*·hay
party (politics) *chama* *cha*·ma
pass *-pita* ·*pee*·ta
passenger *abiria* a·bee·*ree*·a
passionfruit *pasheni* pa·*shay*·nee
passport *pasipoti* pa·see·*poh*·tee
passport number *namba ya pasipoti*
  nam·ba ya pa·see·*poh*·tee
past ⓝ *zamani* za·*ma*·nee
pasta *tambi* *tam*·bee
pastry *kitobosha* kee·toh·*boh*·sha
path *njia* n·*jee*·a
pay *-lipa* ·*lee*·pa
payment *malipo* ma·*lee*·poh
pea *njegere* n·jay·*gay*·ray
peace *amani* a·*ma*·nee
peach *pichi* *pee*·chee
peanut *karanga* ka·*ran*·ga
pear *pea* *pay*·a
pedal *pedeli* pay·*day*·lee
pedestrian *mtembezi* m·taym·*bay*·zee

pen (ballpoint) *kalamu* ka·*la*·moo
pencil *pensili* payn·*see*·lee
penis *mboo* m·*boh*
penknife *kisu cha mfukoni*
  kee·soo cha m·foo·koh·nee
pensioner *mzee* m·*zay*
people *watu* *wa*·too
pepper *pilipili* pee·lee·*pee*·lee
pepper (bell) *pilipili mbichi*
  pee·lee·*pee*·lee m·*bee*·chee
per (day) *kwa* kwa
per cent *asilimia* a·see·lee·*mee*·a
perfect *kamili* ka·*mee*·lee
performance *onyesho* oh·*nyay*·shoh
perfume *marashi* ma·*ra*·shee
period pain *maumivu ya mwezini*
  ma·oo·*mee*·voo ya mway·*zee*·nee
permission *ruhusa* roo·*hoo*·sa
permit *kibali* kee·*ba*·lee
person *mtu* m·*too*
petition *ombi* *ohm*·bee
petrol *mafuta* ma·*foo*·ta
petrol station *kituo cha mafuta*
  kee·*too*·oh cha ma·*foo*·ta
pharmacist *mfamasia* m·fa·ma·*see*·a
pharmacy *duka la dawa* *doo*·ka la *da*·wa
phone book *kitabu cha namba za simu*
  kee·*ta*·boo cha *nam*·ba za *see*·moo
phone box *kibanda cha simu*
  kee·*ban*·da cha *see*·moo
phonecard *kadi ya simu za vibandani*
  ka·dee ya *see*·moo za vee·ban·*da*·nee
photo *picha* *pee*·cha
photographer *mpigapicha*
  m·pee·ga·*pee*·cha
photography *upigaji picha*
  oo·pee·*ga*·jee *pee*·cha
phrasebook *kitabu cha misemo*
  kee·*ta*·boo cha mee·*say*·moh
pickaxe *sururu* soo·*roo*·roo
pickles *achari* a·*cha*·ree
picnic *mandari* man·*da*·ree
pie *pai* *pa*·ee
piece *kipande* kee·*pan*·day
pig *nguruwe* n·goo·roo·*way*
pill *kidonge* kee·*dohn*·gay
(the) pill *kidonge cha kuzuia mimba*
  kee·*dohn*·gay cha koo·zoo·*ee*·a
  meem·ba
pillow *mto* m·*toh*
pillowcase *foronya* foh·*roh*·nya
pineapple *nanasi* na·*na*·see
pink *pinki* *peen*·kee

place *mahali* ma·ha·lee
place of birth *mahali pa kuzaliwa* ma·ha·lee pa koo·za·lee·wa
plane *ndege* n·day·gay
planet *sayari* sa·ya·ree
plant *mmea* m·may·a
plastic *plastiki* pla·stee·kee
plate *sahani* sa·ha·nee
plateau *uwanda wa juu* oo·wan·da wa joo
platform *jukwaa* joo·kwa
play (in theatre) *mchezo wa kuigiza* m·chay·zoh wa koo·ee·gee·za
play cards *-cheza karata* ·chay·za ka·ra·ta
play guitar *-cheza gitaa* ·chay·za gee·taa
plug (bath) *kizibo* kee·zee·boh
plug (electricity) *plagi* pla·gee
plum *plamu* pla·moo
poached (game) *ujangili* oo·jan·gee·lee
pocket *mfuko* m·foo·koh
pocket knife *kisu cha mfukoni* kee·soo cha m·foo·koh·nee
poetry *shairi* pl sha·ee·ree
point (n) *nukta* nook·ta
point (v) *-elekeza* ·ay·lay·kay·za
poisonous *yenye sumu* yay·nyay soo·moo
police *polisi* poh·lee·see
police officer *polisi* poh·lee·see
police station *kituo cha polisi* kee·too·oh cha poh·lee·see
policy *sera* say·ra
politician *mwanasiasa* mwa·na·see·a·sa
politics *siasa* see·a·sa
pollen *chavua* cha·voo·a
pollution *uchafuzi* oo·cha·foo·zee
pool (game) *biliadi* bee·lee·a·dee
pool (swimming) *bwawa* bwa·wa
poor *maskini* mas·kee·nee
popular *ya kupendwa* ya koo·payn·dwa
pork *nyama nguruwe* nya·ma n·goo·roo·way
port (sea) *bandari* ban·da·ree
positive *ya hakika* ya ha·kee·ka
possible *ya kuwezekana* ya koo·way·zay·ka·na
postage *stempu* staym·poo
postcard *postikadi* poh·stee·ka·dee
post code *simbo ya posta* seem·boh ya poh·sta
poster *bango* ban·goh
post office *posta* poh·sta
pot (ceramics) *chungu* choon·goo
pot (dope) *bangi* ban·gee
potato *kiazi* kee·a·zee

pottery *vyombo vya udongo* vyohm·boh vya oo·dohn·goh
pound (money, weight) *paundi* pa·oon·dee
poverty *umaskini* oo·ma·skee·nee
powder *poda* poh·da
power *nguvu* n·goo·voo
prawn *kamba* kam·ba
pray *-sali* ·sa·lee
prayer *sala* sa·la
prefer *-pendelea* ·payn·day·lay·a
pregnancy test kit *upimaji mimba* oo·pee·ma·jee meem·ba
pregnant *mjamzito* m·ja·m·zee·toh
premenstrual tension *zingizi* zeen·gee·zee
prepare *-andaa* ·an·da
prescription *agizo la daktari* a·gee·zoh la dak·ta·ree
present (gift) *zawadi* za·wa·dee
present (time) *sasa* sa·sa
president *rais* ra·ees
pressure *shinikizo* shee·nee·kee·zoh
pretty *ya kupendeza* ya koo·payn·day·za
price *bei* bay
priest *padri* pa·dree
prime minister *waziri mkuu* wa·zee·ree m·koo
printer (computer) *printa* preen·ta
prison *gereza* gay·ray·za
prisoner *mfungwa* m·foon·gwa
private *binafsi* bee·naf·see
profit *faida* fa·ee·da
program *mradi* m·ra·dee
projector *projekta* proh·jayk·ta
promise *-ahidi* ·a·hee·dee
prostitute *malaya* ma·la·ya
protect *-kinga* ·keen·ga
protected species *spishi zilizo hifadhiwa* spee·shee zee·lee·zoh hee·fa·dhee·wa
protest (n) *maandamano* ma·an·da·ma·noh
protest (v) *-pinga* ·peen·ga
provisions *maakuli* ma·a·koo·lee
prune *plamu kavu* pla·moo ka·voo
pub (bar) *baa* ba·a
public relations *uhusiano wa jamii* oo·hoo·see·a·noh wa ja·mee
public telephone *simu ya mtaani* see·moo ya m·ta·nee
public toilet *choo cha hadhara* choh cha ha·dha·ra
pull *-vuta* ·voo·ta

pump ⓝ *pampu* pam·poo
pumpkin *boga* boh·ga
puncture *pancha* pan·cha
pure *halisi* ha·lee·see
purple *zambarau* zam·ba·ra·oo
purse *mkoba* m·koh·ba
push -*sukuma* ·soo·koo·ma
put -*weka* ·way·ka

Q

qualifications *sifa za kielimu*
    see·fa za kee·ay·lee·moo
quality *sifa* see·fa
quarantine *karantini* ka·ran·tee·nee
quarter *robo* roh·boh
queen *malkia* mal·kee·a
question *swali* swa·lee
queue *mstari* m·sta·ree
quick *nyepesi* nyay·pay·see
quiet -*tulivu* ·too·lee·voo
quit -*acha* ·a·cha

R

rabbit *sungura* soon·goo·ra
race (sport) *shindano* sheen·da·noh
racetrack *uwanja wa mbio*
    oo·wan·ja wa m·bee·oh
racing bike *baisikeli ya mashindano*
    ba·ee·see·kay·lee ya ma·sheen·da·noh
racism *ubaguzi wa rangi*
    oo·ba·goo·zee wa ran·gee
racquet *raketi* ra·kay·tee
radiator *kinururishi* kee·noo·roo·ree·shee
radio *redio* ray·dee·oh
radish *figili* fee·gee·lee
railway station *stesheni ya treni*
    stay·shay·nee ya tray·nee
rain *mvua* m·voo·a
raincoat *koti la mvua* koh·tee la m·voo·a
raisin *zabibu kavu* za·bee·boo ka·voo
rally (public meeting) *mkutano wa*
    hadhara m·koo·ta·noh wa ha·dha·ra
rape ⓝ *ubakaji* oo·ba·ka·jee
rape ⓥ -*baka* ·ba·ka
rare (food) *ya kuiva kidogo*
    ya koo·ee·va kee·doh·goh
rare (uncommon) *nadra* na·dra
rash *upele* oo·pay·lay
rat *panya* pa·nya
raw -*bichi* ·bee·chee

razor *wembe* waym·bay
razor blade *wembe* waym·bay
read -*soma* ·soh·ma
reading *somo* soh·moh
ready *tayari* ta·ya·ree
real estate agent *wakala wa maeneo*
    wa·ka·la wa ma·ay·nay·oh
rear (location) *nyuma* nyoo·ma
reason (explanation) *sababu* sa·ba·boo
receipt *risiti* ree·see·tee
recently *hivi karibuni*
    hee·vee ka·ree·boo·nee
recommend -*pendekeza* ·payn·day·kay·za
record (music) -*rekodi (muziki)*
    ·ray·koh·dee (moo·zee·kee)
recording (musical) *kanda* kan·da
recyclable *ya kurejeleza*
    ya koo·ray·jay·lay·za
red *nyekundu* nyay·koon·doo
referee *mwamuzi* mwa·moo·zee
reference *marejeo* ma·ray·jay·oh
refrigerator *friji* free·jee
refugee *mkimbizi* m·keem·bee·zee
refund *kurudisha pesa*
    koo·roo·dee·sha pay·sa
refuse -*kataa* ·ka·ta
regional *ya mkoa* ya m·koh·a
registered mail/post *barua ya rejista*
    ba·roo·a ya ray·jee·sta
rehydration salts *dawa ya kuongeza*
    maji mwilini da·wa ya koo·ohn·gay·za
    ma·jee mwee·lee·nee
relationship *uhusiano* oo·hoo·see·a·noh
relax -*jiburudisha* ·jee·boo·roo·dee·sha
relic *mabaki* ma·ba·kee
religion *dini* dee·nee
religious *ya kidini* ya kee·dee·nee
remote *mbali* m·ba·lee
remote control *rimoti* ree·moh·tee
rent -*kodi* ·koh·dee
repair -*tengeneza* ·tayn·gay·nay·za
republic *jamhuri* jam·hoo·ree
reservation (booking) *buking* boo·keeng
rest -*pumzika* ·poom·zee·ka
restaurant *mgahawa* m·ga·ha·wa
résumé (CV) *muhtasari* mooh·ta·sa·ree
retired *aliyestaafu* a·lee·yay·sta·a·foo
return (come back) -*rudi* ·roo·dee
return ticket *tiketi ya kwenda na kurudi*
    tee·kay·tee ya kwayn·da na koo·roo·dee
review *mapitio* ma·pee·tee·oh
rhinoceros *kifaru* kee·fa·roo
rhythm *mahadhi* ma·ha·dhee

rib *ubavu* oo·ba·voo
rice (cooked) *wali* wa·lee
rice (uncooked) *mchele* m·chay·lay
rich (wealthy) *tajiri* ta·jee·ree
ride ⓝ *lifti* leef·tee
ride (horse) ⓥ *-panda (farasi)* ·pan·da (fa·ra·see)
right (correct) *sawa* sa·wa
right (direction) *kulia* koo·lee·a
right-wing *mrengo wa kulia* m·rayn·goh wa koo·lee·a
ring (on finger) *pete* pay·tay
ring (phone) *-piga simu* ·pee·ga see·moo
rip-off *wizi* wee·zee
risk *hatari* ha·ta·ree
river *mto* m·toh
road *barabara* ba·ra·ba·ra
road map *ramani* ra·ma·nee
rob *-iba* ·ee·ba
rock *jiwe* jee·way
rock climbing *upandaji miamba* oo·pan·da·jee mee·am·ba
rock group *kundi ya roki* koon·dee ya roh·kee
rock music *roki* roh·kee
roll (bread) *skonzi* skohn·zee
romantic *kwa wapenzi* kwa wa·payn·zee
room *chumba* choom·ba
room number *namba ya chumba* nam·ba ya choom·ba
rope *kamba* kam·ba
round *duara* doo·a·ra
roundabout *kiplefti* keep·layf·tee
route *njia* n·jee·a
rowing *kuvuta makasia* koo·voo·ta ma·ka·see·a
rubbish *takataka* ta·ka·ta·ka
rug *zulia* zoo·lee·a
rugby *ragbi* rag·bee
ruins *magofu* ma·goh·foo
rule *utawala* oo·ta·wa·la
run *-kimbia* ·keem·bee·a
running *kukimbia* koo·keem·bee·a
Rwanda *Rwanda* r·wan·da

S

sad *masikitiko* ma·see·kee·tee·koh
saddle *tandiko* tan·dee·koh
safe (for money) ⓝ *kasha la fedha* ka·sha la fay·dha
safe ⓐ *salama* sa·la·ma

safe sex *mapenzi salama* ma·payn·zee sa·la·ma
saint *mtakatifu* m·ta·ka·tee·foo
salad *saladi* sa·la·dee
salary *mshahara* m·sha·ha·ra
sale *seli* say·lee
sales tax *kodi ya mauzo* koh·dee ya ma·oo·zoh
salmon *samoni* sa·moh·nee
salt *chumvi* choom·vee
same *sawasawa* sa·wa·sa·wa
sand *mchanga* m·chan·ga
sandal *ndala* n·da·la
sanitary napkin *sodo* soh·doh
sardine *dagaa* da·ga
Saturday *Jumamosi* joo·ma·moh·see
sauce *mchuzi* m·choo·zee
saucepan *sufuria* soo·foo·ree·a
sauna *sauna* sa·oo·na
sausage *soseji* soh·say·jee
say *-sema* ·say·ma
scalp *ngozi ya kichwa* n·goh·zee ya keech·wa
scarf *skafu* ska·foo
school *shule* shoo·lay
science *sayansi* sa·yan·see
scientist *mwanasayansi* mwa·na·sa·yan·see
scissors *mkasi* m·ka·see
score *alama* a·la·ma
scoreboard *ubao wa matokeo* oo·ba·oh wa ma·toh·kay·oh
Scotland *Skotlandi* skoht·lan·dee
scrambled eggs *mayai yaliyovurugwa* ma·ya·ee ya·lee·yoh·voo·roog·wa
sculpture *uchongaji* oo·chohn·ga·jee
sea *bahari* ba·ha·ree
seasickness *kichefuchefu cha bahrini* kee·chay·foo·chay·foo cha ba·ha·ree·nee
seaside *ufukwe* oo·fook·way
season *majira* ma·jee·ra
seat (place) *kiti* kee·tee
seatbelt *mkanda wa kiti* m·kan·da wa kee·tee
second (time unit) *sekundi* say·koon·dee
second ⓐ *ya pili* ya pee·lee
second class *daraja la pili* da·ra·ja la pee·lee
second-hand *mitumba* mee·toom·ba
second-hand shop *duka la mitumba* doo·ka la mee·toom·ba
secretary *karani* ka·ra·nee

see -ona ·oh·na
self-employed ya kujiajiri
ya koo·jee·a·jee·ree
selfish mwenye choyo
mway·nyay choh·yoh
self service ya kujihuduma
ya koo·jee·hoo·doo·ma
sell -uza ·oo·za
send -peleka ·pay·lay·ka
sensible yenye busara yay·nyay boo·sa·ra
sensual ya kutamanisha
ya koo·ta·ma·nee·sha
separate mbalimbali m·ba·lee·m·ba·lee
September mwezi wa tisa
mway·zee wa tee·sa
serious makini ma·kee·nee
service huduma hoo·doo·ma
service charge malipo ya huduma
ma·lee·poh ya hoo·doo·ma
service station kituo cha petroli
kee·too·oh cha pay·troh·lee
serviette kitambaa cha mkono
kee·tam·ba cha m·koh·noh
several kadhaa ka·dha
sew -shona ·shoh·na
sex (gender) jinsia jeen·see·a
sex (intercourse) mapenzi ma·payn·zee
sexism ubaguzi wa kijinsia
oo·ba·goo·zee wa kee·jeen·see·a
sexy ya kuchochea ashiki
ya koo·choh·chay·a a·shee·kee
shade kivuli kee·voo·lee
shadow kivuli kee·voo·lee
shampoo shampuu sham·poo
shape umbo oom·boh
share (a dorm etc) -gawana ·ga·wa·na
share (with) -shirikiana ·shee·ree·kee·a·na
shave -nyoa ·nyoh·a
shaving cream sabuni ya kunyolea
sa·boo·nee ya koo·nyoh·lay·a
she yeye yay·yay
sheep kondoo kohn·doh
sheet (bed) shuka shoo·ka
shelf rafu ra·foo
shingles (illness) moto ya mungu
moh·toh ya moon·goo
shiny almasi al·ma·see
ship meli may·lee
shirt shati sha·tee
shoe kiatu kee·a·too
shoe shop duka la viatu
doo·ka la vee·a·too
shoes viatu vee·a·too

shoot -piga risasi ·pee·ga ree·sa·see
shop ⓝ duka doo·ka
shop ⓥ -nunua ·noo·noo·a
shopping ununuzi oo·noo·noo·zee
shopping centre madukani
ma·doo·ka·nee
short (height) fupi foo·pee
shortage upungufu oo·poon·goo·foo
shorts kaptura kap·too·ra
shoulder bega bay·ga
shout -piga kelele ·pee·ga kay·lay·lay
show ⓝ onyesho oh·nyay·shoh
show ⓥ -onyesha ·oh·nyay·sha
shower bafuni ba·foo·nee
shrine ziara zee·a·ra
shut ⓐ kufungwa koo·foon·gwa
shy ya aibu ya a·ee·boo
sick mgonjwa m·gohn·jwa
side upande oo·pan·day
sign alama a·la·ma
signature sahihi sa·hee·hee
silk ⓝ hariri ha·ree·ree
silver fedha fay·dha
silver shop duka la fedha doo·ka la fay·dha
SIM card kadi ya simu (ya mikononi)
ka·dee ya see·moo (ya mee·koh·noh·nee)
similar yenye kufanana
yay·nyay koo·fa·na·na
simple rahisi ra·hee·see
since (May) tangu (Mei) tan·goo (may·ee)
sing -imba ·eem·ba
Singapore Singapore seen·ga·poh·ray
singer mwimbaji mweem·ba·jee
single (person) kapera ka·pay·ra
single room chumba kwa mtu mmoja
choom·ba kwa m·too m·moh·ja
singlet fulana ya ndani
foo·la·na ya n·da·nee
sister dada da·da
sit -kaa ·ka
size (general) saizi sa·ee·zee
skate -teleza ·tay·lay·za
skateboarding ubao wa kuteleza
oo·ba·oh wa koo·tay·lay·za
ski -skii ·skee
skiing kuskii koo·skee
skim milk machunda ma·choon·da
skin ngozi n·goh·zee
skirt skati ska·tee
skull fuvu foo·voo
sky mbingu m·been·goo
sleep -sinzia ·seen·zee·a
sleeping bag mfuko wa kulalia
m·foo·koh wa koo·la·lee·a

sleeping berth *kitanda katika behewa*
kee·*tan*·da ka·*tee*·ka bay·*hay*·wa

sleeping car *gari la vitanda*
ga·ree la vee·*tan*·da

sleeping pills *vidonge vya usingizi*
vee·*dohn*·gay vya oo·seen·*gee*·zee

sleepy *mwenye usingizi*
mway·nyay oo·seen·*gee*·zee

slice ⓝ *slaisi* sla·*ee*·see

slide film *filamu ya slaidi*
fee·*la*·moo ya sla·ee·dee

slow *taratibu* ta·ra·*tee*·boo

slowly *polepole* poh·lay·*poh*·lay

small *-dogo* ·doh·goh

smaller *-dogo zaidi* ·doh·goh za·ee·dee

smallest *-dogo kabisa* ·doh·goh ka·*bee*·sa

smart *hodari* hoh·*da*·ree

smell ⓝ *harufu* ha·*roo*·foo

smile *-tabasamu* ·ta·ba·sa·moo

smoke *-vuta sigara* ·voo·ta see·*ga*·ra

snack *kumbwe* koom·bway

snail *konokono* koh·noh·*koh*·noh

snake *nyoka* *nyoh*·ka

snow *theluji* thay·*loo*·jee

soap *sabuni* sa·*boo*·nee

soccer *soka* *soh*·ka

social welfare *ustawi wa jamii*
oo·*sta*·wee wa ja·*mee*

socialist *soshalisti* soh·sha·*lee*·stee

socks *soksi* *sohk*·see

soft drink *soda* *soh*·da

soft-boiled egg *yai lililuchemshwa kidogo* *ya*·ee lee·lee·loh·*chaym*·shwa kee·*doh*·goh

soldier *askari* a·*ska*·ree

Somalia *Somalia* soh·*ma*·lee·a

some *kadhaa* ka·*dha*

someone *fulani* foo·*la*·nee

something *kitu* *kee*·too

sometimes *wakati mwingine*
wa·*la*·ee ya ma·*zee*·wa ya m·*teen*·dee

son *mwana* mwa·na

song *wimbo* *weem*·boh

soon *sasa hivi* sa·sa *hee*·vee

sore *mwenye kuuma* *mway*·nyay koo·oo·ma

soup *supu* *soo*·poo

sour cream *malai ya maziwa ya mtindi*
ma·*la*·ee ya ma·*zee*·wa ya m·*teen*·dee

south *kusini* koo·*see*·nee

South Africa *Afrika ya Kusini*
a·*free*·ka ya koo·*see*·nee

souvenir *kumbukumbu*
koom·boo·*koom*·boo

souvenir shop *duka la kumbukumbu*
doo·ka la koom·boo·*koom*·boo

soy milk *maziwa ya soya*
ma·*zee*·wa ya *soh*·ya

soy sauce *mchuzi wa soya*
m·*choo*·zee wa *soh*·ya

(outer) space *angani* an·*ga*·nee

Spain *Uhispania* oo·hee·*spa*·nee·a

speak *-sema* ·*say*·ma

special *maalum* ma·*a*·loom

specialist *mtaalamu* m·ta·a·*la*·moo

speed (velocity) *mwendo* *mwayn*·doh

speed limit *kikomo cha mwendo*
kee·*koh*·moh cha *mwayn*·doh

speedometer *spidomita* spee·doh·*mee*·ta

spider *buibui* boo·ee·*boo*·ee

spinach *mchicha* m·*chee*·cha

spoilage *uharibifu* oo·ha·ree·*bee*·foo

spoke *spoki* *spoh*·kee

spoon *kijiko* kee·*jee*·koh

sport *michezo* mee·*chay* zoh

sports shop *duka la vifaa vya michezo*
doo·ka la vee·*fa* vya mee·*chay*·zoh

sportsperson *mwanamichezo*
mwa·na·mee·*chay*·zoh

sprain *mteguko* m·tay·*goo*·koh

spring (coil) *springi* *spreen*·gee

spring (season) *majira ya kuchipua*
ma·*jee*·ra ya koo·chee·*poo*·a

square (town) *uwanja* oo·*wan*·ja

stadium *uwanja wa michezo*
oo·*wan*·ja wa mee·*chay*·zoh

stairway *ngazi* n·*ga*·zee

stale *ya zamani* ya za·*ma*·nee

stamp *stempu* *staym*·poo

stand-by ticket *tiketi kutumia kama nafasi ikipatikana* tee·*kay*·tee koo·too·*mee*·a ka·ma na·*fa*·see ee·kee·pa·tee·*ka*·na

star *nyota* *nyoh*·ta

start ⓝ *mwanzo* mwan·zoh

start ⓥ *-anza* ·an·za

station *stesheni* stay·*shay*·nee

stationer *duka la vifaa vya ofisi*
doo·ka la vee·*fa* vya o·*fee*·see

statue *sanamu* sa·na·moo

stay (at a hotel) *-kaa* ·ka

stay (in one place) *-baki* ·*ba*·kee

steak (beef) *mnofu* m·*noh*·foo

steal *-iba* ·ee·ba

steep *ya mwinuko mkali*
ya mway·*noo*·koh m·*ka*·lee

step *hatua* ha·*too*·a

stereo *stirio* stee-*ree*-oh
still water *maji baridi* ma-jee ba-*ree*-dee
stockings *soksi ndefu* sohk-see n-*day*-foo
stolen *ya kuibwa* ya koo-ee-bwa
stomach *tumbo* toom-boh
stomachache *maumivu ya tumbo*
  ma-oo-*mee*-voo ya toom-boh
stone *jiwe* jee-way
stoned (drugged) -*lewa* -*lay*-wa
stop (bus, etc) ⓝ *kituo* kee-too-oh
stop (cease) ⓥ -*simama* -*see*-ma-ma
stop (prevent) ⓥ -*zuia* -zoo-ee-a
storm *dhoruba* dho-roo-ba
story *hadithi* ha-*dee*-thee
stove *jiko* jee-koh
straight *moja kwa moja*
  moh-ja kwa moh-ja
strange *ya kigeni* ya kee-*gay*-nee
stranger *mgeni* m-*gay*-nee
stream *kijito* kee-jee-toh
street *njia* n-jee-a
street children *watoto wa mtaani*
  wa-toh-toh wa m-ta-a-nee
street hawker *mchuuzi* m-choo-oo-zee
street market *soko la mtaani*
  soh-koh la m-ta-a-nee
strike *mgomo* m-goh-moh
string *uzi* oo-zee
stroke (health) *kiharusi* kee-ha-roo-see
stroller (pram) *kigari cha mtoto*
  kee-*ga*-ree cha m-*toh*-toh
strong *madhubuti* ma-dhoo-boo-tee
stubborn *mbishi* m-bee-shee
student *mwanafunzi* mwa-na-*foon*-zee
studio *studio* stoo-dee-oh
stupid *pumbavu* poom-*ba*-voo
style *mtindo* m-*teen*-doh
subtitles *maandishi chini*
  ma-an-*dee*-shee chee-nee
suburb *pembezoni mwa mji*
  paym-bay-*zoh*-nee mwa m-jee
Sudan *Sudan* soo-*dan*
sugar *sukari* soo-*ka*-ree
suitcase *mzigo* m-zee-goh
sultanas *zabibu nyeupe zilizokaushwa*
  za-*bee*-boo nyay-oo-pay
  zee-lee-zoh-ka-*oosh*-wa
summer *majira ya joto*
  ma-*jee*-ra ya *joh*-toh
sun *jua* joo-a
sunblock *dawa la kukinga jua*
  da-wa la koo-*keen*-ga joo-a
sunburn *kuchomwa kwa jua*
  koo-*chom*-wa kwa joo-a

Sunday *Jumapili* joo-ma-*pee*-lee
sunglasses *miwani ya jua*
  mee-*wa*-nee ya joo-a
sunny *ya jua* ya joo-a
sunrise *macheo* ma-*chay*-oh
sunset *machweo* ma-*chway*-oh
sunstroke *ugonjwa wa kuchomwa kwa*
  jua oo-gohn-jwa wa koo-*chohm*-wa
  kwa joo-a
supermarket *duka kubwa*
  doo-ka koob-wa
superstition *ushirikina* oo-shee-ree-*kee*-na
supporter (politics) *mwungaji mkono*
  mwoon-*ga*-jee m-*koh*-noh
supporter (sport) *mshabiki*
  m-sha-*bee*-kee
surface mail (land) *barua kwa lori*
  ba-*roo*-a kwa *loh*-ree
surface mail (sea) *barua kwa meli*
  ba-*roo*-a kwa *may*-lee
surfboard *ubao wa kutelezea*
  oo-*ba*-oh wa koo-tay-lay-*zay*-a
surfing *kuteleza* koo-tay-*lay*-za
surname *jina la baba* jee-na la *ba*-ba
surprise *mshangao* m-shan-*ga*-oh
sweater *sweta* sway-ta
Sweden *Uswidi* oo-*swee*-dee
sweet ⓐ *tamu* ta-moo
sweets *peremende* pay-ray-*mayn*-day
swelling *uvimbe* oo-*veem*-bay
swim -*ogelea* -oh-gay-*lay*-a
swimming (sport) *kuogelea*
  koo-oh-gay-*lay*-a
swimming pool *bwawa la kuogelea*
  bwa-wa la koo-oh-gay-*lay*-a
swimsuit *vazi la kuogelea*
  va-zee la koo-oh-gay-*lay*-a
Switzerland *Uswisi* oo-*swee*-see
synagogue *kanisa ya kiyahudi*
  ka-*nee*-sa ya kee-ya-hoo-dee
synthetic *ya usanisia* ya oo-sa-nee-*see*-a
syringe *sindano* seen-*da*-noh

T

table *meza* may-za
tablecloth *kitambaa cha meza*
  kee-tam-*ba* cha may-za
table tennis *mpira wa meza*
  m-pee-ra wa may-za
tail *mkia* m-*kee*-a
tailor *mshonaji* m-shoh-*na*-jee

take -chukua ·choo·koo·a
take a photo -piga picha ·pee·ga pee·cha
talk -sema ·say·ma
tall mrefu m·ray·foo
tampon sodo soh·doh
tanning lotion dawa la kugeuza rangi
    kwenye jua da·wa la koo·gay·oo·za
    ran·gee kway·nyay joo·a
Tanzania Tanzania tan·za·nee·a
tap bomba bohm·ba
tap water maji ya bomba
    ma·jee ya bohm·ba
tasty tamu ta·moo
tax kodi koh·dee
taxi teksi tayk·see
taxi stand kituo cha teksi
    kee·too·oh cha tayk·see
tea chai cha·ee
teacher mwalimu mwa·lee·moo
team timu tee·moo
teaspoon kijiko cha chai
    kee·jee·koh cha cha·ee
technique mbinu m·bee·noo
teeth meno may·noh
telecom centre telekom tay·lay·kohm
telegram telegramu tay·lay·gra·moo
telephone ⓝ simu see·moo
telephone ⓥ -piga simu ·pee·ga see·moo
telephone box kibanda cha simu
    kee·ban·da cha see·moo
telephone centre kituo cha simu
    kee·too·oh cha see·moo
telescope darubini da·roo·bee·nee
television televisheni
    tay·lay·vee·shay·nee
tell -ambia ·am·bee·a
temperature (fever) homa hoh·ma
temperature (weather) halijoto
    ha·lee·joh·toh
temple hekalu hay·ka·loo
tennis tenesi tay·nay·see
tennis court kiwanja cha tenesi
    kee·wan·ja cha tay·nay·see
tent hema hay·ma
tent peg banzi la hema ban·zee la hay·ma
terrible mbaya sana m·ba·ya sa·na
test mtihani m·tee·ha·nee
thank -shukuru ·shoo·koo·roo
that (person) huyo hoo·yoh
that (thing) hiyo hee·yoh
theatre ukumbi wa maonyesho
    oo·koom·bee wa ma·oh·nyay·shoh
their yao ya·oh

there huko hoo·koh
they wao wa·oh
thick -zito ·zee·toh
thief mwizi mwee·zee
thin mwembamba mwaym·bam·ba
think -fikiri fee·kee·ree
third ya tatu ya ta·too
(to be) thirsty (-sikia) kiu
    (·see·kee·a) kee·oo
this (person) huyu hoo·yoo
this (thing) hii hee
thread uzi oo·zee
throat koo koh
thrush (health) ugonjwa wa upele
    oo·gohn·jwa wa oo·pay·lay
thunderstorm dhoruba ya radi
    dhoh·roo·ba ya ra·dee
Thursday Alhamisi al·ha·mee·see
ticket tiketi/tikiti tee·kay·tee/tee·kee·tee
ticket collector mkusanyaji wa tiketi
    m·koo·sa·nya·jee wa tee·kay·tee
tIcket machine mashine ya tiketi
    ma·shee·nay ya tee·kay·tee
ticket office ofisi ya tiketi
    o·fee·see ya tee·kay·tee
tide maji ya kujaa na kupwa
    ma·jee ya koo·ja na koop·wa
tight ya kubana ya koo·ba·na
time saa sa
time difference tofauti ya wakati
    to·fa·oo·tee ya wa·ka·tee
timetable ratiba ra·tee·ba
tin (can) mkebe/kopo m·kay·bay/koh·poh
tin opener kifungua kopo
    kee·foon·goo·a koh·poh
tiny ndogo sana n·doh·goh sa·na
tip (gratuity) bakshishi bak·shee·shee
tire tairi ta·ee·ree
tired ya kuchoka ya koo·choh·ka
tissues karatasi za shashi
    ka·ra·ta·see za sha·shee
to hadi ha·dee
toast slaisi sla·ee·see
toaster mashine ya kubanika mkate
    ma·shee·nay ya koo·ba·nee·ka m·ka·tay
tobacco tumbaku toom·ba·koo
tobacconist duka la tumbaku
    doo·ka la toom·ba·koo
today leo lay·oh
toe kidole cha mguu
    kee·doh·lay cha m·goo
together pamoja pa·moh·ja
toilet choo choh

toilet paper *karatasi ya choo* ka·ra·ta·see ya choh
tomato *nyanya* nya·nya
tomato sauce *mchuzi wa nyanya* m·choo·zee wa nya·nya
tomorrow *kesho* kay·shoh
tomorrow afternoon *kesho mchana* kay·shoh m·cha·na
tomorrow evening *kesho jioni* kay·shoh jee·oh·nee
tomorrow morning *kesho asubuhi* kay·shoh a·soo·boo·hee
tongue *ulimi* oo·lee·mee
tonight *usiku huu* oo·see·koo hoo
too (expensive etc) *mno* m·noh
tooth *jino* jee·noh
toothache *maumivu ya jino* ma·oo·mee·voo ya jee·noh
toothbrush *mswaki* m·swa·kee
toothpaste *dawa la meno* da·wa la may·noh
toothpick *kijiti cha meno* kee·jee·tee cha may·noh
torch (flashlight) *tochi* toh·chee
touch *-gusa* ·goo·sa
tour *safari ya kutalii* sa·fa·ree ya koo·ta·lee
tourist *mtalii* m·ta·lee
tourist office *ofisi ya watalii* o·fee·see ya wa·ta·lee
towards *kuelekea* koo·ay·lay·kay·a
towel *taulo* ta·oo·loh
tower *mnara* m·na·ra
toxic waste *taka za sumu* ta·ka za soo·moo
toy shop *duka la vitu vya kuchezea* doo·ka la vee·too vya koo·chay·zay·a
track (path) *njia* n·jee·a
track (sport) *michezo ya kukimbia* mee·chay·zoh ya koo·keem·bee·a
trade *biashara* bee·a·sha·ra
tradesperson *mfanyabiashara* m·fa·nya·bee·a·sha·ra
traffic *magari mengi* ma·ga·ree mayn·gee
traffic light *taa ya barabarani* ta ya ba·ra·ba·ra·nee
trail *njia* n·jee·a
train *treni* tray·nee
train station *stesheni ya treni* stay·shay·nee ya tray·nee
transit lounge *chumba cha kupumzikia kwa wanaosafiri choom·ba* cha koo·poom·zee·kee·a kwa wa·na·oh·sa·fee·ree

translate *-tafsiri* ·taf·see·ree
transport *usafirishaji* oo·sa·fee·ree·sha·jee
travel *-safiri* ·sa·fee·ree
travel agency *uwakala wa safari* oo·wa·ka·la wa sa·fa·ree
travellers cheque *hundi ya msafiri* hoon·dee ya m·sa·fee·ree
travel sickness *kichefuchefu cha safari* kee·chay·foo·chay·foo cha sa·fa·ree
tree *mti* m·tee
trip (journey) *safari* sa·fa·ree
trousers *suruali* soo·roo·a·lee
truck *lori* loh·ree
trust *-amini* ·a·mee·nee
try (attempt) *-jaribu* ·ja·ree·boo
try (taste) *-onja* ·ohn·ja
T-shirt *tishati* tee·sha·tee
tube (tyre) *tyubu* tyoo·boo
Tuesday *Jumanne* joo·ma·n·nay
tumour *uvimbe* oo·veem·bay
tuna *jodari* joh·da·ree
tune *wimbo* weem·boh
turkey *bata mzinga* ba·ta m·zeen·ga
turn *-geuza* ·gay·oo·za
TV *televisheni* tay·lay·vee·shay·nee
tweezers *twiza* twee·za
twice *mara mbili* ma·ra m·bee·lee
twin beds *vitanda viwili* vee·tan·da vee·wee·lee
twins *mapacha* ma·pa·cha
two *mbili* m·bee·lee
type *aina* a·ee·na
typical *ya mfano hasa* ya m·fa·noh ha·sa
tyre *tairi* ta·ee·ree

U

Uganda *Uganda* oo·gan·da
ultrasound *kupiga picha ya mtoto tumboni* koo·pee·ga pee·cha ya m·toh·toh toom·boh·nee
umbrella *mwamvuli* mwam·voo·lee
uncomfortable *bila raha* bee·la ra·ha
understand *-elewa* ·ay·lay·wa
underwear *chupi* choo·pee
unemployed *asiye na kazi* a·see·yay na ka·zee
unfair *jeuri* jay·oo·ree
uniform ⓝ *nguo rasmi* n·goo·oh ras·mee
universe *ulimwengu* oo·lee·mwayn·goo
university *chuo kikuu* choo·oh kee·koo
unleaded *isiyo na risasi* ee·see·yoh na ree·sa·see

unsafe *ni hatari* nee ha·*ta*·ree
until *mpaka* m·*pa*·ka
unusual *siyo kawaida* see·yoh ka·wa·ee·da
up *juu* joo
uphill *mwinuko* mwee·*noo*·koh
urgent *muhimu sana* moo·hee·moo *sa*·na
urinary infection *ambukizo la mfumo wa mkojo* am·boo·kee·zoh la m·*foo*·moh wa m·*koh*·joh
USA *Marekani* ma·ray·ka·nee
useful *yenye manufaa* yay·nyay ma·noo·*fa*

V

vacancy *nafasi* na·*fa*·see
vacant *tupu* too·poo
vacation *likizo* lee·*kee*·zoh
vaccination *chanjo* chan·joh
vagina *kuma* koo·ma
validate *-thibitisha* ·thee·bee·*tee*·sha
valley *bonde* *boh*n·day
valuable *ya thamani* ya *tha*·ma·nee
value (price) *thamani* tha·ma·nee
veal *nyama ya ndama* nya·ma ya n·*da*·ma
vegetable *mboga* m·*boh*·ga
vegetarian *mlaji wa mboga za majani tu* m·*la*·jee wa m·*boh*·ga za ma·*ja*·nee too
vein *mshipa* m·*shee*·pa
venereal disease *ugonjwa wa zinaa* oo·*gohn*·jwa wa zee·*na*
venue *mahali* ma *ha*·lee
very *sana* *sa*·na
video recorder *kemra ya video* *kaym*·ra ya vee·*day*·oh
video tape *mkanda wa video* m·*kan*·da wa vee·*day*·oh
view *mandhari* man·*dha*·ree
village *kijiji* kee·*jee*·jee
vine (grape) *mzabibu* m·za·*bee*·boo
vinegar *siki* *see*·kee
vineyard *shamba la mizabibu* *sham*·ba la mee·za·*bee*·boo
virus *virusi* vee·*roo*·see
visa *viza/visa* vee·za/vee·sa
visit *-tembelea* taym·bay·*lay*·a
vitamins *vitamini* vee·ta·*mee*·nee
voice *sauti* *sa*·oo·tee
volleyball (sport) *mpira wa wavu* m·*pee*·ra wa *wa*·voo
volume (sound) *sauti* *sa*·oo·tee
vote *-piga kura* ·*pee*·ga koo·ra
vulture *tumbusi* toom·*boo*·see

W

wage *mshahara* m·sha·*ha*·ra
wait *-subiri* ·soo·*bee*·ree
wait for *-ngojea* ·n·*goh*·jay·a
waiter *mhudumu* m·hoo·*doo*·moo
waiting room *chumba cha wanaosubiri* *choom*·ba cha wa·na·oh·soo·*bee*·ree
wake up *-amka* ·*am*·ka
wake someone up *-amsha* ·*am*·sha
walk *-tembea* taym·*bay*·a
wall (outer) *ukuta* oo·*koo*·ta
want *-taka* ·*ta*·ka
war *vita* *vee*·ta
wardrobe *kabati ya nguo* ka·*ba*·tee ya n·*goo*·oh
warm *ya joto* ya joh·toh
warn *-onya* ·*oh*·nya
wash (oneself) *-oga* ·*oh*·ga
wash (something) *-osha* ·*oh*·sha
wash cloth (flannel) *kitambaa cha uso* kee·*tam*·ba cha oo·soh
washing machine *mashine ya kufulia* ma·*shee*·nay ya koo·foo·*lee*·a
watch *saa* sa
watch *-tazama* ·ta·*za*·ma
water *maji* *ma*·jee
water bottle (hot) *chupa ya maji (ya moto)* *choo*·pa ya *ma*·jee (ya moh·toh)
waterfall *maporomoko ya maji* ma·poh·roh·*moh*·koh ya *ma*·jee
watermelon *tikiti maji* tee·*kee*·tee *ma*·jee
waterproof *kutopenyesha maji* koo·to·pay·nyay·sha *ma*·jee
wave *wimbi* *weem*·bee
way *njia* n·*jee*·a
we *sisi* see·see
weak *hafifu* ha·*fee*·foo
wealthy *tajiri* ta·*jee*·ree
wear *-vaa* ·va
weather *hali ya hewa* *ha*·lee ya *hay*·wa
wedding *arusi* a·*roo*·see
wedding cake *keki ya arusi* *kay*·kee ya a·*roo*·see
wedding present *zawadi ya arusi* za·*wa*·dee ya a·*roo*·see
Wednesday *Jumatano* joo·ma·*ta*·noh
week *wiki* *wee*·kee
weekend *wikendi* wee·*kayn*·dee
weigh *-pima uzito* ·*pee*·ma oo·*zee*·toh
weight *uzito* oo·*zee*·toh

welcome *-karibisha* ·ka·ree·*bee*·sha
welfare *ustawi* oo·*sta*·wee
well *vizuri* vee·*zoo*·ree
west *magharibi* ma·gha·*ree*·bee
West Afrika *Afrika ya Magharibi*
   a·*free*·ka ya mag·ha·*ree*·bee
wet ⓐ *-bichi bee*·chee
what *nini* nee·nee
wheel *gurudumu* goo·roo·*doo*·moo
wheelchair *kiti cha magurudumu*
   kee·tee cha ma·goo·roo·*doo*·moo
when *wakati* wa·*ka*·tee
when *lini* lee·nee
where *wapi* wa·pee
which *gani* ga·nee
white *nyeupe* nyay·*oo*·pay
who *nani* na·nee
why *kwa nini* kwa nee·nee
wide *pana* pa·na
wife *mke* m·kay
wildebeest *nyumbu* nyoom·boo
win *-shinda sheen*·da
wind *upepo* oo·*pay*·poh
window *dirisha* dee·*ree*·sha
windscreen *kiwambo upepo*
   kee·*wam*·boh oo·*pay*·poh
windsurfing *kuteleza na tanga*
   koo·tay·*lay*·za na *tan*·ga
wine *mvinyo* m·vee·nyoh
wings *mabawa* ma·*ba*·wa
winner *mshindi* m·*sheen*·dee
winter *majira ya baridi*
   ma·*jee*·ra ya ba·*ree*·dee
wire *waya* wa·ya
wish *-tumaini* ·too·ma·ee·nee
with *na* na
without *bila* bee·la
woman *mwanamke* mwan·*am*·kay
wonderful *ya ajabu* ya a·*ja*·boo
wood *mbao* m·*ba*·oh
woodcarver's market
   soko la wachonga vinyago
   soh·koh la wa·*chohn*·ga vee·*nya*·goh
wool *sufu* soo·foo
word *neno* nay·noh
work ⓝ *kazi* ka·zee
work ⓥ *-fanya kazi* ·*fa*·nya ka·zee
work experience *uzoefu wa kazi*
   oo·zoh·*ay*·foo wa ka·zee
workout *mazoezi* ma·zoh·*ay*·zee

work permit *ruhusa ya kazi*
   roo·*hoo*·sa ya ka·zee
workshop (place) *karakana* ka·ra·*ka*·na
workshop (meeting) *warsha* war·sha
world *dunia* doo·nee·a
World Cup *Kombe la Dunia*
   kohm·bay la doo·nee·a
worms *minyoo* mee·nyoh
worried *mwenye wasiwasi*
   mway·nyay wa·see·wa·see
worship *-abudu* ·a·*boo*·doo
wrist *kiwiko* kee·*wee*·koh
write *-andika* ·an·dee·ka
writer *mwandishi* mwan·*dee*·shee
wrong *kosa* koh·sa

x-ray *eksirei* ayk·see·*ray*·ee

year *mwaka* mwa·ka
yellow *manjano* man·*ja*·noh
yes *ndiyo* n·*dee*·yoh
yesterday *jana* ja·na
yogurt *maziwa ganda* ma·zee·wa *gan*·da
you sg *wewe* way·way
you pl *nyinyi* nyee·nyee
young *ya kijana* ya kee·*ja*·na
your sg *yako* ya·koh
your pl *yenu* yay·noo
youth hostel *hosteli ya vijana*
   hoh·*stay*·lee ya vee·*ja*·na

Zaire *Jamhuri ya Kidemokrasia ya Kongo*
   jam·*hoo*·ree ya kee·day·moh·kra·*see*·a
   ya *kohn*·goh
Zambia *Zambia* zam·bee·a
Zanzibar City *Mji Mkongwe*
   m·jee m·*kohn*·gway
Zanzibar Island *Unguja* oon·*goo*·ja
zebra *punda milia* poon·da mee·*lee*·a
zip/zipper *zipu* zee·poo
zodiac *zodiaki* zoh·dee·*a*·kee
zoo *hifadhi ndogo ya wanyama*
   hee·*fa*·dhee n·*doh*·goh ya wa·*nya*·ma

Verbs are shown in the dictionary in their root forms, with a hyphen in front. To express a series of functions in a sentence, the verb can have several prefixes, infixes and suffixes. Some adjectives will also have a hyphen in front as they take different prefixes depending on certain characteristics of the thing being described. For more details on verbs and adjectives, see the **phrasebuilder**. You'll also find words marked as adjective ⓐ, noun ⓝ, verb ⓥ, singular sg, plural pl, adverb adv and preposition prep where necessary. A Swahili dictionary is also available online at www.yale.edu/swahili.

A

a/c ay-see *air conditioning*
abiria a-bee-*ree*-a *passenger*
-abudu ·a-*boo*-doo *worship*
-acha ·a-cha *quit*
achari a-*cha*-ree *pickles*
adapta a-*dap*-ta *adaptor*
afadhali a-fa-*dha*-lee *better*
afya af-ya *health*
-agiza ·a-*gee*-za *order* ⓥ
agizo a-*gee*-zoh *order* ⓝ
   — la daktari la dak-*ta*-ree *prescription*
-ahidi ·a-*hee*-dee *promise*
aibu a-*ee*-boo *embarrassment*
aina a-*ee*-na *type*
   — ya damu ya *da*-moo *blood group*
aiskrimu a-ee-*skree*-moo *ice cream*
ajali a-*ja*-lee *accident*
akaunti a-ka-*oon*-tee *account*
   — ya benki ya *bayn*-kee *bank account*
akiba za chakula a-*kee*-ba za cha-*koo*-la *food supplies*
alama a-*la*-ma *score • sign*
Alhamisi al-ha-*mee*-see *Thursday*
aliyestaafu a-lee-yay-sta-*a*-foo *retired*
almasi al-*ma*-see *shiny*
amana a-*ma*-na *deposit (bank)*
amani a-*ma*-nee *peace*
-ambia ·am-*bee*-a *tell*
ambukizo am-boo-*kee*-zoh *infection*
   — la mfumo wa mkojo la m-*foo*-moh wa m-*koh*-joh *urinary infection*
amekufa a-may-*koo*-fa *dead*
-amini ·a-*mee*-nee *trust*
-amka ·am-ka *wake up*

-amsha ·am-sha *wake someone up*
-amua ·a-*moo*-a *decide*
anasa a-*na*-sa *luxury*
-andaa ·an-*da* *prepare*
-andika ·an-*dee*-ka *write*
-angalia ·an-ga-*lee*-a *look*
angani an-*ga*-nee *airspace • outer space*
-anguka ·an-*goo*-ka *fall (down)*
anwani an-*wa*-nee *address*
-anza ·*an*-za *start*
ardhi ar-dhee *land*
arusi a-*roo*-see *wedding*
asali a-*sa*-lee *honey*
asante a-*san*-tay *thank you*
asilimia a-see-lee-*mee*-a *per cent*
asiye na hatia a-*see*-yay na ha-*tee*-a *innocent*
asiye na kazi a-*see*-yay na *ka*-zee *unemployed*
askari a-*ska*-ree *soldier*
aspirini a-*spee-ree*-nee *aspirin*
asubuhi a-soo-*boo*-hee *morning*
au a-oo *or*

B

baa ba *bar (pub)*
baada ya ba-*a*-da ya *after*
baadaye ba-a-*da*-yay *later*
baba *ba*-ba *father*
babamkwe ba-ba-m-kway *father-in-law*
babu *ba*-boo *grandfather*
-badilisha ·ba-dee-*lee*-sha *exchange*
   — hela *hay*-la *change (money)*
bado *ba*-doh *not yet*
bafu *ba*-foo *bath*

bafuni ba·foo·nee
bathroom (for bathing) • *shower*
bahari ba·ha·ree *ocean* • *sea*
bahasha ba·ha·sha *envelope*
bahati ba·ha·tee *luck*
baisikeli ba·ee·see·kay·lee *bicycle*
— **kwenye gia** kway·nyay gee·a
mountain bike
— **ya mashindano**
ya ma·sheen·da·noh *racing bike*
bajeti ba·jay·tee *budget*
-**baka** ·ba·ka *rape*
-**baki** ·ba·kee *stay (in one place)*
bakshishi bak·shee·shee *tip (gratuity)*
bakuli ba·koo·lee *bowl*
balbu ya taa bal·boo ya ta *light bulb*
balozi ba·loh·zee *ambassador*
balungi ba·loon·gee *grapefruit*
bandari ban·da·ree *harbour* • *port (sea)*
bangi ban·gee
hash • *marijuana* • *pot (dope)*
bango ban·goh *poster*
banzi la hema ban·zee la hay·ma *tent peg*
bao la kukatia ba·oh la koo·ka·tee·a
chopping board
barabara ba·ra·ba·ra
avenue • *highway* • *motorway* • *road*
— **kuu** koo *main road*
barabara ba·ra·ba·ra *excellent*
barafu ba·ra·foo *ice*
baridi ba·ree·dee *cold* ⓐ
barua ba·roo·a *letter* • *mail*
— **kwa haraka** kwa ha·ra·ka
(by) express mail
— **kwa lori** kwa loh·ree
surface mail (land)
— **kwa meli** kwa may·lee
surface mail (sea)
— **kwa ndege** kwa n·day·gay *airmail*
— **pepe** pay·pay *email*
— **ya rejista** ya ray·jee·sta
(by) registered mail/post
basi ba·see *bus (intercity)* • *coach*
bata ba·ta *duck*
— **mzinga** m·zeen·ga *turkey*
-**beba** ·bay·ba *carry*
bega bay·ga *shoulder*
bei bay *price*
— **ya kuingia** ya koo·een·gee·a
cover charge • *admission (price)*
bekoni bay·koh·nee *bacon*
bendera bayn·day·ra *flag*
benki bayn·kee *bank*

betri bay·tree *battery*
Bi bee *Mrs* • *Madam*
bia bee·a *beer*
biashara bee·a·sha·ra *business* • *trade*
bibi bee·bee *grandmother*
Bibi bee·bee *Ms* • *Miss*
Biblia beeb·lee·a *Bible*
-**bichi** ·bee·chee *fresh* • *raw* • *wet*
bila bee·la *without*
— **nyumba** nyoom·ba *homeless*
— **raha** ra·ha *uncomfortable*
bili bee·lee *cheque (bill)*
biliadi bee·lee·a·dee *pool (game)*
bima bee·ma *insurance*
binafsi bee·naf·see *private*
binti been·tee *daughter*
biri bee·ree *cigar*
biringani bee·reen·ga·nee
aubergine • *eggplant*
-**bisha** ·bee·sha *argue*
biskuti bee·skoo·tee *biscuit* • *cookie*
bizari bee·za·ree *curry*
blanketi blan·kay·tee *blanket*
blue bandi bloo·ban·dee *margarine*
boga boh·ga *pumpkin*
bogi la kulia chakula
boh·gee la koo·lee·a cha·koo·la *dining car*
bomba bohm·ba *faucet* • *tap*
bonde bohn·day *valley*
boti boh·tee *boat*
brandi bran·dee *brandy*
breki bray·kee *brakes*
bubu boo·boo *mute*
bucha boo·cha *butcher* • *butcher's shop*
buibui boo·ee·boo·ee *spider*
buking boo·keeng *reservation* • *booking*
buluu boo·loo *blue*
bunduki boon·doo·kee *gun*
bunge boon·gay *parliament*
-**buni** ·boo·nee *guess*
burashi boo·ra·shee *brush*
— **ya nywele** ya nyway·lay *hairbrush*
bure boo·ray *complimentary (free)*
burudani boo·roo·da·nee *fun*
bustani boo·sta·nee *garden*
— **ya kibotania** ya kee·boh·ta·nee·a
botanic garden
busu boo·soo *kiss*
-**busu** ·boo·soo *kiss*
Bwana bwa·na *Mr* • *Sir*
bwawa la kuogelea bwa·wa la
koo·oh·gay·lay·a *swimming pool*

C

chache *cha·chay*
few · less · little (not much)
chafu *cha·foo* dirty
-chagua *-cha·goo·a* choose
chai *cha·ee* tea
— **ya asubuhi** ya a·soo·*boo*·hee
breakfast
chakula *cha·koo·la* dish · food
— **cha jioni** cha jee·oh·nee dinner
— **cha mchana** cha m·*cha*·na lunch
— **cha mtoto mchanga**
cha m·*toh*·toh m·*chan*·ga baby food
chama *cha·ma* party (politics)
chandarua chan·da·roo·a mosquito net
-changanyika *-chan·ga·nyee·ka* mix
chanjo *chan·joh* vaccination
chanuo cha·*noo·oh* comb
chavua cha *voo·a* pollen
chawa *cha·wa* lice
chaza *cha·za* oyster
-cheka *-chay·ka* laugh
chekechea chay·kay·*chay·a*
kindergarten
chenji *chayn·jee* change
chenza *chayn·za* mandarin
cheti *chay·tee* certificate
— **cha kuzaliwa** cha koo·za·lee·wa
birth certificate
-cheza *-chay·za* play (guitar, cards etc)
-cheza densi *-chay·za dayn·see* dance
chini *chee·nee*
below · bottom (position) · down · low
chokoleti choh·koh·*lay·tee* chocolate
-choma sindano *-choh·ma seen·da·noh*
inject
chombo cha kusaidia kusikia
*chohm·*boh cha koo·sa·ee·*dee·a*
koo·see·*kee·a* hearing aid
chombo cha majivu
chohm·boh cha ma·*jee·voo* ashtray
chomboni chohm·*boh·nee* aboard
choo *choh* bathroom (toilet)
— **cha hadhara** cha ha·*dha·ra*
public toilet
choroa choh·*roh·a* oryx
-choshwa *-choh·shwa* bored
chui *choo·ee* leopard
-chukua *-choo·koo·a* take

chumba *choom·ba* room
— **cha dobi** cha *doh·bee*
laundry (room)
— **cha kubadilisha nguo**
cha koo·ba·dee·*lee·sha* n·*goo·oh*
changing room (in shop)
— **cha kulala** cha koo·*la·la* bedroom
— **cha kupumzikia kwa wanaosafiri**
cha koo·poom·zee·*kee·a* kwa
wa·na·oh·sa·*fee·ree* transit lounge
— **cha kuwekea mizigo**
cha koo·way·*kay·a* mee·zee·goh
left-luggage office
— **cha makoti** cha ma·*koh·tee* cloakroom
— **cha mali ya kuokota** cha *ma·lee* ya
koo·oh·*koh·ta* lost property office
— **cha wanaosubiri** cha
wa·na·oh·soo·*bee·ree* waiting room
— **kwa watu wawili**
kwa *wa*·too wa·*wee·lee* double room
— **kwa mtu mmoja**
kwa m·too m·*moh·ja* single room
chumvi *choom·vee* salt
chungu *choon·goo*
bitter ⓐ · pot (ceramics) ⓝ
chuo *choo·oh* college
— **kikuu** kee·*koo* university
chupa *choo·pa* bottle · jar
— **ya maji** (ya moto)
ya *ma·jee* (ya *moh·toh*) water bottle (hot)
chupi *choo·pee* boxer shorts · underwear

D

dada *da·da* sister
dadu *da·doo* dice
daftari daf·*ta·ree* notebook
dagaa da·*ga* sardine
daima da·*ee·ma* always
dakika da·*kee·ka* minute
daktari dak·*ta·ree* doctor
— **wa akina mama** wa a·*kee·na ma·ma*
gynaecologist
— **wa macho** wa *ma*·choh optometrist
— **wa meno** wa *may·noh* dentist
daladala Tan da·*la·da·la* bus (city)
damu *da·moo* blood
daraja da·*ra·ja* bridge
— **la kwanza** la *kwan·za* first class
— **la pili** la *pee·lee* second class
— **la tatu** la *ta·too* economy class
— **la wafanyabiashara**
la wa·fa·nya·bee·a·*sha·ra* business class

darubini da-roo-bee-nee
binoculars • telescope
dau da-oo bet
dawa da-wa drug • medicine
— **la kuendesha** la koo-ayn-day-sha
laxative
— **la kugeuza rangi kwenye jua**
la koo-gay-oo-za ran-gee kway-nyay
joo-a tanning lotion
— **la kukinga jua** la koo-keen-ga joo-a
sunblock
— **la kukohoa** la koo-koh-hoh-a
cough medicine
— **la meno** la may-noh toothpaste
— **la midomo** la mee-doh-moh
lip balm
— **la sindano** la seen-da-noh
injection
— **la kuboresha nywele**
la koo-boh-ray-sha nyway-lay
conditioner (hair)
— **la kuongeza maji mwilini**
la koo-ohn-gay-za ma-jee mwee-lee-nee
rehydration salts
— **la kusafisha jeraha**
la koo-sa-fee-sha jay-ra-ha antiseptic ⓝ
demokrasia day-moh-kra-see-a
democracy
dengu dayn-goo lentil
densi dayn-see dancing
dhahabu dha-ha-boo gold
dhamana dha-ma-na guarantee
dharura dha-roo-ra emergency
dhidi ya nyuklia dhee-dee ya nyoo-klee-a
antinuclear
dhoruba dho-roo-ba storm
— **ya radi** ya ra-dee thunderstorm
dini dee-nee religion
diodorani dee-oh-doh-ra-nee
deodorant
dira dee-ra compass
dirisha dee-ree-sha window
disketi dees-kay-tee disk (floppy)
diski dee-skee disk (CD-ROM)
disko dees-koh disco
dobi doh-bee launderette
-dogo -doh-goh small
— **kabisa** ka-bee-sa smallest
— **zaidi** za-ee-dee smaller
dola doh-la dollar
dozi kubwa mno ya dawa doh-zee
koob-wa m-noh ya da-wa overdose
duara doo-a-ra round

duka doo-ka shop
— **kubwa** koob-wa supermarket
— **la aiskrimu** la a-ee-skree-moo
ice-cream parlour
— **la baisikeli** la ba-ee-see-kay-lee
bike shop
— **la bidhaa mbalimbali** la bee-dha
m-ba-lee-m-ba-lee convenience store
— **la bidhaa za umeme**
la bee-dha za oo-may-may electrical store
— **la dawa** la da-wa chemist • pharmacy
— **la fedha** la fay-dha silver shop
— **la keki** la kay-kee cake shop
— **la kemra** la kaym-ra camera shop
— **la kumbukumbu**
la koom-boo-koom-boo souvenir shop
— **la magazeti** la ma-ga-zay-tee
newsstand
— **la maua** la ma-oo-a florist
— **la mboga** la m-boh-ga greengrocer
— **la mitumba** la mee-toom-ba
second-hand shop
— **la mkate** la m-ka-tay bakery
— **la muziki** la moo-zee-kee music shop
— **la nguo** la n-goo-oh clothing store
— **la pombe kali** la pohm-bay ka-lee
bottle shop • liquor store
— **la samaki** la sa-ma-kee fish shop
— **la tumbaku** la toom-ba-koo tobacconist
— **la viatu** la vee-a-too shoe shop
— **la vifaa vya kambi**
la vee-fa vya kam-bee camping store
— **la vifaa vya michezo**
la vee-fa vya mee-chay-zoh sports store
— **la vifaa vya ofisi**
la vee-fa vya o-fee-see stationer (shop)
— **la vifaa vya ujenzi**
la vee-fa vya oo-jayn-zee hardware store
— **la vipuli** la vee-poo-lee jewellery store
— **la vitabu** la vee-ta-boo bookshop
— **la vitu vya kuchezea**
la vee-too vya koo-chay-zay-a toy shop
— **lenye vitu vingi** lay-nyay vee-too
veen-gee department store
duma doo-ma cheetah
Dunia doo-nee-a Earth
dunia doo-nee-a world

E

-egesha -ay-gay-sha park (a car)
ekspres ayk-sprays express ⓐ
ekstasi ayk-sta-see ecstacy (drug)

elasto *ay·la·stoh Band-Aid*
-elekeza *ay·lay·kay·za point*
-elewa *·ay·lay·wa understand*
elimu *ay·lee·moo education*
embe *aym·bay mango*
— **mafuta** *ma·foo·ta avocado*
-enda *·ayn·da go*
— **dukani** *doo·ka·nee go shopping*
— **nje** *n·jay go out*
-endesha *·ayn·day·sha drive*
eskaleta *ays·ka·lay·ta escalator*
euro *ay·oo·roh euro*
eutanasia *ay·oo·ta·na·see·a euthanasia*

F

-fa *·fa die*
faida *fa·ee·da profit*
faini *fa·ee·nee fine (penalty)*
faksi *fak·see fax machine*
falaki *fa·la·kee horoscope*
familia *fa·mee·lee·a family*
-fanya *·fa·nya do*
— **buking** *boo·keeng make a booking*
— **kazi** *ka·zee work*
farasi *fa·ra·see horse*
faulo *fa·oo·loh foul*
fedha *fay·dha cash · silver*
feni *fay·nee fan (machine)*
fenicha *fay·nee·cha furniture*
figili *fee·gee·lee radish*
figo *fee·goh kidney*
-fika *·fee·ka arrive*
-fikiri *·fee·kee·ree think*
-fikisha *·fee·kee·sha deliver*
filamu *fee·la·moo film (cinema)*
— **ya hali halisi** *ya ha·lee ha·lee·see documentary (film)*
— **ya slaidi** *ya sla·ee·dee slide film*
fisi *fee·see hyena*
fleti *flay·tee flat (apartment)*
fluu *floo flu (influenza)*
forodha *foh·roh·dha customs*
foronya *foh·roh·nya pillowcase*
friji *free·jee fridge*
-fuata *·foo·a·ta follow*
fulana ya ndani *foo·la·na ya n·da·nee singlet*
fulani *foo·la·nee someone*
fundi *foon·dee mechanic*
funga *foon·ga close*
-funga kwa ufunguo *·foon·ga kwa oo·foon·goo·oh lock*

fungate *foon·ga·tay honeymoon*
-fungua *·foon·goo·a open*
fupi *foo·pee short (height)*
-furahia *·foo·ra·hee·a enjoy (oneself) · have fun*
fursa sawa *foor·sa sa·wa equal opportunity*
furushi *foo·roo·shee package*
-futa *·foo·ta cancel*
futbol ya kimarekani *foot·bohl ya kee·ma·ray·ka·nee American football*
fuvu *foo·voo skull*

F

G

-ganda *·gan·da freeze*
gani *ga·nee which*
gari *ga·ree car*
— **la hospitali** *la hoh·spee·ta·lee ambulance*
— **la vitanda** *la vee·tan·da sleeping car*
-gawa *·ga·wa deal (cards)*
-gawana *·ga·wa·na share (a dorm etc)*
gazeti *ga·zay·tee magazine · newspaper*
gereji *gay·ray·jee garage (to park a car)*
gereza *gay·ray·za jail*
gesti *gay·stee guesthouse · hotel · motel*
-geuza *·gay·oo·za turn*
ghali *ga·lee expensive*
gharama *ga·ra·ma cost*
— **kwa mpigiwa simu** *kwa m·pee·gee·wa see·moo collect call*
ghorofa *go·ro·fa floor · storey*
giza *gee·za dark*
glesi *glay·see glass*
godolo *goh·doh·loh mattress*
goli *goh·lee goal*
goti *goh·tee knee*
gramu *gra·moo gram*
gundi *goon·dee glue*
-gundua *·goon·doo·a find*
gurudumu *goo·roo·doo·moo wheel*
-gusa *·goo·sa touch*

H

habari *ha·ba·ree news*
hadhi ya kindoa *ha·dhee ya kee·n·doh·a marital status*
hadi *ha·dee to*
hadithi *ha·dee·thee story*
— **kama riwaya** *ka·ma ree·wa·ya drama*

hafifu ha-*fee*-foo *weak*
haiwezekani ha-ee-*way*-zay-ka-nee
  impossible
haki ya kisheria ya mmiliki wa gari
  ha-kee ya kee-*shay*-ree-a ya
  m-mee-*lee*-kee wa *ga*-ree
  car owner's title
haki za binadamu
  ha-kee za been-a-*da*-moo
  civil rights • human rights
-hakikisha (buking) -ha-kee-*kee*-sha
  (*boo*-keeng) *confirm (a booking)*
hakimu ha-*kee*-moo *judge*
hakuna ha-*koo*-na *none*
  — kitu *kee*-too *nothing*
  — nafasi na-*fa*-see
  booked out • no vacancy
  — sigara see-*ga*-ra *nonsmoking*
halali ha-*la*-lee *halal • kosher • legal*
hali asili *ha*-le a-*see*-lee *nature*
hali ya hewa ha-lee y-*hay*-wa *weather*
halijoto ha-lee-*joh*-toh
  temperature (weather)
halisi ha-*lee*-see *pure*
hamna *ham*-na *none*
hapa *ha*-pa *here*
hapana ha-*pa*-na *no • not*
hapo jirani *ha*-poh jee-*ra*-nee *nearby*
hapo karibuni
  ha-poh ka-ree-*boo*-nee *nearby*
hariri ha-*ree*-ree *silk*
harufu ha-*roo*-foo *smell*
hatari ha-*ta*-ree *dangerous • risk*
hatua ha-*too*-a *step*
hedhi *hay*-dhee *menstruation*
hekalu hay-*ka*-loo *temple*
hela *hay*-la *money*
helmeti hayl-*may*-tee *helmet*
hema *hay*-ma *tent*
herini hay-*ree*-nee *earrings*
heroe hay-roh-*ay* *flamingo*
heroini hay-roh-ee-*nee* *heroin*
-hesabu -hay-*sa*-boo *count*
hewa *hay*-wa *air (outside) • atmosphere*
hifadhi hee-*fa*-dhee *park*
  — ndogo ya wanyama
  n-*doh*-goh ya wa-*nya*-ma *zoo*
  — ya wanyama ya wa-*nya*-ma
  game park • national park
hii hee *it • this (thing)*
-hisi -*hee*-see *feel (touch)*
hisia hee-*see*-a *a feeling (physical) • feelings*
historia hee-stoh-*ree*-a *history*
-hitaji -hee-*ta*-jee *need*

hivi karibuni
  hee-vee ka-ree-*boo*-nee *recently*
hiyo *hee*-yoh *that (thing)*
hodari hoh-*da*-ree *brilliant (smart)*
hoki ya barafuni
  hoh-kee ya ba-ra-*foo*-nee *ice hockey*
homa *hoh*-ma *fever (temperature)*
  — ya matezi ya ma-*tay*-zee
  glandular fever
  — ya mzio ya m-*zee*-oh *hay fever*
hongera hohn-*gay*-ra *congratulations*
honi *hoh*-nee *horn*
hospitali hoh-spee-*ta*-lee *hospital*
hosteli ya vijana
  hoh-*stay*-lee ya vee-*ja*-na
  youth hostel
huduma hoo-*doo*-ma *service*
huko *hoo*-koh *there*
hundi *hoon*-dee *cheque (banking)*
  — ya msafiri ya m-sa-*fee*-ree
  travellers cheque
huru *hoo*-roo *free (not bound)*
husuni hoo-*soo*-nee *castle*
huyo *hoo*-yoh *that (person)*
huyu *hoo*-yoo *this (person)*

I

-iba -*ee*-ba *rob*
ijayo ee-*ja*-yoh *next*
Ijumaa ee-joo-*ma* *Friday*
-imba -*eem*-ba *sing*
imevunjika ee-may-voon-*jee*-ka
  out of order
-ingia -*een*-gee-a *enter*
ini *ee*-nee *liver*
injini een-*jee*-nee *engine*
intanet kafe een-ta-*nayt* ka-*fay*
  Internet café
-ishi -*ee*-shee *live (somewhere)*
isiyo na risasi
  ee-*see*-yoh na ree-*sa*-see *unleaded*
-ita -*ee*-ta *call*

J

-ja -ja *come*
jaketi ja-*kay*-tee *jacket*
  — la kuokolea la koo-oh-koh-*lay*-a
  life jacket
jamhuri jam-*hoo*-ree *republic*
jamu *ja*-moo *jam*
  — ya machungwa ya ma-*choon*-gwa
  marmalade

jana *ja*·na yesterday
jangwa *jan*·gwa desert
jani *ja*·nee leaf
-jaribu *ja·ree*·boo try (attempt)
-jaza *ja*·za fill
-jenga *jayn*·ga build
jengo *jayn*·goh building
jeraha jay·*ra*·ha bruise • injury
— la moto la *moh*·toh burn
jeshi *jay*·shee military
jeuri jay·*oo*·ree unfair
jibini jee·*bee*·nee cheese
jibu *jee*·boo answer
-jiburudisha ·jee·boo·roo·*dee*·sha relax
jicho *jee*·choh eye
-jifunza ·jee·*foon*·za learn
jiko *jee*·koh kitchen • stove
jina *jee*·na name
— la baba la *ba*·ba surname
— la familia la fa·mee·*lee*·a
family name
— la kwanza la *kwan*·za Christian name
— la utani la oo·*ta*·nee nickname
jino *jee*·noh tooth
jinsia jeen·*see*·a sex (gender)
jinzi jeen·zee jeans
jioni jee·oh·nee evening
jipi *jee*·pee jeep
jirani jee·*ra*·nee beside • near
jiwe *jee*·way rock • stone
jodari joh·*da*·ree tuna
joko *joh*·koh oven
— la mikrowevu la mee·kroh·*way*·voo
microwave (oven)
joto *joh*·toh heat ⑩ • heating ⑩ • hot ⓐ
jua *joo*·a sun
-jua ·*joo*·a know
jukwaa *joo*·kwa platform
Jumamosi joo·ma·*moh*·see Saturday
Jumanne joo·ma·*n*·nay Tuesday
Jumapili joo·ma·*pee*·lee Sunday
Jumatano joo·ma·*ta*·noh Wednesday
Jumatatu joo·ma·*ta*·too Monday
jumba *joom*·ba palace
— la opera la oh·*pay*·ra opera house
jumuiya ya masista joo·moo·*ee*·ya ya
ma·*see*·sta convent
jusi *joo*·see juice
juu *joo*·high • up
juu ya joo ya above ⓐ • on adv
juzi *joo*·zee day before yesterday

K

-kaa ·ka sit • stay (at a hotel)
-kaanga ·ka·*an*·ga fry
kabati ka·*ba*·tee cupboard
— ya nguo ya n·*goo*·oh wardrobe
kabichi ka·*bee*·chee cabbage
kabla *ka*·bla before
kaburi ka·*boo*·ree grave
kabuti ka·*boo*·tee overcoat
kadhaa ·*dha* several • some
kadi ya benki *ka*·dee ya *bayn*·kee
credit card
kadi ya simu (ya mikononi) *ka*·dee ya
see·moo (ya mee·koh·*noh*·nee) SIM card
kadi ya simu za vibandani *ka*·dee ya
see·moo za vee·ban·*da*·nee phonecard
-kagua ·ka·*goo*·a check
kahawa ka·*ha*·wa coffee
kahawia ka·ha·*wee*·a brown
kaka *ka*·ka brother
kakao ka·*ka*·oh cocoa
kalamu ka·*la*·moo pen (ballpoint)
kalenda ka·*layn*·da calendar
kama *ka*·ma if
-kamata ·ka·*ma*·ta arrest
kamba *kam*·ba prawn • rope
— ya kukausha nguo
ya koo·ka·oo·sha n·*goo*·oh clothesline
— za viatu za vee·*a*·too laces
kamili ka·*mee*·lee exactly adv • perfect ⓐ
kamisheni ka·mee·*shay*·nee commission
kampuni kam·poo·nee company
— ya ndege ya n·*day*·gay airline
kamusi ka·*moo*·see dictionary
kamwe *kam*·way never
kanda *kan*·da cassette
— ya musiki ya moo·*zee*·kee
musical recording
kando ya *kan*·doh ya next to
kanisa ka·*nee*·sa church
— kuu koo cathedral
— ya kiyahudi ya kee·ya·*hoo*·dee
synagogue
kansa *kan*·sa cancer
kapera ka·*pay*·ra single (person)
kaptura kap·*too*·ra shorts
karakana ka·ra·*ka*·na
workshop (to make things)
karanga ka·*ran*·ga groundnut • peanut
karani ka·*ra*·nee secretary

karantini ka·ran·*tee*·nee *quarantine*
karata ka·*ra*·ta *playing cards*
karatasi ka·ra·*ta*·see *paper*
  — ya choo ya choh *toilet paper*
  — za shashi za *sha*·shee *tissues*
-karibisha ·ka·ree·*bee*·sha *invite • welcome*
karibu ka·*ree*·boo *close (near)*
  — na na *almost*
  — zaidi za·ee·dee *nearest*
karoti ka·*roh*·tee *carrot*
kasha la fedha ka·sha la *fay*·dha *safe (for money)*
kasino ka·*see*·noh *casino*
kaskazini kas·ka·*zee*·nee *north*
-kata ·ka·ta *cut*
-kataa ·ka·ta *refuse*
katika ka·*tee*·ka *in*
  — muda wa (saa moja) moo·da wa (sa moh·ja) *within (an hour)*
katikati ka·tee·*ka*·tee *between* adv • *centre* ⓝ
  — ya mji ya *m*·jee *city centre*
katoni ka·*toh*·nee *carton*
kaunta ka·*oon*·ta *counter (at bar)*
-kausha ·ka·*oo*·sha *dry*
kavu ka·voo *dry*
kawaida ka·wa·*ee*·da *ordinary*
kazi ka·zee *job • work*
  — kwenye baa *kway*·nyay ba *bar work*
  — ya mikono ya mee·*koh*·noh *handicrafts*
  — ya nyumbani ya nyum·*ba*·nee *housework*
  — ya ukarani ya oo·ka·*ra*·nee *paperwork*
kebo za kuwashia *kay*·boh za koo·wa·*shee*·a *jumper leads*
kejekeje kay·jay·*kay*·jay *loose*
keki *kay*·kee *cake*
  — ya arusi ya a·*roo*·see *wedding cake*
kemra *kaym*·ra *camera*
keshia kay·*shee*·a *cashier*
kesho *kay*·shoh *tomorrow*
  — asubuhi a·soo·*boo*·hee *tomorrow morning*
  — jioni jee·oh·nee *tomorrow evening*
  — kutwa *koot*·wa *the day after tomorrow*
  — mchana *m*·*cha*·na *tomorrow afternoon*
kiambato kee·am·*ba*·toh *ingredient*
kiasi gani kee·*a*·see *ga*·nee *how much*
kiatu kee·*a*·too *shoe*
kiazi kee·*a*·zee *potato*

kiazisukari kee·a·zee·soo·*ka*·ree *beetroot*
kibali kee·*ba*·lee *permit*
kibanda cha simu kee·*ban*·da cha *see*·moo *telephone box*
kibandiko cha chupi kee·ban·*dee*·koh cha *choo*·pee *panty liners*
kibarua kee·ba·*roo*·a *casual work • part-time*
kibiriti kee·bee·*ree*·tee *lighter (match)*
kibofu kee·*boh*·foo *bladder*
kiboko kee·*boh*·koh *hippopotamus*
kibole kee·*boh*·lay *appendix (body)*
kichapishi kee·cha·*pee*·shee *keyboard*
kichefuchefu kee·chay·foo·*chay*·foo *nausea*
  — cha asubuhi cha a·soo·*boo*·hee *morning sickness*
  — cha baharini cha ba·ha·*ree*·nee *seasickness*
  — cha safari cha sa·*fa*·ree *travel sickness*
kichwa *keech*·wa *head*
kidole kee·*doh*·lay *finger*
  — cha mguu cha m·*goo* *toe*
kidonge kee·*dohn*·gay *pill*
  — cha kuzuia mimba cha koo·zoo·ee·a *meem*·ba *the pill*
kifafa kee·*fa*·fa *epilepsy*
kifaru kee·*fa*·roo *rhinoceros*
kifiko kee·*fee*·koh *destination*
kifungo kee·*foon*·goh *button*
kifungua chupa kee·foon·*goo*·a *choo*·pa *bottle opener*
kifungua kopo kee·foon·*goo*·a *koh*·poh *tin opener*
kifurushi kee·foo·*roo*·shee *parcel*
kigari cha mtoto kee·*ga*·ree cha m·*toh*·toh *stroller • pram*
kiharusi kee·ha·*roo*·see *stroke (health)*
Kiingereza kee·een·gay·*ray*·za *English (language)*
kijani kee·*ja*·nee *green*
kijiji kee·*jee*·jee *village*
kijiko kee·*jee*·koh *spoon*
  — cha chai cha *cha*·ee *teaspoon*
kijitabu kee·jee·*ta*·boo *brochure*
kijiti cha meno kee·*jee*·tee cha *may*·noh *toothpick*
kijiti cha pamba safi kee·*jee*·tee cha *pam*·ba *sa*·fee *cotton buds*
kijito kee·*jee*·toh *stream*
kijivu kee·*jee*·voo *grey*
kikaango kee·ka·*an*·goh *frying pan*
kikapu kee·*ka*·poo *basket*

kikohozi kee-koh-*hoh*-zee *cough*
kikokotoo kee-koh-koh-*toh*-oh *calculator*
kikombe kee-*kohm*-bay *cup*
kikomo cha mwendo kee-*koh*-moh cha *mwayn*-doh *speed limit*
kikundi kee-*koon*-dee *band (music)*
kila *kee*-la *each • every*
kila kitu *kee*-la *kee*-too *everything*
kila siku *kee*-la *see*-koo *daily*
kilainishio kee-la-ee-nee-*shee*-oh *lubricant*
kilele kee-*lay*-lay *peak (mountain)*
kilema kee-*lay*-ma *paraplegic*
kilevi kee-*lay*-vee *alcohol*
kilimo kee-*lee*-moh *agriculture*
   — cha bustani cha boo-*sta*-nee *gardening*
kilio kee-*lee*-oh *funeral*
kilo *kee*-loh *kilogram*
kilomita kee-loh-*mee*-ta *kilometre*
-kimbia -*keem*-bee-a *run*
kimo *kee*-moh *altitude*
-kinga -*keen*-ga *protect*
kingamimba keen-ga-*meem*-ba *contraceptives*
kinururishi kee-noo-roo-*ree*-shee *radiator*
kinyozi kee-*nyoh*-zee *barber*
kinyume kee-*nyoo*-may *opposite*
kinywaji kee-*nywa*-jee *drink*
kiondoa maumivu kee-ohn-*doh*-a ma-oo-*mee*-voo *painkiller*
kiongozi kee-ohn-*goh*-zee *guide (person) • leader*
kionyeshi kee-oh-*nyay*-shee *indicator*
kioo kee-*oh* *mirror*
kioski kee-*oh*-skee *kiosk*
kipa *kee*-pa *goalkeeper*
kipandauso kee-pan-da-*oo*-soh *migraine*
kipande kee-*pan*-day *piece*
   — cha namba ya gari cha *nam*-ba ya *ga*-ree *numberplate*
kipasha moto kee-*pa*-sha moh-toh *heater*
kipepeo kee-pay-*pay*-oh *butterfly*
kipima mwanga kee-*pee*-ma *mwan*-ga *light meter*
kipimo cha damu kee-*pee*-moh cha *da*-moo *blood test*
kipindi cha baridi kidogo kee-*peen*-dee cha ba-*ree*-dee kee-*doh*-goh *fall (autumn)*
kiplefti keep-*layf*-tee *roundabout*
kipodozi kee-poh-*doh*-zee *make-up*

kipofu kee-*poh*-foo *blind*
kirekebisho moyo kee-ray-kay-*bee*-shoh *moh*-yoh *pacemaker*
kemra ya video *kaym*-ra ya vee-*day*-oh *video recorder*
kiroboto kee-roh-*boh*-toh *flea*
kisanduku cha huduma ya kwanza kee-san-*doo*-koo cha hoo-*doo*-ma ya *kwan*-za *first-aid kit*
kishota cha kukatia barafu kee-*shoh*-ta cha koo-ka-*tee*-a ba-*ra*-foo *ice axe*
kisiwa kee-*see*-wa *island*
kisu *kee*-soo *knife*
   — cha mfukoni cha m-*foo*-*koh*-nee *penknife • pocket knife*
kisukari kee-soo-*ka*-ree *diabetes*
kitabu kee-*ta*-boo *book*
   — cha kumbukumbu cha koom-boo-*koom*-boo *diary*
   — cha misemo cha mee-*say*-moh *phrasebook*
   — cha mwongozo cha mwohn-*goh*-zoh *guidebook*
   — cha namba za simu cha *nam*-ba za *see*-moo *phone book*
kitambaa kee-tam-*ba* *fabric*
   — cha meza cha *may*-za *tablecloth*
   — cha mkono cha m-*koh*-noh *face cloth • handkerchief • napkin*
   — cha uso cha oo-*soh* *wash cloth (flannel)*
kitambulisho kee-tam-boo-*lee*-shoh *identification • identification card (ID)*
kitanda kee-*tan*-da *bed*
   — cha watu wawili cha *wa*-too wa-*wee*-lee *double bed*
   — katika behewa ka-*tee*-ka bay-*hay*-wa *sleeping berth*
kitani kee-*ta*-nee *linen (material)*
kitanzi cha kuzuia kuzaa kee-*tan*-zee cha koo-zoo-*ee*-a koo-*za* *IUD*
kiti *kee*-tee *chair • seat (place)*
   — cha magurudumu cha ma-goo-roo-*doo*-moo *wheelchair*
   — cha mtoto cha m-*toh*-toh *child seat*
   — juu cha mtoto joo cha m-*toh*-toh *highchair*
kitindamlo kee-teen-da-*m*-loh *dessert*
kitobosha kee-toh-*boh*-sha *pastry*
kitu *kee*-too *something*
kitunguu kee-toon-*goo* *onion*
   — saumu sa-*oo*-moo *garlic*

K

swahili–english

233

kituo kee·*too*·oh *stop (bus etc)*
— **cha basi** cha ba·see *bus stop*
— **cha mafuta** cha ma·*foo*·ta *petrol station*
— **cha petroli** cha pay·*troh*·lee *service station*
— **cha polisi** cha poh·*lee*·see *police station*
— **cha simu** cha see·moo *telephone centre*
— **cha teksi** cha tayk·see *taxi stand*
— **cha ukaguzi** cha oo·ka·*goo*·zee *checkpoint*
(-sikia) kiu (·see·*kee*·a) *kee*·oo *(be) thirsty*
kiuavijasumu kee·oo·a·vee·ja·*soo*·moo *antibiotic*
kiungo kee·*oon*·goh *connection*
kivuko kee·*voo*·koh *ferry*
kivuli kee·*voo*·lee *shade · shadow*
kiwambo cha kizuia mimba kee·*wam*·boh cha kee·zoo·*ee*·a *meem*·ba *diaphragm (contraceptive)*
kiwambo upepo kee·*wam*·boh oo·*pay*·poh *windscreen*
kiwanda kee·*wan*·da *factory · industry*
kiwango cha kubadilisha fedha kee·*wan*·goh cha koo·ba·dee·lee·*shee*·a *fay*·dha *exchange rate*
kiwanja cha kupiga kambi kee·*wan*·ja cha kuu·pee·*gee*·a *kam*·bee *campsite*
kiwanja cha tenesi kee·*wan*·ja cha tay·*nay*·see *tennis court*
kiwashio kee·wa·*shee*·oh *cigarette lighter*
kiwiko kee·*wee*·koh *wrist*
— **cha mguu** cha m·*goo* *ankle*
kizibo kee·*zee*·boh *plug (bath)*
kizibuo kee·zee·boo·oh *corkscrew*
kizuizi kee·zoo·ee·zee *blockage*
kizunguzungu kee·zoon·goo·*zoon*·goo *dizzyness*
— **cha saa kutokana na kusafiri kwa ndege** cha sa koo·toh·*ka*·na na koo·sa·*fee*·ree kwa n·*day*·gay *jet lag*
klabu ya usiku *kla*·boo ya oo·see·koo *nightclub*
klachi *kla*·chee *clutch (car)*
koboko koh·*boh*·koh *cobra*
-kodi ·koh·dee *hire (rent)*
kodi koh·dee *tax*
— **ya mapato** ya ma·*pa*·toh *income tax*
— **ya mauzo** ya ma·oo·zoh *sales tax*
— **ya uwanja wa ndege** ya oo·*wan*·ja wa n·*day*·gay *airport tax*
kofia koh·*fee*·a *hat*

kokeini koh·kay·*ee*·nee *cocaine*
kokteli kohk·*tay*·lee *cocktail*
kokwa *kohk*·wa *nut*
koliflawa koh·lee·*fla*·wa *cauliflower*
Kombe la Dunia *kohm*·bay la doo·*nee*·a *World Cup*
kome *koh*·may *mussel*
kompyuta kohm·*pyoo*·ta *computer*
— **ya kubeba** ya koo·*bay*·ba *laptop*
komunyo kohm·*moo*·nyoh *communion*
kona *koh*·na *corner*
kondom kohn·dohm *condom*
kondoo kohn·*doh* *sheep*
konokono koh·noh·*koh*·noh *snail*
koo koh *throat*
-kopa koh·pa *borrow*
kopo *koh*·poh *can · tin*
korosho koh·roh·shoh *cashew*
kosa *koh*·sa *(someone's) fault* ⓝ · *mistake* ⓝ · *wrong* ⓐ
-kosa ·koh·sa *miss (feel absence of)*
koti *koh*·tee *coat*
— **la mvua** la m·*voo*·a *raincoat*
kriketi kree·*kay*·tee *cricket (sport)*
krimu ya kulainisha ngozi *kree*·moo ya koo·la·ee·*nee*·sha n·*goh*·zee *moisturiser*
kuandikwa kitu kimoja kimoja koo·an·*deek*·wa kee·too kee·*moh*·ja kee·*moh*·jah *itemised*
kubadilisha hela koo·ba·dee·lee·sha *hay*·la *currency exchange*
-kubali ·koo·ba·lee *agree*
kubwa *koob*·wa *big (large)*
— **kabisa** ka·*bee*·sa *biggest*
— **sana** sa·na *huge*
— **zaidi** za·ee·dee *bigger*
kucha *koo*·cha *dawn*
kuchomwa kwa jua koo·*chom*·wa kwa *joo*·a *sunburn*
kuchuliwa koo·choo·*lee*·wa *massage*
kuelekea koo·ay·lay·*kay*·a *towards*
kufua koo·*foo*·a *chest (body)*
kufuli koo·*foo*·lee *lock · padlock*
— **ya baisikeli** ya ba·ee·see·*kay*·lee *bike lock*
kufungwa koo·*foon*·gwa *shut*
kuhara koo·*ha*·ra *diarrhoea*
kuharibu mimba koo·ha·*ree*·boo *meem*·ba *miscarriage*
kuharibu misitu koo·ha·*ree*·boo mee·see·*too* *deforestation*
kuhusu koo·*hoo*·soo *about*
kujeruhiwa koo·jay·roo·*hee*·wa *injured*

kukata nywele koo·*ka*·ta *nyway*·lay haircut

kukimbia koo·keem·*bee*·a running

— **taratibu** ta·ra·*tee*·boo jogging

kukodi gari koo·*koh*·dee *ga*·ree car hire

kuku *koo*·koo chicken

kulia koo·*lee*·a right (direction)

kuma *koo*·ma vagina

-kumbatia ·koom·ba·*tee*·a a hug

kumbukumbu koom·*boo*·koom·boo souvenir

kumbwe *koom*·bway snack

kumi na mbili *koo*·mee na m·*bee*·lee dozen

kuna mawingu *koo*·na ma·*ween*·goo cloudy

kundekunde koon·*day*·koon·day legume

kundi ya roki *koon*·dee ya *roh*·kee rock group

kuni *koo*·nee firewood

kuogelea koo·oh·gay·*lay*·a swimming (sport)

kuondoka koo·ohn·*doh*·ka departure

kupanda baisikeli koo·*pan*·da ba·ee·see·*kay*·lee cycling

kupanda farasi koo·*pan*·da fa·*ra*·see horse riding

kupanda milima koo·*pan*·da mee·*lee*·ma mountaineering

kupatikana koo·pa·tee·*ka*·na free (available)

kupiga picha ya mtoto tumboni koo·*pee*·ga *pee*·cha ya m·*toh*·toh toom·*boh*·nee ultrasound

kupiga simu moja kwa moja koo·*pee*·ga see·moo *moh*·ja kwa *moh*·ja direct-dial

kupika koo·*pee*·ka cooking

kuponi koo·*pohn*·ee coupon

kurudisha pesa koo·roo·*dee*·sha *pay*·sa refund

kushambuliwa na maradhi ya moyo koo·sham·boo·*lee*·wa na ma·*ra*·dhee ya *moh*·yoh heart attack

kushoto koo·*shoh*·toh left (direction)

kusimama kwa mapigo ya moyo koo·see·*ma*·ma kwa ma·*pee*·goh ya *moh*·yoh cardiac arrest

kusini koo·*see*·nee south

kuskii koo·*skee* skiing

-kuta ·koo·ta meet

kutaamali koo·ta·a·*ma*·lee meditation

kutalikiwa koo·ta·lee·*kee*·wa divorced

kuteleza koo·tay·*lay*·za surfing

— **na tanga** na *tan*·ga windsurfing

kutembea porini koo·taym·*bay*·a poh·*ree*·nee hiking

kutengenezwa kwa mkono koo·tayn·gay·*nayz*·wa kwa m·*koh*·noh handmade

kutoa mimba koo·*toh*·a *meem*·ba abortion

kutoka koo·*toh*·ka exit ⓝ • from prep

kutopenyesha maji koo·to·pay·*nyay*·sha ma·*jee* waterproof

kutumikia jeshi koo·too·mee·*kee*·a *jay*·shee military service

-kuu ·koo·koo main

kuuza madawa ya kulevya koo·oo·za ma·*da*·wa ya koo·*lay*·vya drug trafficking

kuvimba kibofu koo·*veem*·ba kee·*boh*·foo cystitis

kuvimbiwa koo·veem·*bee*·wa indigestion

kuvuna matunda koo·*voo*·na ma·*toon*·da fruit picking

kuvuta makasia koo·*voo*·ta ma·ka·*see*·a rowing

kuwahi koo·*wa*·hee on time • early

kuzamia koo·za·*mee*·a diving

kwa kwa per (day)

kwa haraka kwa ha·*ra*·ka in a hurry

kwa heri kwa *hay*·ree goodbye

kwa kuteremka kwa koo·tay·*raym*·ka downhill

kwa nini kwa *nee*·nee why

kwa sababu kwa sa·*ba*·boo because

kwa sauti kwa sa·*oo*·tee loud

kwa usiku mmoja kwa oo·*see*·koo m·*moh*·ja overnight

kwa wapenzi kwa wa·*payn*·zee romantic

kwenye *kway*·nyay at • to

— **a/c** ay·*see* air-conditioned

L

-la ·la eat

labda *lab*·da maybe

laiseni la·ee·*say*·nee license

lakini la·*kee*·nee but

-lala ·*la*·la lie (not stand)

-lalamika ·la·la·*mee*·ka complain

lalamiko la·la·*mee*·koh complaint

laza la·za admit

lazima la·*zee*·ma necessary

lengelenge layn·gay·*layn*·gay blister

lenzi mboni *layn*·zee m·*boh*·nee
contact lenses

leo *lay*·oh today

leseni ya kuendesha gari lay·*say*·nee ya koo·ayn·*day*·sha *ga*·ree drivers license

-leta *·lay*·ta bring

-lewa *·lay*·wa drunk • stoned (drugged)

lifti *leef*·tee lift • elevator • ride

likizo lee·*kee*·zoh holidays • vacation

limau lee·*ma*·oo lemon

lindo *leen*·doh lookout

lini *lee*·nee when

-lipa *·lee*·pa pay

-lipwa fedha kwa kutoa hundi *·leep*·wa fay·dha kwa koo·*toh*·a *hoon*·dee cash (a cheque)

-lisha *·lee*·sha feed

lori *loh*·ree truck
— **la wasafiri** la wa·sa·*fee*·ree caravan

losheni baada ya kunyoa ndevu loh·*shay*·nee ba·*a*·da ya koo·*nyoh*·a n·*day*·voo aftershave

lozi *loh*·zee almond

lugha *loo*·gha language

M

maakuli ma·a·*koo*·lee provisions

maalum ma·a·*loom* special

maandamano ma·an·da·*ma*·noh demonstration • protest

maandishi chini ma·an·*dee*·shee *chee*·nee subtitles

maarufu ma·a·*roo*·foo famous

mabaki ma·*ba*·kee relic

mabawa ma·*ba*·wa wings

mabuti ma·*boo*·tee boots (footwear)
— **ya kutembea porini** ya koo·taym·*bay*·a poh·*ree*·nee hiking boots

machela ma·*chay*·la hammock

macheo ma·*chay*·oh sunrise

macho ma·*choh* eyes

machumbwichumbwi ma·choom·bwee·*choom*·bwee mumps

machunda ma·*choon*·da skim milk

machweo ma·*chway*·oh sunset

madawa (ya kulevya) ma·*da*·wa (ya koo·*lay*·vya) (illegal) drugs

madhahabu ma·dha·*ha*·boo altar

madhubuti ma·dhoo·*boo*·tee strong

madukani ma·doo·*ka*·nee
shopping centre

maelezo binafsi ya ujuzi ma·ay·*lay*·zoh bee·*naf*·see ya oo·joo·zee CV • résumé

mafuriko ma·foo·*ree*·koh flood

mafusha ya pamba ma·*foo*·sha ya *pam*·ba cotton balls

mafuta ma·*foo*·ta gas (petrol) • oil
— **ya taa** ya ta gas (for cooking)
— **ya zaituni** ya za·ee·*too*·nee olive oil

magari mengi ma·*ga*·ree *mayn*·gee traffic

magharibi ma·gha·*ree*·bee west

maglavu ma·*gla*·voo gloves

magofu ma·*goh*·foo ruins

mahadhi ma·*ha*·dhee rhythm

mahakama ma·ha·*ka*·ma court (legal)

mahali ma·*ha*·lee place • venue
— **pa kuzaliwa** pa koo·za·*lee*·wa place of birth

maharagwe ma·ha·*rag*·way beans

mahindi ma·*heen*·dee corn

mahojiano ma·hoh·jee·*a*·noh interview

maisha ma·ee·*sha* life

majaribio ya nyuklia ma·ja·ree·*bee*·oh ya nyook·lee·a nuclear testing

maji *ma*·jee water
— **baridi** ba·*ree*·dee still water
— **ya bomba** ya bohm·ba tap water
— **ya kujaa na kupwa** ya koo·*ja* na *koop*·wa tide
— **ya limau** ya lee·*ma*·oo lemonade
— **ya machungwa** ya ma·*choon*·gwa orange juice
— **ya madini** ya ma·*dee*·nee mineral water
— **ya moto** ya moh·toh hot water

majira ma·*jee*·ra season
— **ya baridi** ya ba·*ree*·dee winter
— **ya joto** ya joh·toh summer
— **ya kuchipua** ya koo·chee·*poo*·a spring

makaburini ma·ka·boo·*ree*·nee cemetery

makini ma·*kee*·nee serious

maktaba mak·*ta*·ba library

makumbusho ma·koom·*boo*·shoh museum

malai ya maziwa ya mtindi ma·*la*·ee ya ma·*zee*·wa ya m·*teen*·dee sour cream

malaya ma·*la*·ya prostitute

malazi ma·*la*·zee accommodation

malipo ma·*lee*·poh payment
— **ya huduma** ya hoo·*doo*·ma service charge

-maliza ·ma·*lee*·za finish

malkia mal·*kee*·a queen

mama *ma*·ma mother

mamamkwe ma·ma·*m*·kway mother-in-law

mamba *mam*·ba crocodile

mandari man·*da*·ree picnic

mandhari man·*dha*·ree view

manjano man·*ja*·noh yellow

maoni ma·*oh*·nee opinion

maonyesho ma·oh·*nyay*·shoh exhibition

mapacha ma·*pa*·cha twins

mapema ma·*pay*·ma early

mapenzi ma·*payn*·zee sex (intercourse)

— **salama** sa·*la*·ma safe sex

mapitio ma·pee·*tee*·oh review

mapokezi ma·poh·*kay*·zee check-in (desk)

maporomoko ya maji ma·poh·roh·*moh*·koh ya *ma*·jee waterfall

mapumziko ma·poom·*zee*·koh intermission

mara mbili *ma*·ra m·*bee*·lee twice

mara moja *ma*·ra *moh*·ja once

mara nyingi *ma*·ra *nyeen*·gee often

maradhi ma·*ra*·dhee disease

marashi ma·*ra*·shee perfume

marejeo ma·ray·*jay*·oh reference

Marekani ma·ray·*ka*·nee USA

masaa ya kufunguliwa ma·*sa* ya koo·foon·goo·*lee*·wa opening hours

mashariki ma·sha·*ree*·kee east

mashindano ya ubingwa ma·sheen·*da*·noh ya oo·*been*·gwa championships

mashine ma·*shee*·nay machine

— **ya kubanika mkate** ya koo·ba·*nee*·ka m·*ka*·tay toaster

— **ya kufulia** ya koo·foo·*lee*·a washing machine

— **ya kutolea pesa** ya koo·toh·*lay*·a *pay*·sa automated teller machine (ATM)

— **ya tiketi** ya tee·*kay*·tee ticket machine

mashuka ma·*shoo*·ka linen (sheets etc)

masikitiko ma·see·kee·*tee*·koh sad

maskini mas·*kee*·nee poor

mastadi ma·*sta*·dee mustard

matako ma·*ta*·koh bottom (body)

matatu ma·*ta*·too bus (city)

matibabu asilia ma·tee·*ba*·boo a·see·*lee*·a naturopathy

matone ya macho ma·*toh*·nay ya *ma*·choh eye drops

matope ma·*toh*·pay mud

matukio ya leo ma·too·*kee*·oh ya *lay*·oh current affairs

matunda yaliyokaushwa ma·*toon*·da ya·lee·yoh·ka·*oosh*·wa dried fruit

mauaji ma·oo·*a*·jee murder

maumivu ma·oo·*mee*·voo pain

— **ya jino** ya *jee*·noh toothache

— **ya kichwa** ya *keech*·wa headache

— **ya mwezini** ya mway·*zee*·nee period pain

maumivu ya tumbo ma·oo·*mee*·voo ya *toom*·boh stomachache

mawasiliano ma·wa·see·lee·*a*·noh communications (profession)

mawe za mizani *ma*·way za mee·*za*·nee weights

mayai yaliyovurugwa ma·*ya*·ee ya·lee·yoh·voo·*roog*·wa scrambled eggs

mayonezi ma·yoh·*nay*·zee mayonnaise

mazingira ma·zeen·*gee*·ra environment

maziwa ma·*zee*·wa milk

— **ganda** *gan*·da yoghurt

— **ya soya** ya *soh*·ya soy milk

mazoezi ma·zoh·*ay*·zee workout

mbali m·*ba*·lee far • remote

mbalimbali m·ba·lee·m·*ba*·lee separate

mbao m·*ba*·oh wood

mbaya m·*ba*·ya bad • off (spoiled)

mbaya sana m·*ba*·ya *sa*·na awful • terrible

mbele m·*bay*·lay ahead

— **ya** m·*bay*·lay ya in front of

mbeleni m·bay·*lay*·nee future

mbili m·*bee*·lee both • two

mbilimbili m·bee·lee·m·*bee*·lee double

mbingu m·*been*·goo sky

mbinu m·*bee*·noo technique

mbishi m·*bee*·shee stubborn

mboga m·*boh*·ga vegetable

— **za majani** za ma·*ja*·nee herbs

mboni m·*boh*·nee lens (eye)

mboo m·*boh* penis

mbu *m*·boo mosquito

Mbudisti m·boo·*dee*·stee Buddhist

mbuni m·*boo*·nee ostrich

mbuzi m·*boo*·zee goat

mbwa m·*bwa* dog

— **wa kuongoza** wa koo·ohn·*goh*·za guide dog

mchana m·*cha*·na afternoon

mchanga m·*chan*·ga sand
mchele m·*chay*·lay rice (uncooked)
mchemuo m·*chay*·moo·oh exhaust (car)
mchezo m·*chay*·zoh game (sport)
　— **kwenye kompyuta**
　kway·nyay kom·*pyoo*·ta computer game
　— **wa kuigiza** wa koo·ee·*gee*·za
　play (theatre)
　— **wa soka** wa soh·ka football • soccer
mchicha m·*chee*·cha spinach
mchonga vinyago
　m·*chohn*·ga vee·*nya*·goh woodcarver
mchuaji m·choo·*a*·jee masseur/masseuse
mchumba m·*choom*·ba fiancé/fiancée
mchuuzi m·choo·oo·zee street hawker
　— **wa samaki** wa sa·*ma*·kee
　fish monger
mchuzi m·*choo*·zee sauce
　— **wa nyanya** wa *nya*·nya
　tomato sauce • ketchup
　— **wa pilipili hoho**
　wa pee·lee·*pee*·lee hoh·hoh chilli sauce
　— **wa soya** wa soh·ya soy sauce
mdanganyi m·dan·*ga*·nyee cheat
mdomo m·*doh*·moh mouth
mdudu m·*doo*·doo bug
-mea ·*may*·a grow
mechi may·chee match (sports)
meli may·lee ship
mende mayn·day cockroach
meneja may·*nay*·ja
　manager (restaurant, hotel)
meno may·noh teeth
menyu may·nyoo menu
metali may·*ta*·lee metal ⓝ
meza may·za table
　— **kujihudumia**
　koo·jee·hoo·doo·*mee*·a buffet
mfalme m·*fal*·may king
mfamasia m·fa·ma·*see*·a
　chemist (person) • pharmacist
mfano m·*fa*·noh example
mfanyabiashara m·fa·nya·bee·a·*sha*·ra
　business person • tradesperson
mfanyakazi m·fa·nya·*ka*·zee
　employee • labourer
　— **ofisini** o·fee·*see*·nee office worker
　— **wa kiwandani** kee·wan·*da*·nee
　factory worker
　— **wa kutumia mikono** koo·too·*mee*·a
　mee·*koh*·noh manual worker
mfuko m·*foo*·koh bag • pocket

　— **wa kiunoni** wa kee·oo·*noh*·nee
　bumbag
　— **wa kulalia** wa koo·la·*lee*·a
　sleeping bag
mfumo wa matabaka
　m·*foo*·moh wa ma·ta·*ba*·ka
　class system
mfungwa m·*foon*·gwa prisoner
mfupa m·*foo*·pa bone
mgahawa m·ga·*ha*·wa café • restaurant
mganga wa madawa ya kienyeji
　m·*gan*·ga wa ma·*da*·wa ya
　kee·ay·*nyay*·jee herbalist
mgeni m·*gay*·nee stranger
mgomo m·*goh*·moh strike
mgongano m·gohn·*ga*·noh crash
mgongo m·*gohn*·goh back (body)
mgonjwa m·*gohn*·jwa ill • sick
mguu m·*goo* foot • leg
mhadhiri m·ha·*dhee*·ree lecturer
mhamisishaji m·ha·mee·see·*sha*·jee
　activist
mhandisi m·han·*dee*·see engineer
Mhindu m·*heen*·doo Hindu
mhudumu m·hoo·doo·moo waiter • waitress
mhuni m·*hoo*·nee hoodlum
mia *mee*·a hundred
miadi mee·*a*·dee date (appointment)
miche ya maharagwe mee·chay ya
　ma·ha·*rag*·way beansprouts
michezo mee·*chay*·zoh sport
　— **ya kukimbia** ya koo·keem·*bee*·a
　track (sport)
　— **ya riadha** ya ree·*a*·dha athletics
Michezo ya Olimpiki mee·*chay*·zoh ya
　oh·leem·*pee*·kee Olympic Games
midomo mee·*doh*·moh lips
mieleka mee·ay·*lay*·ka martial arts
mikutano mee·koo·*ta*·noh
　conference (big)
mila *mee*·la custom
milele mee·*lay*·lay forever
milimita mee·lee·*mee*·ta millimetre
milioni mee·lee·oh·nee million
mimi *mee*·mee I • me
minyoo mee·*nyoh* worms
misa *mee*·sa mass (Catholic)
mita *mee*·ta metre
mitumba mee·*toom*·ba second-hand
miwani mee·*wa*·nee glasses (spectacles)
　— **ya jua** ya *joo*·a sunglasses
　— **ya kuogelea** ya koo·oh·gay·*lay*·a
　goggles (swimming)

mizigo mee-*zee*-goh *baggage (luggage)*
— **iliyowekwa** ee-lee-yoh-*wayk*-wa *left luggage*
— **ziada** zee-*a*-da *excess baggage*
mjamzito m-ja-m-*zee*-toh *pregnant*
mjenzi m-*jayn*-zee *builder*
mji m-*jee city*
mjinga m-*jeen*-ga *idiot*
mjukuu m-joo-*koo grandchild*
mjusi m-*joo*-see *lizard*
mkalimani m-ka-lee-*ma*-nee *interpreter*
mkamba m-*kam*-ba *bronchitis*
mkanda wa feni m-*kan*-da wa *fay*-nee *fanbelt*
mkanda wa kiti m-*kan*-da wa *kee*-tee *seatbelt*
mkanda wa picha m-*kan*-da wa *pee*-cha *film (for camera)*
mkanda wa video m-*kan*-da wa vee-*day*-oh *video tape*
mkarimu m-ka-*ree*-moo *kind (nice)*
mkasi m-*ka*-see *scissors*
mkasi wa kucha m-*ka*-see wa *koo*-cha *nail clippers*
mkataba m-ka-*ta*-ba *contract*
mkate m-*ka*-tay *bread*
— **mkavu** m-*ka*-voo *cracker (biscuit)*
— **wa ngano asilia** wa n-*ga*-noh a-*see*-lee-a *wholemeal bread*
mke m-*kay wife*
— **anayekaa nyumbani** a-na-yay-*ka* nyoom-*ba*-nee *homemaker*
mkebe m-*kay*-bay *can • tin*
mkeka m-*kay*-ka *mat*
Mkesha wa Krismasi m-*kay*-sha wa krees-*ma*-see *Christmas Eve*
Mkesha wa Mwaka Mpya m-*kay*-sha wa *mwa*-ka m-*pya New Year's Eve*
mkia m-*kee*-a *tail*
mkimbizi m-keem-*bee*-zee *refugee*
mkoba m-*koh*-ba *briefcase • handbag • purse*
mkondo m-*kohn*-doh *current (electricity)*
mkono m-*koh*-noh *arm • hand*
mkopo m-*koh*-poh *credit*
Mkristo m-*kree*-stoh *Christian*
mkufu m-*koo*-foo *necklace*
mkulima m-koo-*lee*-ma *farmer*
mkurugenzi m-koo-roo-*gayn*-zee *director • manager*
mkusanyaji wa tiketi m-koo-sa-*nya*-jee wa tee-*kay*-tee *ticket collector*

mkutano m-koo-*ta*-noh *conference (small)*
— **wa hadhara** wa ha-*dha*-ra *rally • public meeting*
mlaji wa mboga za majani tu m-*la*-jee wa m-*boh*-ga za ma-*ja*-nee too *vegetarian* (n)
mlango m-*lan*-goh *door • gate (airport etc)*
— **wa kuondoka** wa koo-ohn-*doh*-ka *departure gate*
mlima m-*lee*-ma *hill • mountain*
mlio wa simu m-lee-oh wa *see*-moo *dial tone*
mlo m-*loh diet • meal*
mmea m-*may*-a *plant*
mnada m-*na*-da *fleamarket*
mnara m-*na*-ra *monument • tower*
mno m-*noh too (expensive etc)*
mnofu m-*noh*-foo *steak*
mnyama m-*nya*-ma *animal*
mnyororo m-nyoh-*roh*-roh *chain*
— **wa baisikeli** wa ba-ee-see-*kay*-lee *bike chain*
moja *moh*-ja *one*
— **kwa moja** kwa *moh*-ja *direct • straight*
motaboti moh-ta-*boh*-tee *motorboat*
moto *moh*-toh *fire*
— **ya mungu** ya *moon*-goo *shingles (illness)*
moyo *moh*-yoh *heart*
mpaka m-*pa*-ka *border* (n) *• until* prep
mpanda baisikeli m-*pan*-da ba-ee-see-*kay*-lee *cyclist*
mpenzi m-*payn*-zee *boyfriend • girlfriend • lover*
mpigapicha m-pee-ga-*pee*-cha *photographer*
mpira m-*pee*-ra *ball • chewing gum • gum*
— **wa gofu** wa goh-*foo golf ball*
— **wa kikapu** wa kee-*ka*-poo *basketball*
— **wa meza** wa *may*-za *table tennis*
— **wa mikono** wa mee-*koh*-noh *handball*
— **wa wavu** wa *wa*-voo *volleyball*
— **wa wavu ufukoni** wa *wa*-voo oo-foo-*koh*-nee *beach volleyball*
mpishi m-*pee*-shee *chef • cook*
mpya m-*pya new*
mradi m-*ra*-dee *program*
mrefu m-*ray*-foo *tall*

mrembo m·*raym*·boh handsome
mrengo wa kulia
  m·*rayn*·goh wa koo·*lee*·a right-wing
mrengo wa kushoto
  m·*rayn*·goh wa koo·*shoh*·toh left-wing
mruko m·*roo*·koh flight (of a bird)
msaada m·sa·*a*·da help
msagaji m·sa·*ga*·jee lesbian
msalaba m·sa·*la*·ba cross (religious)
msanifu wa majengo
  m·sa·*nee*·foo wa ma·*jayn*·goh
  architect
msanii m·sa·*nee* artist
  — wa rangi wa ran·gee painter
msenge m·*sayn*·gay gay (homosexual)
mshabiki m·sha·*bee*·kee fan (sport, etc)
  — wa utawala huria
  wa oo·ta·*wa*·la hoo·*ree*·a anarchist
mshahara m·sha·*ha*·ra salary · wage
mshangao m·shan·*ga*·oh surprise
mshindi m·*sheen*·dee winner
mshipa m·*shee*·pa vein
mshonaji m·shoh·*na*·jee tailor
mshtuko wa ubongo m·*shtoo*·koh wa
  oo·*bohn*·goh concussion
mshumaa m·shoo·*ma* candle
mshushio m·shoo·*shee*·oh orgasm
msichana m·see·*cha*·na girl
msikiti m·see·*kee*·tee mosque
msitu m·*see*·too forest
mstari m·*sta*·ree queue
msusi m·*soo*·see hairdresser
mswaki m·*swa*·kee toothbrush
mtaalamu m·ta·a·*la*·moo specialist
mtabiri m·ta·*bee*·ree fortune teller
mtakatifu m·ta·ka·*tee*·foo saint
mtalii m·ta·*lee* tourist
mtandao wa kompyuta
  m·tan·*da*·oh wa kohm·*pyoo*·ta
  Internet
mtawa m·*ta*·wa monk
mteguko m·tay·*goo*·koh sprain
mteja m·*tay*·ja client
mtembezi m·taym·*bay*·zee pedestrian
mti m·tee tree
mtihani m·tee·*ha*·nee test
mtindi m·*teen*·dee cream
mtindo m·*teen*·doh fashion · style
mto m·toh pillow · river
mtoto m·*toh*·toh child
  — mchanga m·*chan*·ga baby
mtu m·too person
  — mzima m·*zee*·ma adult ⓝ

mtumiaji wa madawa ya kulevya
  m·too·mee·*a*·jee wa ma·*da*·wa ya
  koo·*lay*·vya drug user
mtungi wa gesi m·*toon*·gee wa *gay*·see
  gas cartridge
mtunza bustani m·*toon*·za boo·*sta*·nee
  gardener
muhafidhina moo·ha·fee·*dhee*·na
  conservative
muhimu moo·*hee*·moo important
  — sana sa·na urgent
muhtasari mooh·*ta*·sa·ree résumé (CV)
mume moo·may husband
mumunye ya kula moo·moo·nyay ya
  koo·la courgette · zucchini
Mungu *moon*·goo God
musuli moo·*soo*·lee muscle
muziki moo·*zee*·kee music
mvinyo m·*vee*·nyoh wine
  — mwenye povu mway·nyay poh·voo
  sparkling wine
mvivu m·*vee*·voo lazy
mvua m·*voo*·a rain
mvulana m·voo·*la*·na boy
mwajiri mwa·*jee*·ree employer
mwaka mwa·ka year
  — huu mwa·ka this year
mwalimu mwa·*lee*·moo
  instructor · teacher
mwamba mwam·ba cliff · ledge
mwamuzi mwa·moo·zee referee
mwamvuli mwam·*voo*·lee umbrella
mwana mwa·na son
mwanachama mwa·na·*cha*·ma member
mwanafunzi mwa·na·*foon*·zee student
mwanakondoo mwa·na·kohn·*doh* lamb
mwanamichezo mwa·na·mee·*chay*·zoh
  sportsperson
mwanamke mwan·*am*·kay woman
mwanamume mwa·na·*moo*·may man
mwanamuziki mwa·na·moo·*zee*·kee
  musician
mwanasayansi mwa·na·sa·*yan*·see
  scientist
mwanasesere mwa·na·say·*say*·ray doll
mwanasheria mwa·na·shay·*ree*·a lawyer
mwanasiasa mwa·na·see·*a*·sa politician
mwandishi mwan·*dee*·shee writer
  — wa habari wa ha·ba·ree journalist
mwanga *mwan*·ga light ⓝ
mwanzo mwan·zoh start
mwasho mwa·shoh itch
mwema *mway*·ma nice

mwembamba mwaym-*bam*-ba *thin*
mwendo mwayn-doh *speed (velocity)*
— **wa mkanda** wa m-*kan*-da
film speed
mwenye *mway*-nyay *owner*
— **bahati** ba-*ha*-tee *lucky*
— **choyo** choh-yoh *selfish*
— **furaha** foo-*ra*-ha *happy*
— **haiba** ha-*ee*-ba *charming*
— **hasira** ha-*see*-ra *angry*
— **hatia** ha-*tee*-a *guilty*
— **hisia** hee-*see*-a *emotional*
— **kichaa** kee-*cha* *crazy*
— **kuuma** koo-oo-ma *sore*
— **nyumba** nyoom-ba
landlady/landlord
— **shughuli nyingi**
shoo-*goo*-lee nyeen-gee *busy (person)*
— **shukrani** shook-*ra*-nee *grateful*
— **usingizi** oo-seen-*gee*-zee *sleepy*
— **wasiwasi** wa-see-*wa*-see *worried*
— **wivu** wee-voo *jealous*
mwenyekiti mway-nyay-kee-tee *mayor*
mwenzi *mwayn*-zee *companion*
— **wangu** wan-goo *colleague*
mwezi *mway*-zee *month • moon*
— **wa kumi** wa koo-mee *October*
— **wa kumi na mbili**
wa koo-mee na m-bee-lee *December*
— **wa kumi na moja**
wa koo-mee na moh-ja *November*
— **wa kwanza** wa *kwan*-za *January*
— **wa nane** wa na-nay *August*
— **wa nne** wa n-nay *April*
— **wa pili** wa pee-lee *February*
— **wa saba** wa sa-ba *July*
— **wa sita** wa see-ta *June*
— **wa tano** wa ta-noh *May*
— **wa tatu** wa ta-too *March*
— **wa tisa** wa tee-sa *September*
mwigizaji mwee-gee-*za*-jee *actor*
mwili *mwee*-lee *body*
mwimbaji mweem-*ba*-jee *singer*
— **barabarani** ba-ra-ba-*ra*-nee *busker*
mwingilio mween-gee-*lee*-oh *entry (access)*
mwinuko mwee-*noo*-koh *uphill*
mwisho *mwee*-shoh *end (finish)*
Mwislamu mwee-*sla*-moo *Muslim*
mwizi *mwee*-zee *thief*
mwombaji mwohm-*ba*-jee *beggar*
mwongo *mwohn*-goh *liar*
mwongozo (wa sauti) mwohn-*goh*-zoh
(wa sa-oo-tee) *(audio) guide*

mwongozo wa burudani
mwohn-*goh*-zoh wa boo-roo-*da*-nee
entertainment guide
mwuguzi mwoo-*goo*-zee *nurse*
mwungaji mkono mwoon-*ga*-jee
m-*koh*-noh *supporter (politics)*
mwuzaji wa chakula
mwoo-*za*-jee wa cha-*koo*-la
food vendor
mwuzaji wa madawa ya kulevya
mwoo-*za*-jee wa ma-*da*-wa ya
koo-*lay*-vya *drug dealer*
mwuzaji wa magazeti mwoo-*za*-jee wa
ma-ga-*zay*-tee *newspaper vendor*
Myahudi m-ya-*hoo*-dee *Jewish*
myeyuko wa lenzi mboni
m-yay-*yoo*-koh wa layn-zee m-*boh*-nee
contact lens solution
mzabibu m-za-*bee*-boo *vine (grape)*
mzawa m-*za*-wa *descendent*
mzee m-*zay* *old person • pensioner*
mzigo m-*zee*-goh *suitcase*
mzio m-*zee*-oh *allergy*

N

na na *and • with*
nadra na-dra *rare (uncommon)*
nafaka na-*fa*-ka *cereal*
nafasi na-*fa*-see *chance • vacancy*
namba nam-ba *number*
— **ya chumba** ya choom-ba
room number
— **ya gari** ya ga-ree
license plate number
— **ya pasipoti** ya pa-see-*poh*-tee
passport number
namna nam-na *how*
nanasi na-*na*-see *pineapple*
nani na-nee *who*
nauli na-oo-lee *fare*
nazi na-zee *coconut*
nchi n-chee *country*
— **za nje** za n-jay *abroad (overseas)*
ndala n-*da*-la *sandal*
ndani n-*da*-nee *indoor • inside*
— **yake** ya-kay *included*
ndefu n-*day*-foo *long*
ndege n-day-gay
airplane • bird • flight (scheduled)
ndimu n-dee-moo *lime*
ndiyo n-*dee*-yoh *yes*

0

ndizi n-*dee*·zee *banana*
ndoa n-*doh*·a *marriage*
ndogo sana n-*doh*·goh *sa*·na *tiny*
ndondi n-*dohn*·dee *boxing*
ndoo n-*doh* *bucket*
ndoto n-*doh*·toh *dream*
ndovu n-*doh*·voo *elephant*
nene *nay*·nay *fat*
neno *nay*·noh *word*
nepi *nay*·pee *diaper* • *nappy*
neti *nay*·tee *net*
ng'ambo ng-*am*·boh *across*
ng'ombe ng-*ohm*·bay *cow*
ngamia n-ga-*mee*·a *camel*
ngazi n-*ga*·zee *stairway*
-ngoja n-*goh*·ja *wait*
-ngojea -n·goh·*jay*·a *wait for*
ngoma n-*goh*·ma *drum*
  — **ya kuigiza hadithi**
  ya koo·ee·*gee*·za ha·*dee*·thee *ballet*
ngozi n-*goh*·zee *leather* • *skin*
  — **ya kichwa** ya *keech*·wa *scalp*
ngumu n-*goo*·moo *hard (not soft)*
nguo n-*goo*·oh *clothing*
  — **kufua** koo·*foo*·a *laundry (clothes)*
  — **rasmi** *ras*·mee *uniform*
  — **za kuogelea** za koo·oh·*gay*·*lay*·a
  bathing suit
nguruwe n-goo·*roo*·way *pig*
nguvu n-*goo*·voo *power*
ni hatari nee ha·*ta*·ree *unsafe*
nimechumbiwa nee·may·choom·*bee*·wa
  (I'm) engaged
nimeoa nee·may·oh·a *(I'm) married (man)*
nimeolewa nee·may·oh·*lay*·wa
  (I'm) married (woman)
nini *nee*·nee *what*
nishati ya nyuklia
  nee·sha·tee ya *nyook*·lee·a *nuclear energy*
njaa n-*ja* *hunger*
nje n-*jay* *outside*
njegere n-jay·*gay*·ray *pea*
njia n-*jee*·a *aisle (on plane)* • *path* • *route* •
  street • *track* • *way*
  — **mkato** m-*ka*·toh *shortcut*
  — **ya baisikeli** ya ba·ee·see·*kay*·lee
  bike path
  — **ya kupanda mlimani** ya koo·*pan*·da
  m·lee·*ma*·nee *mountain path*
  — **ya kutembea porini**
  ya koo·taym·*bay*·a poh·*ree*·nee
  hiking route
  — **ya miguu** ya mee·*goo* *footpath*

noti *noh*·tee *banknote*
nukta *nook*·ta *point*
-nunua ·noo·noo·a *buy* • *shop*
nusu noo·soo *half*
nyama *nya*·ma *meat*
nyani *nya*·nee *baboon*
nyanya *nya*·nya *tomato*
nyasi *nya*·see *grass*
nyati *nya*·tee *buffalo*
nyekundu nyay·*koon*·doo *red*
nyepesi nyay·*pay*·see
  light (not heavy) • *quick*
nyeupe nyay·oo·pay
  light (of colour) • *white*
nyeusi nyay·oo·see *black* • *dark (of colour)*
  — **na nyeupe** na nyay·oo·pay *B&W (film)*
nyika *nyee*·ka *countryside*
nyingi *nyeen*·gee *a lot* • *many*
nyingine nyeen·*gee*·nay *another* • *other*
nyinyi *nyee*·nyee *you* pl
-nyoa ·*nyoh*·a *shave*
nyoka *nyoh*·ka *snake*
-nyonyesha ·nyoh·*nyay*·sha *breast-feed*
nyonyo bandia *nyoh*·nyoh ban·*dee*·a
  dummy • *pacifier*
nyota *nyoh*·ta *star*
nyuki *nyoo*·kee *bee*
nyuma *nyoo*·ma
  back (position) • *behind* • *rear (seat etc)*
nyumba *nyoom*·ba *house*
  — **ya sanaa** ya sa·*na* *art gallery*
  — **ya utawa wa wanaume**
  ya oo·*ta*·wa wa wa·na·oo·may *monastery*
  — **ya wageni** ya wa·*gay*·nee
  boarding house
nyumbani nyoom·*ba*·nee *home*
nyumbu nyoom·boo *wildebeest*
nyundo nyoon·doh *hammer*
nyuzi nyoo·zee *degrees (temperature)*
-nywa ·*nywa* *drink*
nywele nyway·lay *hair*
nzito n-*zee*·toh *heavy*
nzuri n-*zoo*·ree *fine* • *good*
  — **kabisa** ka·*bee*·sa *best*
  — **sana** *sa*·na *great (fantastic)*

O

-oa ·*oh*·a *marry (man)*
ofisi oh·*fee*·see *office*
  — **ya tiketi** ya tee·*kay*·tee *ticket office*
  — **ya watalii** ya wa·ta·*lee* *tourist office*

-oga *oh*·ga wash (oneself)
-ogelea *oh*·gay·*lay*·a swim
okestra oh·*kay*·stra orchestra
oksijeni ohk·see·*jay*·nee oxygen
-olewa *oh*·*lay*·wa marry (woman)
-omba *ohm*·ba ask (for something)
— lifti *leef*·tee hitchhike
ombi *ohm*·bee petition
omlet *ohm*·layt omelette
-ona *oh*·na see
-ondoka *ohn*·*doh*·ka depart
-onja *ohn*·ja try (taste)
-onya *oh*·nya warn
-onyesha *oh*·*nyay*·sha show
onyesho *oh*·*nyay*·shoh
gig (musical) · performance · show
— la muziki la moo·*zee*·kee concert
opareta oh·pa·*ray*·ta operator
opena ya kopo oh·*pay*·na ya *koh*·poh
can opener
opera *oh*·*pay*·ra opera
operesheni oh·*pay*·ray·*shay*·nee
operation (medical)
-osha *oh*·sha wash (something)
ovari oh·*va*·ree ovary

P

-pa *·pa give
padri *pa*·dree priest
pafu *pa*·foo lung
paka *pa*·ka cat
pakiti pa·*kee*·tee packet (general)
palahala pa·la·*ha*·la antelope
pamba *pam*·ba cotton
pamoja pa·*moh*·ja together
pampu *pam*·poo pump
pana *pa*·na wide
pancha *pan*·cha puncture
-panda *·pan*·da
board (a plane, ship etc) · climb
— baisikeli ba·ee·see·*kay*·lee cycle
— farasi fa·*ra*·see ride a horse
pango *pan*·goh cave
panya *pa*·nya mouse · rat
Pasaka pa·*sa*·ka Easter
pasheni pa·*shay*·nee passionfruit
pasi *pa*·see iron (for clothes)
pasi ya kupanda ndege *pa*·see ya
koo·*pan*·da n·*day*·gay boarding pass
pasipoti pa·see·*poh*·tee passport
-pata *·pa*·ta earn · get

pauda kwa mtoto
pa·*oo*·da kwa m·*toh*·toh baby powder
paundi pa·*oon*·dee pound (money, weight)
pea *pay*·a pear
pedeli pay·*day*·lee pedal
pekee pay·*kay* alone
-peleka *·pay*·*lay*·ka send
pembezoni mwa mji
paym·bay·*zoh*·nee mwa m·jee suburb
-penda *·payn*·da like · love
-pendekeza *·payn*·day·*kay*·za recommend
-pendelea *·payn*·day·*lay*·a prefer
pensili payn·*see*·lee pencil
peremende pay·ray·*mayn*·day sweets
pesa *pay*·sa change
— kichele kee·*chay*·lay loose change
pete *pay*·tay ring (on finger)
pia *pee*·a also
picha *pee*·cha painting (a work) · photo
pichi *pee*·chee peach
-piga kambi *·pee*·ga *kam*·bee camp
-piga kelele *·pee*·ga kay·*lay*·lay shout
-piga kura *·pee*·ga koo·ra vote
-piga picha *·pee*·ga *pee*·cha take a photo
-piga risasi *·pee*·ga ree·*sa*·see shoot
-piga simu *·pee*·ga *see*·moo ring (phone)
-piga teke *·pee*·ga *tay*·kay kick
pigano pee·*ga*·noh fight
-pika *·pee*·ka cook
pikipiki pee·kee·*pee*·kee motorcycle
pilipili pee·lee·*pee*·lee pepper
— hoho pee·lee·*pee*·lee *hoh*·hoh
capsicum · chilli
— mbichi pee·lee·*pee*·lee m·*bee*·chee
pepper (bell)
-pima uzito *·pee*·ma oo·*zee*·toh weigh
-pinda *·peen*·da turn
-pinga *·peen*·ga protest
pinki *peen*·kee pink
pipa la taka *pee*·pa la *ta*·ka garbage can
pipi *pee*·pee candy (lollies)
-pita *·pee*·ta pass
plagi *pla*·gee plug (electricity)
plamu *pla*·moo plum
— kavu *ka*·voo prune
plasta *pla*·sta bandage
plastiki pla·*stee*·kee plastic
poda *poh*·da powder
polepole poh·*lay*·poh·*lay slowly
polisi poh·*lee*·see police · police officer
pombe *pohm*·bay drink (alcoholic)
— ya kienyeji ya ka·ee·*nyay*·jee
home brew

posho *poh*-shoh *dole*
posta *poh*-sta
  mail (postal system) • *post office*
postikadi poh-stee-*ka*-dee *postcard*
-potea -poh-*tay*-a *lose*
printa *preen*-ta *printer (computer)*
projekta proh-*jayk*-ta *projector*
pua *poo*-a *nose*
  — yenye makamasi
  yay-nyay ma-ka-*ma*-see *runny nose*
pumbavu poom-*ba*-voo *stupid*
pumu *poo*-moo *asthma*
-pumua -poo-*moo*-a *breathe*
-pumzika -poom-*zee*-ka *rest*
punda milia poon-da mee-*lee*-a *zebra*
punguzo poon-*goo*-zoh *discount*
pwani *pwa*-nee *coast*

R

rafiki ra-*fee*-kee *friend*
-rafikiana -ra-fee-kee-*a*-na *go out with*
rafu *ra*-foo *shelf*
ragbi *rag*-bee *rugby*
rahisi ra-*hee*-see *cheap* • *easy* • *simple*
raia ra-*ee*-a *nationality*
rais ra-*ees* *president*
raketi ra-*kay*-tee *racquet*
ramani ra-*ma*-nee *map* • *road map*
rangi *ran*-gee *colour*
  — ya machungwa ya ma-*choon*-gwa
  orange (colour)
  — ya mdomo ya m-*doh*-moh *lipstick*
rasimu ra-*see*-moo *design*
ratiba ra-*tee*-ba *timetable*
  — ya safari ya sa-*fa*-ree *itinerary*
redio ray-*dee*-oh *radio*
-refu -*ray*-foo *deep*
-rejeleza -ray-jay-*lay*-za *recycle*
rejista ray-*gee*-sta *cash register*
-rekodi -ray-*koh*-dee *record*
rimoti ree-*moh*-tee *remote control*
risiti ree-*see*-tee *receipt*
robo *roh*-boh *quarter*
roki *roh*-kee *rock (music)*
Romani roh-*ma*-nee
  Catholic (denomination)
-rudi -*roo*-dee *return (come back)*
ruhusa roo-*hoo*-sa *permission*
  — ya kazi ya *ka*-zee *work permit*
-ruhusiwa -roo-hoo-*see*-wa
  can (have permission)
-ruka -*roo*-ka *fly* • *jump*

S

saa sa *clock* • *hour* • *time* • *watch*
  — sita mchana *see*-ta m-*cha*-na
  midday (noon)
  — sita usiku *see*-ta oo-*see*-koo
  midnight
  — yenye kengele
  yay-nyay kayn-*gay*-lay *alarm clock*
sababu sa-*ba*-boo *reason*
sabuni sa-*boo*-nee *soap*
  — ya kunyolea ya koo-nyoh-*lay*-a
  shaving cream
safari sa-*fa*-ree *trip (journey)*
  — kwa biashara kwa bee-a-*sha*-ra
  business trip
  — ya kutalii ya koo-ta-*lee* *tour*
  — yenye kiongozi
  yay-nyay kee-ohn-*goh*-zee
  guided tour
safi *sa*-fee *clean*
-safiri -sa-*fee*-ree *travel*
-safisha -sa-*fee*-sha *clean*
safu ya milima *sa*-foo ya mee-*lee*-ma
  mountain range
sahani sa-*ha*-nee *plate*
-sahau -sa-*ha*-oo *forget*
sahihi sa-*hee*-hee *signature*
-saidia -sa-ee-*dee*-a *help*
saizi sa-*ee*-zee *size (general)*
sakafu sa-*ka*-foo *floor*
sakitu sa-*kee*-too *frost*
sala *sa*-la *prayer*
salama sa-*la*-ma *safe*
-sali -*sa*-lee *pray*
saloni sa-*loh*-nee *beauty salon*
samaki sa-*ma*-kee *fish*
-samehe -*sa*-may-hay *forgive*
sana *sa*-na *very*
sanaa sa-*na* *art*
  — ya uchoraji wa rangi
  ya oo-choh-ra-jee wa *ran*-gee
  painting (the art)
sanamu sa-*na*-moo *statue*
sanduku san-*doo*-koo *box*
— la kuhifadhia mizigo
  la koo-hee-fa-*dhee*-a mee-*zee*-goh
  luggage locker
— la posta la *poh*-sta *mailbox*
sarafu sa-*ra*-foo *change (coins)*
sarakasi sa-ra-*ka*-see *circus* • *gymnastics*
sarara sa-*ra*-ra *fillet*

sasa *sa*·sa *now • present (time)*
— hivi *hee*·vee *soon*
sataranji sa·ta·*ran*·jee *chess*
sauna sa·*oo*·na *sauna*
sauti sa·*oo*·tee *voice • volume (sound)*
sawa *sa*·wa *right (correct)*
sawasawa *sa*·wa·*sa*·wa *same*
sayansi sa·*yan*·see *science*
— za jamii za ja·*mee* *humanities*
sayari sa·*ya*·ree *planet*
sebule say·*boo*·lay *foyer*
sehemu say·*hay*·moo *part (component)*
— ya kuchukulia mizigo
ya koo·choo·koo·*lee*·a mee·*zee*·goh
baggage claim
— ya kuegeshea magari
ya koo·ay·gay·*shay*·a ma·*ga*·ree *car park*
sekundi say·*koon*·dee *second (time unit)*
seli *say*·lee *sale*
-sema ·*say*·ma *say • speak • talk*
senti *sayn*·tee *cent*
sentimita sayn·tee·*mee*·ta *centimetre*
sera *say*·ra *policy*
seremala say·*ray*·ma·la *carpenter*
serikali say·ree·*ka*·lee *government*
shaba *sha*·ba *copper*
shairi pl sha·*ee*·ree *poetry*
shamba *sham*·ba *farm*
— la mizabibu la mee·za·*bee*·boo
vineyard
shampeni *sham*·nay·nee *champagne*
shampuu *sham*·poo *shampoo*
shangazi shan·*ga*·zee *aunt*
shanta *shan*·ta *backpack*
shashi *sha*·shee *gauze*
shati *sha*·tee *shirt*
shayiri sha·*yee*·ree *oats*
sherehe shay·*ray*·hay
celebration • party (night out)
sheria shay·*ree*·a
legislation • law (study, profession)
shifta *sheef*·ta *derailleur*
-shinda ·*sheen*·da *win*
shindano sheen·*da*·noh *race (sport)*
shinikizo shee·nee·*kee*·zoh *pressure*
— la damu la *da*·moo *blood pressure*
shirika la habari shee·*ree*·ka la ha·*ba*·ree
newsagency
-shirikiana ·shee·ree·kee·*a*·na *share (with)*
-shona ·*shoh*·na *sew*
shuka *shoo*·ka *bed linen • sheet*
— na tandiko na tan·*dee*·koh *bedding*
-shuka ·*shoo*·ka *get off (a train, etc)*

-shukuru ·shoo·*koo*·roo *thank*
shule *shoo*·lay *school*
— ya msingi ya m·*seen*·gee *high school*
shupavu shoo·*pa*·voo *brave*
siagi see·*a*·gee *butter*
siasa see·*a*·sa *politics*
sidiria see·dee·*ree*·a *bra*
sifa *see*·fa *quality*
— za kielimu za kee·ay·*lee*·moo
qualifications
sigara see·*ga*·ra *cigarette*
siki *see*·kee *vinegar*
-sikia ·see·*kee*·a *hear*
-sikiliza ·see·kee·*lee*·za *listen*
-sikilizia ·see·kee·lee·*zee*·a *listen to*
sikio see·*kee*·oh *ear*
siku *see*·koo *day*
Siku ya Krismasi *see*·koo ya krees·*ma*·see
Christmas Day
Siku ya Mwaka Mpya
see·koo ya *mwa*·ka m·pya
New Year's Day
sikukuu see·koo·*koo* *holiday*
— ya kuzaliwa ya koo·za·*lee*·wa
birthday
-simama ·see·*ma*·ma *stop (cease)*
simba *seem*·ba *lion*
simbo ya posta *seem*·boh ya *poh*·sta
post code
simu *see*·moo *telephone*
— ya mkononi ya m·koh·*noh*·nee
cell phone • mobile phone
— ya mtaani ya m·*ta*·nee
public telephone
sindano (ya dawa)
seen·*da*·noh (ya *da*·wa) *needle (syringe)*
sindano (ya kushonea) seen·*da*·noh (ya
koo·shoh·*na*·a) *needle (sewing)*
sinema see·*nay*·ma *cinema*
-sinzia ·seen·*zee*·a *sleep*
sisi *see*·see *we*
sista *see*·sta *nun*
siyo kawaida *see*·yoh ka·wa·*ee*·da
unusual
skafu *ska*·foo *scarf*
skati *ska*·tee *skirt*
-skii ·skee *ski*
skonzi *skohn*·zee *bread rolls*
slaidi sla·*ee*·dee *slide (film)*
soda *soh*·da *soft drink*
sodo *soh*·doh *sanitary napkin • tampon*
soga *soh*·ga *joke*
soka *soh*·ka *football (soccer)*

soko *soh*-koh *market*
— **la mtaani** la m-ta-*a*-nee *street market*
— **la wachonga vinyago** la wa-*chohn*-ga vee-*nya*-goh *woodcarver's market*
soksi *sohk*-see *socks* • *condom (slang)*
— **ndefu** n-*day*-foo *stockings*
-soma -*soh*-ma *read*
somo *soh*-moh *reading*
soshalisti soh-sha-*lee*-stee *socialist*
spidomita spee-doh-*mee*-ta *speedometer*
spishi zilizo hatarini *spee*-shee *lee*-zoh ha-ta-*ree*-nee *endangered species*
spishi zilizo hifadhiwa *spee*-shee *lee*-zoh hee-fa-*dhee*-wa *protected species*
spoki *spoh*-kee *spoke*
springi *spreen*-gee *spring (coil)*
stempu *staym*-poo *postage* • *stamp*
stendi ya basi *stayn*-dee ya *ba*-see *bus station*
steseheni stay-*shay*-nee *station*
— **ya treni** ya *tray*-nee *railway station*
stirio *stee*-ree-oh *stereo*
studio *stoo*-dee-oh *studio*
-subiri -*soo*-bee-ree *wait*
sufu *soo*-foo *wool*
sufuria soo-*foo*-ree-a *saucepan*
sukari soo-*ka*-ree *sugar*
-sukuma -*soo*-koo-ma *push*
sungura soon-*goo*-ra *rabbit*
sungusungu soon-goo-*soon*-goo *ant*
supu *soo*-poo *soup*
surua soo-*roo*-a *measles*
suruali soo-roo-*a*-lee *pants (trousers)*
sururu soo-*roo*-roo *pickaxe*
swala *swa*-la *gazelle*
swalapala swa-la-*pa*-la *impala*
swali *swa*-lee *question*
sweta *sway*-ta *jumper (sweater)*

T

taa ta *light (lamp)*
— **ya barabarani** ya ba-ra-ba-*ra*-nee *traffic light*
— **za mbele** za m-*bay*-lay *headlights*

taarifa ta-a-*ree*-fa *information*
tabaka ta-*ba*-ka *class (category)*
— **la hewa ya ozoni** la *hay*-wa ya oh-*zoh*-nee *ozone layer*
-tabasamu -ta-ba-*sa*-moo *smile*
tabibu wa maungo ta-*bee*-boo wa ma-*oon*-goh *chiropractor*
-tafsiri taf-*see*-ree *translate*
-tafuta -ta-*foo*-ta *look for*
tairi ta-ee-*ree* *tyre*
tajiri ta-*jee*-ree *rich (wealthy)*
-taka -*ta*-ka *want*
taka za sumu *ta*-ka za *soo*-moo *toxic waste*
takataka ta-ka-*ta*-ka *garbage*
— **za nyuklia** za *nyook*-lee-a *nuclear waste*
tamasha ta-*ma*-sha *festival*
tambalale tam-ba-*la*-lay *flat* Ⓐ
tambi *tam*-bee *noodles* • *pasta*
tamu *ta*-moo *sweet* • *tasty*
tandiko tan-*dee*-koh *saddle*
tangazo tan-*ga*-zoh *advertisement*
tango *tan*-goh *cucumber*
tangu (Mei) *tan*-goo (*may*-ee) *since (May)*
taratibu ta-ra-*tee*-boo *slow*
tarehe ta-*ray*-hay *date (day)*
— **ya kuzaliwa** ya koo-za-*lee*-wa *date of birth*
taulo ta-*oo*-loh *towel*
taya *ta*-ya *jaw*
tayari ta-*ya*-ree *already* adv • *ready* Ⓐ
-tazama -ta-*za*-ma *watch*
teknolojia ya maarifa tayk-noh-loh-*jee*-a ya ma-a-*ree*-fa *IT*
teksi *tayk*-see *taxi*
telegramu tay-lay-*gra*-moo *telegram*
telekom *tay*-lay-kohm *telecom centre*
televisheni tay-lay-vee-*shay*-nee *television*
-teleza -tay-*lay*-za *skate*
-tembea -taym-*bay*-a *walk*
— **porini** poh-*ree*-nee *hike*
-tembelea -taym-bay-*lay*-a *visit*
tembo *taym*-boh *elephant*
tena *tay*-na *again*
tende *tayn*-day *date (fruit)*
tenesi tay-*nay*-see *tennis*
-tengeneza -tayn-gay-*nay*-za *make* • *repair*
tetekuwanga tay-tay-koo-*wan*-ga *chicken pox*

tetemeko la ardhi
 tay·tay·*may*·koh la *ar*·dhee earthquake
thamani tha·*ma*·nee value (price)
theluji thay·*loo*·jee snow
-thibitisha ·thee·bee·*tee*·sha validate
tiba ya harufu tee·ba ya ha·*roo*·foo
 aromatherapy
tiba ya kuchoma na sindano
 tee·ba ya koo·*choh*·ma na seen·*da*·noh
 acupuncture
tiketi tee·*ke*·tee ticket
 — **kutumia kama nafasi ikipatikana**
 koo·too·*mee*·a ka·ma na·*fa*·see
 ee·kee·pa·tee·*ka*·na stand-by ticket
 — **ya kwenda tu** ya *kwayn*·da too
 one-way (ticket)
 — **ya kwenda na kurudi** ya *kwayn*·da
 na koo·*roo*·dee return (ticket)
 — **ya mzigo** ya m·*zee*·goh luggage tag
tikiti tee·*kee*·tee ticket
timu tee·moo team
tini tee·nee fig
tishati tee·sha·tee T-shirt
titi tee·tee breast (body)
-toa rushwa ·*toh*·a roosh·wa bribe
tochi toh·chee torch (flashlight)
tofaa to·fa apple
tofauti to·fa·*oo*·tee different
 — **ya wakati** ya wa·*ka*·tee time difference
treni *tray*·nee train
tu too only
-tulivu ·too·*lee*·voo quiet
-tumaini ·too·ma·*ee*·nee wish
tumbaku toom·*ba*·koo tobacco
tumbili toom·*bee*·lee monkey
tumbo toom·boh stomach
tumbusi toom·*boo*·see vulture
tunda *toon*·da fruit
-tunza ·*toon*·za
 care (for someone) • look after
tupu too·poo empty • vacant
twiga *twee*·ga giraffe
twiza *twee*·za tweezers
tyubu *tyoo*·boo inner tube • tyre

U

ua oo·*a* flower
-ua ·oo·*a* murder
ubaguzi oo·ba·*goo*·zee discrimination
 — **wa kijinsia** wa kee·jeen·*see*·a sexism
 — **wa rangi** wa *ran*·gee racism

ubakaji oo·ba·*ka*·jee rape
ubalozi oo·ba·*loh*·zee embassy
 — **mdogo** m·doh·goh consulate
ubao wa kuteleza oo·*ba*·oh wa
 koo·tay·*lay*·za skateboarding
ubao wa kutelezea
 oo·*ba*·oh wa koo·tay·lay·*zay*·a surfboard
ubao wa matokeo
 oo·*ba*·oh wa ma·toh·*kay*·oh scoreboard
ubao wa sataranji
 oo·*ba*·oh wa sa·ta·*ran*·jee chessboard
ubaraza oo·ba·*ra*·za balcony
ubatizo oo·ba·*tee*·zoh baptism
ubavu oo·*ba*·voo rib
uchafuzi oo·cha·*foo*·zee pollution
uchaguzi oo·cha·*goo*·zee election
ucheleweshaji oo·chay·lay·way·*sha*·jee
 delay
uchongaji oo·chohn·*ga*·jee sculpture
uchumba oo·*choom*·ba engagement
udaktari oo·dak·*ta*·ree
 medicine (study, profession)
udobi oo·*doh*·bee laundry (place)
udongo oo·*dohn*·goh clay
uelekeo oo·ay·lay·*kay*·oh direction
ufinyanzi oo·fee·*nyan*·zee ceramics
ufukwe oo·*fook*·way beach • seaside
ufunguo oo·*foon*·goo·oh key
ugonjwa wa kuchomwa kwa jua
 oo·*gohn*·jwa wa koo·*chohm*·wa kwa
 joo·a sunstroke
ugonjwa wa moyo oo·*gohn*·jwa wa
 moh·yoh heart condition
ugonjwa wa upele oo·*gohn*·jwa wa
 oo·*pay*·lay thrush (health)
ugonjwa wa zinaa
 oo·*gohn*·jwa wa zee·*na* venereal disease
uhamiaji oo·ha·mee·*a*·jee immigration
uhandisi oo·han·*dee*·see engineering
uharibifu oo·ha·ree·bee·foo spoilage
uhusiano oo·hoo·see·*a*·noh relationship
 — **wa jamii** wa ja·*mee* public relations
ujangili oo·jan·*gee*·lee poached (game)
ujao oo·*ja*·oh next
ujenzi oo·*jayn*·zee architecture
ujumbe oo·*joom*·bay message
ukarimu oo·ka·*ree*·moo hospitality
ukimwi oo·*keem*·wee AIDS
ukumbi oo·*koom*·bee gym (place)
 — **wa maonyesho**
 wa ma·oh·*nyay*·shoh theatre
ukungu oo·*koon*·goo fog
ukurasa oo·koo·*ra*·sa page

ukurutu oo·koo·*roo*·too *eczema*

ukuta oo·*koo*·ta *wall (outer)*

Ulaya vee·a·*la*·ya *Europe*

ulezi wa mtoto oo·*lay*·zee wa m·*toh*·toh *childminding*

ulimi oo·*lee*·mee *tongue*

ulimwengu oo·lee·*mwayn*·goo *universe*

-uliza ·oo·*lee*·za *ask (a question)*

uma *oo*·ma *bite (dog, insect)* • *fork*

-uma ·oo·ma *hurt*

umaskini oo·ma·*skee*·nee *poverty*

umbo oom·*boh* *shape*

umeme oo·*may*·may *electricity*

umri oom·*ree* *age*

ungamo oon·*ga*·moh *confession*

ununuzi oo·noo·*noo*·zee *shopping*

uongezaji wa visa oo·ohn·*gay*·za·jee wa *vee*·sa *extension (visa)*

upandaji miamba oo·pan·*da*·jee mee·*am*·ba *rock climbing*

upande oo·*pan*·day *side*

upele oo·*pay*·lay *rash*

— **wa nepi** wa *nay*·pee *nappy rash*

upendo oo·*payn*·doh *love*

upepo oo·*pay*·poh *air (in a tyre)* • *wind*

upigaji picha oo·pee·*ga*·jee *pee*·cha *photography*

upimaji mimba oo·pee·*ma*·jee meem·ba *pregnancy test kit*

upungufu oo·poon·*goo*·foo *shortage*

— **wa damu** wa *da*·moo *anaemia*

uraia oo·ra·*ee*·a *citizenship*

urari oo·*ra*·ree *balance (account)*

usafi oo·*sa*·fee *cleaning*

usafirishaji oo·sa·fee·ree·*sha*·jee *transport*

usajili wa gari oo·sa·*jee*·lee wa *ga*·ree *car registration*

usawa oo·*sa*·wa *equality*

ushauri oo·*sha*·oo·ree *advice*

ushirikina oo·shee·ree·*kee*·na *superstition*

usiku oo·*see*·koo *night*

— **huu** huu *tonight*

— **nje** n·jay *night out*

usimamizi oo·see·ma·*mee*·zee *administration*

uso *oo*·soh *face*

ustawi oo·*sta*·wee *welfare*

— **wa jamii** wa ja·*mee* *social welfare*

usukani pl oo·soo·*ka*·nee *handlebars*

usumbufu oo·soom·*boo*·foo *harassment*

utawala oo·ta·*wa*·la *rule*

utegemezi wa madawa ya kulevya oo·*tay*·gay·*may*·zee wa ma·*da*·wa ya koo·*lay*·vya *drug addiction*

utumiaji oo·too·mee·*a*·jee *exploitation*

uvimbe oo·*veem*·bay *inflammation* • *lump* • *swelling* • *tumour*

— **wa mboni** wa m·*boh*·nee *conjunctivitis*

— **wa ovari** wa oh·*va*·ree *ovarian cyst*

uvimbi wa ini oo·*veem*·bee wa *ee*·nee *hepatitis*

uvuvi oo·*voo*·vee *fishing*

uwakala wa safari oo·wa·*ka*·la wa sa·*fa*·ree *travel agency*

uwanda wa juu oo·*wan*·da wa joo *plateau*

uwanja oo·*wan*·ja *square (town)*

— **wa gofu** wa goh·foo *golf course*

— **wa kupigia kambi** wa kuu·pee·*gee*·a *kam*·bee *camping ground*

— **wa mbio** wa m·*bee*·oh *racetrack*

— **wa michezo** wa mee·*chay*·zoh *stadium*

— **wa ndege** wa n·*day*·gay *airport*

uwezo wa watu oo·*way*·zoh wa *wa*·too *human resources*

uwindaji oo·ween·*da*·jee *hunting*

uyabisi wa tumbo oo·ya·*bee*·see wa *toom*·boh *constipation*

uyoga oo·*yoh*·ga *mushroom*

-uza ·oo·za *sell*

uzi oo·zee *string* • *thread*

— **wa meno** wa *may*·noh *dental floss*

uzito oo·*zee*·toh *weight*

— **usiolipiwa** oo·see·oh·lee·*pee*·wa *baggage allowance*

uzoefu oo·zoh·*ay*·foo *experience*

— **wa kazi** wa *ka*·zee *work experience*

uzushi oo·*zoo*·shee *fiction*

V

-vaa ·va *wear*

vazi va·zee *dress*

— **la kuogelea** la koo·oh·*gay*·*lay*·a *swimsuit*

viatu vee·a·too *shoes*

vibiriti vee·bee·*ree*·tee *matches (for lighting)*

vidonge vya usingizi vee·*dohn*·gay vya oo·*seen*·*gee*·zee *sleeping pills*

vifaa vee·*fa* *equipment*

— **vya kuzamia** vya koo·za·*mee*·a *diving equipment*

vigumu vee·*goo*·moo *difficult*

vipengele vee·*payn*·*gay*·lay *details*

vipuli vee·*poo*·lee *jewellery*

virusi vee-*roo*-see *virus*
visa vee-sa *visa*
visu vee-soo *cutlery*
vita vee-ta *war*
vitamini vee-ta-*mee*-nee *vitamins*
vitanda viwili vee-*tan*-da vee-*wee*-lee *twin beds*
vitu vya sanaa vee-too vya sa-*na crafts*
viza vee-za *visa*
vizibo vya masikio vee-*zee*-boh vya ma-see-*kee*-oh *earplugs*
vizuri vee-*zoo*-ree *well*
-vunja -*voon*-ja *break*
-vunjika -*voon*-jee-ka *break down*
-vuta -*voo*-ta *pull*
— **sigara** see-*ga*-ra *smoke*
VVU vee-vee-yoo *HIV*
vyakula vya-*koo*-la *groceries*
vyombo vya habari
vyohm-boh vya ha-*ba*-ree *media*
vyombo vya udongo
vyohm-boh vya oo-*dohn*-goh *pottery*

W

-wa -wa *be*
— **marafiki** ma-ra-*fee*-kee *date (a person)*
— **mgonjwa** m-*gohn*-jwa *have a cold*
— **na** na *have*
— **na deni** na *day*-nee *owe*
wakala wa maeneo wa-*ka*-la wa ma-ay-*nay*-oh *real estate agent*
wakala wa shamba wa-*ka*-la wa *sham*-ba *estate agency*
wakati wa-*ka*-tee *when*
— **mwingine** mween-*gee*-nay *sometimes*
wala wa-la *neither*
wali wa-lee *rice (cooked)*
-wa na maumivu ya tumbo -wa na ma-oo-*mee*-voo ya *toom*-boh *to have a stomachache*
wanaofika wa-na-oh-*fee*-ka *arrivals*
wao wa-oh *they • their*
wapi wa-pee *where*
warsha war-sha *workshop (meeting)*
wasiojiweza wa-see-oh-jee-*way*-za *disabled*
watoto wa-*toh*-toh *children*
— **wa mtaani** wa m-ta-*a*-nee *street children*

watu wa-too *people*
wawili wawili wa-*wee*-lee wa-*wee*-lee *pair (couple)*
waya wa-ya *wire*
wazazi wa-za-zee *parents*
wazi wa-zee *open (premises)*
wazimu wa-zee-moo *hallucination*
waziri mkuu wa-zee-ree m-koo *prime minister*
-weka -*way*-ka *put*
wembe waym-bay *razor • razor blade*
wewe way-way *you* sg
-weza -*way*-za *can (be able)*
wigo wee-goh *fence*
wikendi wee-*kayn*-dee *weekend*
wiki wee-kee *week*
— **iliyopita** ee-lee-yoh-*pee*-ta *last week*
— **mbili** m-bee-lee *fortnight*
wimbi weem-bee *wave*
wimbo weem-boh *song • tune*
wingu ween-goo *cloud*
wizi wee-zee *rip-off*
wote woh-tay *everyone*

Y

ya aibu ya a-*ee*-boo *shy*
ya ajabu ya a-*ja*-boo *wonderful*
ya awali ya a-wa-lee *original*
ya baridi ya ba-*ree*-dee *cool*
ya chujwa ya *chooj*-wa *filtered*
ya elimu kale ya ay-*lee*-moo *ka*-lay *archaeological*
ya hakika ya ha-*kee*-ka *positive*
ya jadi ya *ja*-dee *classical*
ya joto ya *joh*-toh *warm*
ya jua ya *joo*-a *sunny*
ya kabla ya kab-la *last (previous)*
ya kale ya *ka*-lay *ancient*
ya kasi ya *ka*-see *fast*
ya kidini ya kee-*dee*-nee *religious*
ya kienyeji ya kee-ayn-*nyay*-jee *local*
ya kigeni ya kee-*gay*-nee *foreign • strange*
ya kihistoria ya kee-hee-stoh-*ree*-a *historical*
ya kijana ya kee-*ja*-na *young*
ya kike ya kee-kay *female*
ya kimataifa ya ka-ma-ta-*ee*-fa *international*
ya kisasa ya kee-*sa*-sa *modern*
ya kuachwa ya koo-*ach*-wa *excluded*
ya kubana ya koo-*ba*-na *tight*

ya kuchekesha ya koo-chay-*kay*-sha
   comedy • funny
ya kuchelewa ya koo-chay-*lay*-wa late
ya kuchochea ashiki
   ya koo-choh-*chay*-a a-*shee*-kee sexy
ya kuchoka ya koo-*choh*-ka tired
ya kuchomwa ya koo-*chohm*-wa burnt
ya kuchosha ya koo-*choh*-sha boring
ya kufungwa ya koo-*foon*-gwa
   closed • locked
ya kugandwa ya koo-*gan*-dwa frozen
ya kuharibika ya koo-ha-ree-*bee*-ka
   broken down
ya kuibwa ya koo-*ee*-bwa stolen
ya kujaa ya koo-*ja* full
ya kujazana ya koo-ja-*za*-na crowded
ya kujiajiri ya koo-jee-a-*jee*-ree
   self-employed
ya kujihuduma ya koo-jee-hoo-*doo*-ma
   self-service
ya kukana ya koo-*ka*-na negative
ya kukaushwa ya koo-ka-*oosh*-wa dried
ya kula rushwa ya koo-la roosh-wa
   corrupt
ya kupendeza ya koo-payn-*day*-za
   beautiful • pretty
ya kupendwa ya koo-*payn*-dwa popular
ya kupotezwa ya koo-poh-*tayz*-wa lost
ya kurejeleza ya koo-ray-jay-*lay*-za
   recyclable
ya kutamanisha ya koo-ta-ma-*nee*-sha
   sensual
ya kutosha ya koo-*toh*-sha enough
ya kuumiza ya koo-oo-*mee*-za painful
ya kuvunjika ya koo-voon-*jee*-ka broken
   — kirahisi kee-ra-*hee*-see fragile
ya kuvutia ya koo-voo-*tee*-a interesting
ya kuwezekana
   ya koo-way-zay-*ka*-na possible
ya kwanza ya *kwan*-za first
ya mfano hasa ya m-*fa*-noh *ha*-sa typical
ya mkoa ya m-*koh*-a regional
ya moto ya *moh*-toh heated
ya muda kamili ya *moo*-da ka-*mee*-lee
   full-time
ya mwinuko mkali
   ya mwee-*noo*-koh m-*ka*-lee steep
ya mwisho ya mwee-shoh last (final)
ya pili ya *pee*-lee second ⓐ
ya starehe ya sta-*ray*-hay comfortable

ya tatu ya *ta*-too third
ya thamani ya *tha*-ma-nee valuable
ya usanisia ya oo-sa-nee-*see*-a synthetic
ya zamani ya za-*ma*-nee
   antique • old • stale
yai *ya*-ee egg
yake *ya*-kay her • his
yako *ya*-koh your sg
yangu *yan*-goo my
yao *ya*-oh their
yaya *ya*-ya babysitter
yenu *yay*-noo your pl
yenye busara *yay*-nyay boo-*sa*-ra sensible
yenye kelele *yay*-nyay kay-*lay*-lay noisy
yenye kosa *yay*-nyay koh-sa faulty
yenye kufanana *yay*-nyay koo-fa-*na*-na
   similar
yenye manufaa
   yay-nyay ma-noo-*fa* useful
yenye sumu *yay*-nyay soo-moo poisonous
yenye uhalisi *yay*-nyay oo-ha-*lee*-see
   realistic
yetu *yay*-too our
yeye *yay*-yay he • she
yoyote yoh-*yoh*-tay any

Z

zabibu za-*bee*-boo grapes
   — kavu ka-voo raisin
zaidi za-ee-dee more
zaituni za-ee-*too*-nee olive
-zalisha -za-*lee*-sha produce
zamani za-*ma*-nee past
zambarau zam-ba-*ra*-oo purple
zao za-oh crop
zawadi za-*wa*-dee present (gift)
   — ya arusi ya a-*roo*-see
   wedding present
zeze *zay*-zay guitar
ziara zee-*a*-ra shrine
zingizi zeen-*gee*-zee premenstrual tension
zipu *zee*-poo zip/zipper
-zito -zee-toh thick
ziwa *zee*-wa lake
ziwi zee-wee deaf
zodiaki zoh-dee-*a*-kee zodiac
zote *zoh*-tay all
-zuia -zoo-ee-a stop (prevent)
zulia zoo-*lee*-a rug